To Keep or To Change First Past The Post?

To Keep or To Change First Past The Post?

The Politics of Electoral Reform

Edited by

André Blais

OXFORD
UNIVERSITY PRESS

OXFORD
UNIVERSITY PRESS

Great Clarendon Street, Oxford OX2 6DP

Oxford University Press is a department of the University of Oxford.
It furthers the University's objective of excellence in research, scholarship,
and education by publishing worldwide in

Oxford New York

Auckland Cape Town Dar es Salaam Hong Kong Karachi
Kuala Lumpur Madrid Melbourne Mexico City Nairobi
New Delhi Shanghai Taipei Toronto

With offices in

Argentina Austria Brazil Chile Czech Republic France Greece
Guatemala Hungary Italy Japan Poland Portugal Singapore
South Korea Switzerland Thailand Turkey Ukraine Vietnam

Oxford is a registered trade mark of Oxford University Press
in the UK and in certain other countries

Published in the United States
by Oxford University Press Inc., New York

British Library Cataloguing in Publication Data
Data available
Library of Congress Cataloging in Publication Data
Data available

Typeset by SPI Publisher Services, Pondicherry, India
Printed in Great Britain
on acid-free paper by
Biddles Ltd., King's Lynn, Norfolk

ISBN 978–0–19–953939–0

1 3 5 7 9 10 8 6 4 2

Preface

This book is the outcome of a conference held in Montreal in June 2006. First drafts of the chapters were presented and discussed at the conference. The authors substantially revised their chapters on the basis of the discussion at the conference and my own suggestions, and subsequently after having received the referees' comments.

The conference and this book would not have been possible without the collaboration of many persons and institutions. The conference was organized by the Canada Research Chair in Electoral Studies (and most particularly by Daniel Rubenson), with the financial support of CIREQ (Centre interuniversitaire de recherche en économie quantitative) and IRPP (Institute for Research on Public Policy), as part of a two round set of conferences on plurality and multi-round elections organized jointly with Bernie Groffman (Irvine) and Shaun Bowler (California at Riverside). I thank these institutions and persons for their support.

I also thank all authors for their patience in responding to (some of) my suggestions, Agnieszka Dobrzynska for her dedication to preparing the manuscript for publication, and to Dominic Byatt and Aimee Wright from Oxford University Press for their diligent and competent support.

First past the post is one of the oldest institutions of electoral democracies. How representatives should be chosen is one of the most basic issues that have been addressed by all those who care about the quality of democratic life, and whether first past the post is a 'good' or 'bad' system and whether it should be kept or changed has been on the political agenda for at least a century. This book does not directly deal with the normative issue of whether such a system is 'good' or 'bad'. It is concerned with closely related and more empirically oriented questions: Why is impetus for reform sometimes relatively weak and sometimes rather strong? And why do reform attempts sometimes succeed and sometimes fail? The answers... follow.

André Blais

Contents

List of Figures

List of Tables

List of Abbreviations

ADQ	Action Démocratique du Québec
AMS	Additional Member System
AV	alternative vote/alternative voting
BC	British Colombia
CA	Citizens' Assembly
CCF	Cooperative Commonwealth Federation
CVD	Center for Voting and Democracy
ERC	Electoral Reform Coalition
FLQ	Front de Libération du Québec
FPTP	first past the post
FVC	Fair Vote Canada
IRV	instant runoff voting
MDN	Mouvement pour une Démocratie nouvelle
MMP	mixed-member proportional
MPs	members of parliament
NCSL	National Conference of State Legislatures
NDP	New Democratic Party
PEI	Prince Edward Island
PLQ	Quebec Liberal party
PQ	Parti Québécois
PR	proportional representation
PUP	People's United Party
SMD	single-member district
SMP	single-member plurality
STV	single transferable vote
UDP	United Democratic Party

Notes on Contributors

André Blais is a Professor of Political Science at Université de Montréal and he holds a Canada Research Chair in Electoral Studies. He was a principal co-investigator of the Canadian Election Study until 2006. He has published more than 100 articles in outstanding journals of political science. His most important book is *To Vote or Not to Vote? The Merits and Limits of Rational Choice Theory* (2000).

Adrian Blau is a Lecturer in Governance and Policy Analysis at Manchester University. He works on electoral and party systems, as well as on democratic theory more generally.

Shaun Bowler is a Professor of Political Science at the University of California, Riverside. His research interests include comparative electoral systems and voting behaviour. Professor Bowler is the author of *Demanding Choices: Opinion Voting and Direct Democracy* with Todd Donovan (1998).

R. Kenneth Carty is a Professor of Political Science and Brenda & David McLean Chair in Canadian Studies at the University of British Columbia. During 2004, he served as Director of Research for the British Columbia Citizens' Assembly on Electoral Reform. His most recent book is *Politics is Local: National Politics at the Grassroots* (2005).

Todd Donovan is a Professor in the Political Science Department at Western Washington University. His research interests are in the areas of American state politics, direct democracy, election systems, and representation. Professor Donovan's latest books include *Electoral Reform and Minority Representation* with Bowler and Brockington (2003) and *Reforming the Republic: Democratic Institutions for the New America* with Bowler (2004).

Patrick Fournier is an Associate Professor of Political Science at Université de Montréal. He is co-investigator of the 2000, 2004, and upcoming Canadian Election Studies.

Louis Massicotte is a Professor of Political Science at Université Laval, Québec, Canada. He taught previously at the Université de Montréal and was Visiting Professor at American University, Washington, DC. He co-authored *Establishing the Rules of the Game. Election Laws in Democracies* and has published widely about electoral systems. From 2003 to 2005, he worked on electoral reform for the Quebec government.

Matthew Søberg Shugart is a Professor of Political Science and International Relations at the University of California, San Diego. His publications on electoral systems include *Mixed-Member Electoral Systems: The Best of Both Worlds?* (co-edited with Martin P. Wattenberg, 2001).

Jack Vowles is a Professor of Politics at the University of Exeter and Adjunct Professor at the University of Auckland. He leads the New Zealand Election Study and is co-author or co-editor of five books on New Zealand elections since 1990.

Introduction

André Blais

First past the post (FPTP) is one of the oldest and simplest electoral systems. The logic is straightforward. In each district, the candidate with the most votes wins, the party that wins most seats (almost always) forms the government, and the governing party gets to make public policy until the next election.

First past the post is used for all legislative elections (both national and sub-national) in Canada and for national parliamentary elections in the UK and the USA (except in the state of Georgia). It is also the system used for all elections in India and most Caribbean islands. All these countries are former British colonies (Blais and Massicotte 1997).

Such a system seems destined to survive for ever. The party that forms the government has (almost always) benefited from the system in the previous election, that is, its seat share exceeded its vote share. There appears to be no reason why the governing party would want to change the rules under which it had just won. Making the system more proportional, in particular, would make smaller parties stronger and larger parties, including the governing party, weaker.

In spite of such unfavourable auspices, there has been a strong push for replacement of first past the post almost everywhere it prevails, and the system was actually replaced in a number of countries. Sweden and Denmark switched from single-member plurality (SMP) to proportional representation (PR) in 1908 and 1920, respectively, and Australia abandoned first past the vote in favour of the alternative vote in 1918. For its part, Norway went from plurality to two-rounds majority in 1906 before adopting PR in 1921. And Greece switched between plurality and PR three times between 1923 and 1936. More recently, in

1996, New Zealand moved from SMP to a mixed-member proportional system.

The book addresses a simple but basic question: What fosters or hinders reform of first past the post? This simple question can be decomposed into sub-questions: When and why does reform of FPTP emerge on the political agenda? Who proposes and who opposes reform? Why? When and why do reform proposals succeed or fail? What kind of reform tends to be put on the table, that is, which electoral system is proposed to replace FPTP? Why? Are some types of proposal more likely to succeed or fail? Why?

In order for reform to take place, the issue of electoral system must make it on the political agenda. Once it is on the agenda, a decision must be made to keep or to change it, and in the latter case, a choice must be made among many alternatives. Of course, policymakers can also let things drag on for ever, so that they do not have to make a formal decision, thus maintaining the status quo.

The book looks at the conditions under which electoral reform emerges on the political agenda and at the strategies deployed by the actors in the electoral reform game. The analyses reveal when and why electoral reform is most and least likely to occur.

The decision to keep or to change first past the post is not made in isolation. The debate that takes place entails a comparative evaluation of the merits and limits of this voting system versus those of alternative options. Traditionally, the debate has been between first past the post and proportional representation. This was particularly so at the beginning of the twentieth century, which witnessed a widespread shift toward PR (Blais, Dobrzynska, and Indridason 2005).

The basic argument in favour of first past the post is that it produces stability and accountability while PR is advocated because it produces broad and fair representation (Blais 1991; Blais and Massicotte 2002). First past the post usually produces one-party majority governments (Blais and Carty 1987; Lijphart 1994), these governments tend to be more durable (Blais and Kim 2007), and it is easy to get rid of them if they are not performing satisfactorily. Furthermore, the presence of single-member districts provides voters with a close relationship with their representatives.

Proportional representation is argued to be a fairer system because it is intended to give each party a share of seats more or less equal to its vote share. It also allows for a greater diversity of opinions and interests to be expressed in the legislature and government, as more parties are represented in both.

The debate between first past the post and PR is thus very much about which values should get priority. But the debate is not solely about values. Interests also matter. Some parties are bound to do better in one system than the other: first past the post tends to benefit larger parties and PR smaller ones. The question is often which parties' views prevail at the end.

This raises the question of which players are involved in the electoral reform game. I have just mentioned the parties, which can be distinguished on the basis of whether they are large or small and on whether they are in government (and thus able to implement or block reform if they form a majority government). Within the parties, one can also distinguish party leaders and simple members of parliament (MPs), whose interests may sometimes diverge. There may be organized groups or opinion leaders. And there is finally the larger public, who may have views on the matter, which politicians may decide to respond to.

PR is not the only alternative to first past the post. There are also majority systems where an absolute majority is required in order to be elected. There are two types of majority system, two-round systems like France where a second round takes place if no candidate obtains a majority on the first ballot, and the alternative vote like in Australia where voters rank order the candidates and second choices are considered if no candidate obtains a majority of first choices. And indeed first past the post was replaced by the alternative vote in Australia in 1919 and New Zealand in 1908 (New Zealand moved back to first past the post in 1914), and a two-round system in Norway in 1906 (Norway switched to PR in 1921).

More recently, the most popular alternative to first past the post has been a mixed-member proportional system, like Germany, under which some members of parliament are elected under first past the post while others are elected under some PR formula. This was the option that New Zealand adopted in 1996. This is obviously an attempt to have 'the best of both worlds' (Shugart and Wattenberg 2001a), especially to attain 'fair' representation while keeping many single-member districts with individually accounted members of parliament.

It is the case that FPTP has remained in place in Britain (but only for national elections), Canada, the USA, the Caribbean islands, and India, but it has been replaced in Sweden, Denmark, Australia, and New Zealand. The system has proven to be resilient but there has been some change, both at the beginning and at the end of the twentieth century.

The objective of this book is to understand the factors that foster or hinder reform of FPTP. The focus is on recent or contemporary patterns in the UK, the USA, Canada, and New Zealand. We look not only at the final outcome (whether reform actually takes place or not?) but also at the strength or weakness of the reform impetus.

Chapter 1 focuses on the conditions for reform initiation. Shugart argues that two conditions must be met for reform initiation, that is, a process through which an alternative to FPTP is formally considered and put to a referendum or parliamentary vote. The first condition is systemic failure, the incapacity of the electoral system to deliver the normatively expected connection between the vote and the formation of government. The most typical instances of 'inherent' failure are lopsided majorities and plurality reversals (the party with the most seats comes second in votes). But that condition is not sufficient. A 'contingent' condition must also be satisfied. Either the governing party believes that it would do better under a new rule or it thinks that initiating reform will increase its own popularity among voters. When and only when both inherent and contingent conditions are met is reform formally considered by the government.

The following chapters examine in greater detail the politics of electoral reform in the UK, the USA, Canada, and New Zealand. The chapters provide a thorough description and analysis of the debate over electoral systems in each country, of the alternative proposals that have been made, of the major actors involved in the process, and of the strategies utilized to defend their interests and values. On the basis of these thick descriptions, the authors offer their own explanation for why reform was or was not initiated and implemented.

Chapter 2 looks at electoral reform in the UK. Blau indicates that there are four reasons why the leaders of a major party may envisage reform: if they believe that another system is normatively 'better', if this is needed to get a minor party support in a hung parliament, if they think that this might increase the popularity of the party (which Shugart calls 'act contingencies'), and if they believe that the party would actually benefit from the new rule (called 'outcome contingencies' by Shugart). It is one thing to put reform on the political agenda; it is another to put it in the statute book. It is often argued that the major obstacle to reform comes from the incumbency-based self-interest of MPs. But Blau contends that the most crucial hurdle is that it is not obviously in either major party's interests to change the system.

Chapter 3 deals with the American case. It is in the USA that FPTP appears to be most solidly established. There is very little serious discussion of replacing it at the national level (note, however, that substantial experimentation is going on at the local level). Again, the USA seems to be 'exceptional' (Pontusson 2006). Why? Bowler and Donovan make a number of interesting observations. First, the absence of new entrants into the political system in the USA is bound to reduce impetus for reform. Everything else being equal, the more parties there are, the greater the probability of pressure for electoral reform (Benoit 2004; Colomer 2004). So the source of US resistance could be the resilient two-party system. Bowler and Donovan also remind us that there have been lots of changes in the electoral law. So from a broader perspective, the USA is not that exceptional. Or it is exceptional only in the sense that, contrary to most countries, electoral reform has not been directed at changing the electoral formula.

In Chapter 4, Massicotte examines the third wave of electoral system debate in Canada, starting in the 1980s. He suggests that the revival of interest in the issue is concomitant with declining political support (for a similar argument, see Dalton 2004). Massicotte shows that the debate has now spread to all regions of the country, that there is new emphasis on the reform process itself, and that the favourite alternative option is the so-called mixed-member proportional system. Finally he notes that all attempts at reform have failed so far. He observes that the issue has not reached the wide public while most mainstream politicians remain hostile to reform.

Chapter 5 moves to a consideration of the startling experiment conducted in the Canadian province of British Columbia, where an Assembly composed of 'ordinary' citizens chosen through a lottery was invited to propose a new electoral system and where a referendum was held on the Assembly proposal (which was the single transferable vote). What is most remarkable here is that the politicians decided to relinquish their power to decide themselves the rules governing how they are to be elected. The authors argue that the most likely reason was simply that the Premier was convinced that this is how things should be done.

New Zealand is the last case to be examined, and this is the only clear instance of electoral reform 'success'. So what is special about New Zealand? As Vowles notes, New Zealand can be construed as an extreme instance of majoritarian government, with a total lack of restraint (a unitary state, with no constitutional law and no second Chamber). According to Vowles, that system was acceptable provided governments were perceived to be broadly responsive and accountable to public opinion. The succession of three governments that decided to implement radical and widely unpopular policies was just too much to swallow. And so, it would seem that the most important 'cause' of the change was normative. Most New Zealanders had come to the conclusion that democracy was not working as it should, that the excessive power of the Prime Minister and its Cabinet had to be curtailed, and that the best way to achieve this was to move to a more proportional system.

These rich analyses demonstrate that no simple and parsimonious model can explain why electoral reform does or does not emerge on the political agenda, and, when it does, why it sometimes succeeds and, more often, fails. This raises the question of whether there are general lessons to be learnt from these cases. This is the question addressed in the Conclusion.

1

Inherent and Contingent Factors in Reform Initiation in Plurality Systems*

Matthew Søberg Shugart

The first past the post (FPTP) electoral system is one of the earliest mechanisms for electing legislative representatives, and it continues to be used for the lower (or sole elected) legislative chamber of four of the eight largest countries in the world to have been continuously democratic since shortly after the Second World War, including the two largest (India and the USA).[1] By one estimate, just over 43.5% of the world's population that lives in any of the 199 countries with direct legislative elections lives under FPTP (Reynolds, Reilly, and Ellis 2005). Despite its long historical pedigree and its continuing widespread use, it is a system that academic specialists in electoral systems rate as one of the least desirable systems (Bowler and Farrell 2006), and it also does not fare well in competition with other electoral systems when new democracies are choosing their method of electing representatives. Of the many new democracies to have emerged since the mid-1970s (the so-called 'Third Wave') from the end of military, Communist Party, or other authoritarian or imperial rule, almost none have chosen FPTP. Furthermore, in the small 'wave' of reform in established democracies in recent decades, not one country has moved to FPTP. Rather, all reforms have been either from FPTP to some form of proportional representation (PR) (as in New Zealand in 1996) or from some form of PR to a mixed-member system that retains some seats

* I am grateful to André Blais, Adrian Blau, Royce Carroll, Ken Carty, Wilfred Day, David Farrell, Benjamin Nyblade, Alan Siaroff, Rein Taagepera, Jack Vowles, Martin Wattenberg, and participants at a seminar at the University of British Columbia for comments on earlier versions of this chapter. I benefited enormously from research assistance by Royce Carroll and Mónica Pachón-Buitrago. Kashi Tanaka was kind enough to share his data on multi-seat districts in Canada.

elected on a proportional principle even while it entails others elected by FPTP (as, for example, in Italy from 1994 until 2001).

Thus in attempting to understand decisions of various political jurisdictions to keep or change FPTP—the topic of this volume—we are presented with a puzzle. The universe of countries, states, or provinces that we must analyse is one that is using an electoral system roundly rejected by those who supposedly understand such systems best (i.e. political scientists such as the contributors to this volume) and by those actors (politicians, commissioners, and citizens assembly members) who have actually taken the time and effort to consider whether to adopt a new electoral system, whether in a new or ongoing democracy. Yet, to date, only one jurisdiction with an extended period of using FPTP has made a decision to replace it with a form of PR. Thus, as we try to understand keeping or changing FPTP, we need to understand decisions or non-decisions that almost always wind up with 'keep' as their outcome.

If, in building towards an understanding of the 'keep' or 'change' decision, we were to analyse only those cases that changed, we would be left with nothing but the New Zealand case. If we were to consider those where the public voted on whether to change from FPTP, we would add one more case [British Columbia (BC), 2005] thus far, with a third scheduled (Ontario, 2007). Thus we might also include cases where a formal recommendation to keep or change was made by some government-appointed commission. This adds a few more Canadian provinces and the UK to our list. In each of these cases, the recommendation has always been 'change', but the result so far has been 'keep' (again, of course, with the New Zealand exception and the Ontario result pending). Thus we are very much dealing with rare events, whether we define the 'event' as a change in the electoral system or even as a formal decision to recommend a change. To cope with this problem of rarity, I will cast this chapter as explaining not 'electoral reform', per se, but rather *reform processes*.

This chapter seeks to advance our understanding of the conditions under which a government elected by FPTP would open up a process that could lead to the replacement of FPTP by PR. In order to be 'opened up', the process should be one that is at least arms length from the government or its parliamentary majority, because a certain threshold of seriousness has been crossed when a government allows a body outside its direct control to study the electoral system and make a formal recommendation of a new system.

I will regard a reform process as having started when a government empowers a commission or other 'consultative' body (defined below) with reviewing the electoral system and potentially recommending an alternative.

Of course, a reform process can be initiated without ever proceeding to a formal recommendation. I will regard a consultative process on electoral reform as having been completed at the point at which there is either a vote in parliament or a public referendum that pits the existing FPTP system against one or more proposed alternative electoral systems. A reform process could be aborted at any step between its initiation and completion, as those steps are defined here. As we will see, some have been aborted before the final vote on FPTP versus reform. Following Nohlen (1984), as well as Lijphart (1984, 1999), Powell (2000), and numerous others, I take FPTP and PR to be opposing principles of representation, and for this reason, I will confine the analysis to cases where such a wholesale replacement of FPTP with an opposing electoral-system concept is up for debate.

A reform process could be further broken down into its many phases, as Blau (Chapter 2 in this volume) discusses. Electoral-system change can be blocked at any of several decision nodes along the way, but I am focusing on the beginning and end points of the process: whether to open it up in the first place and whether to proceed a final binding vote (whether by referendum or in the legislature) that pits FPTP against at least one PR alternative. I will leave to case studies (including those in the present volume) the task of detailed tracing of the various intermediate steps along the way. My purpose is to determine whether there are any predictable patterns in the performance of FPTP systems that lead one of the two major political parties—the very parties that normally gain the most from FPTP—to make and keep a public commitment to consult with experts and the public on possibly replacing the system with a proportional system.

I argue below that the decision to consider changing the electoral system must be understood as a product of both *inherent* and *contingent* conditions. An inherent condition for reform is poor performance, relative to normative standards for the electoral system in use, that results from the mechanical application of the seat-allocation principle of the existing system. When this poor performance leads to obviously anomalous outcomes, it can be said that the inherent tendencies of the system have generated a *systemic failure*. A failure of the system, however, is certainly not sufficient for a reform process to get underway. In order for the prospect of reform to make it to the government's agenda, a governing party must see an advantage to putting it there. For instance, a party may expect electoral rewards from branding itself as 'reformist' and placing a commitment to review the electoral system in a campaign manifesto. If it wins the election, then a government has been elected with a stated commitment to open up the process (though that still, of course, does guarantee it will follow through). Were it not for the presence of systemic failure, there would be little value to promoting reform, just as without the contingent benefits from promoting reform, the inherent conditions would not be translated into an actual reform process. Thus, the model of the reform process developed here combines both the norms-based and rational-actor approaches (for more on this, see the Conclusion to this volume). Norms matter, in that a given pattern of democracy is expected to perform in a given manner and when it fails, demands for reform may emerge. Norms also matter in that they are not necessarily fixed, in that expectations about how democracy should work may evolve over time, and an existing electoral system may be seen as failing to live up to revised normative expectations (even if it still meets the former expectations that sustained it previously). For the case of New Zealand, Vowles (Chapter 6) suggests that in the period during which electoral reform was under consideration in that country, there was a shift in democratic norms such that FPTP no longer seemed as democratic as PR. It is worth emphasizing, however, that an argument that norms matter does not imply that strategic interests of rational political actors are thrown aside. In fact, it is precisely at the intersection of normative critiques of the existing rules and rational interest of political actors that reform is most likely to occur. If the current system is seen as normatively deficient—whether by failure to meet its own criteria or by failure to meet an emerging consensus centred on different norms—political parties and aspiring leaders may see a strategic advantage in advocating reform, or strategic peril in being seen as attempting to stop it.

1.1. A Theory of Electoral Reform

The causes of not only electoral reform but also other events—social revolutions, accidents, onset of disease, and many others—may be broken down into contingent and inherent factors (Eckstein 1980). Explanations based on inherent factors focus on antecedent conditions, whereas explanations focusing on contingency focus on more immediate triggers of an event. For instance, a wildfire may be explained by the accumulation of dry brush (an inherent factor) or by a lost hunter's signal fire getting out of control. Both explanations are valid, but they are incomplete. Dry brush may accumulate over years or decades without ever catching fire, and numerous lost hunters have set fires to help rescuers spot them without starting conflagrations. Similarly, certain types of electoral systems inherently produce pressures for reform because their actual operation is prone to generate outcomes that violate certain normative expectations for how the electoral system should operate. Yet these electoral systems may remain in place over many electoral cycles, either because the inherent flaws go largely unnoticed or because the actors who could change them prefer not to do so, even in the face of criticisms from other actors. Thus for reform actually to occur, there must be some triggering event or events—contingencies—that lead politicians either to vote to change the rules under which they were elected or that cause them to lose control over the selection of rules.

1.1.1. *The Inherent Tendency for Systemic Failure*

Almost any type of electoral system has some inherent tendency to produce systemic failure. This does not mean, of course, that we are faced with the gloomy prospect that all systems are doomed to fail. Rather, it means that any electoral system trades off some democratic values over others and the failure to meet some values can lead to a perception that something is wrong with the system itself. Shugart and Wattenberg (2001b) introduced the term, systemic failure, as a precondition for major electoral reform, but they left the definition and operationalization of the term incomplete. We may consider a system to have failed if there is general criticism of it, or if opposition parties have campaign platforms calling for the system's abolition and replacement with something dramatically different. But can we identify a priori some conditions that would be theoretically expected to bring about discontent with the institutional status quo? Identifying antecedents for failure in plurality systems is one of the primary purposes of this chapter, but before we can begin to think about what those antecedents might be, we must consider a more basic question: What does it mean to say that an electoral system has failed?

An electoral system allocates political power, by translating votes for parties and candidates into seats in the legislature.[2] The FPTP system is associated, in parliamentary democracies, with a majoritarian pattern of governance in which a single party takes all the executive portfolios (Lijphart 1984, 1999; Powell 2000). The FPTP system is associated with majoritarian governance precisely because its disproportional allocation of parliamentary seats enhances the possibility that one party will win a majority of seats, and hence be in a position to control the executive for the duration of the parliamentary term. The majoritarian model does not assume that the largest party has a majority of votes, but it does assume that the electoral system enhances the clarity of authority, relative to the votes' outcome. That is, normative models of the FPTP electoral system and its attendant majoritarian pattern of governance assume that the incumbent government will be clearly identifiable and accountable, and they further assume that there exists a clear opposition party to which power could be transferred at a subsequent election.

The role of the opposition is almost as critical to the normative model of majoritarian governance as is that of the majority itself. As inherited from British tradition, this model of parliamentary democracy provides an official designation to the opposition, and various abstractions of the model consider the opposition to be the electorate's monitor over the government, given that there is neither power-sharing within the cabinet nor a separately elected institution (e.g. a presidency or a powerful upper house) to check the government (Palmer 1995). The majoritarian (or Westminster) model thus assumes opposition with a capital *O*, as Helms (2004) puts it.

This discussion of the normative theory of majoritarian democracy highlights an important factor in potentially undermining the FPTP system: there must be a jurisdiction-wide (national or provincial) politics and a process by which a government and an opposition can be identified at the jurisdictional level. The more the process of selecting legislators remains local or regional in focus, such that legislators elected in their single-seat districts are seen as delegates of more particularistic interests, the less likely it is that a critique of the majoritarian performance of the electoral system could emerge. I will return to this point below, in discussing case selection. For now, the point is that in order for a normative critique such as 'systemic failure' to impel electoral reform onto the political agenda, it is imperative that it be politically relevant in the given jurisdiction what the relationship is between aggregate vote shares and seat shares in the legislature. In some democratic systems, we can take this for granted, while in others, perhaps we cannot.

As I use the term in this chapter, a systemic failure results when the normative expectations of the current system are not being met. Thus, while an FPTP system might be criticized in some quarters for producing a single-party majority government for a plurality party that did not win even 40% of the vote, such an outcome is not a systemic failure, because the system is in fact doing what it is expected to do: amplify the vote differential between the leading parties in order to ensure single-party government. Systemic failures may be defined as *the incapacity of the electoral system to deliver the normatively expected connection between the vote and the formation of executive authority.*[3] For example, under FPTP, the election of the second largest party (by votes) to a position of full executive power could be considered a systemic failure, as it calls into question the ability of voters either to re-elect or to replace an incumbent government if the outcome after the election is that the party with the most votes is in opposition. Another form of systemic failure in a plurality system would be the decimation of the opposition in the form of an overly lopsided majority for the largest party. As noted above, the majoritarian model of democracy carves out an important role for the opposition as the only institutional monitor—one cannot say 'check'—on the government. The effective absence of an opposition is clearly a major flaw in the system. Lesser systemic failures might include minority governments, on the grounds that they cloud accountability; they do not, however, significantly cloud identifiability in that a single party remains responsible for administration. It is also important to reiterate what is *not* a systemic failure: a majority for a party with well under a majority of the votes. As long as that party has the plurality of votes, the system is performing as expected, by magnifying the lead of the largest party and resulting in its clear responsibility for power.

The inherent conditions for electoral reform have been met, I will argue, when a visible systemic failure has occurred. Systemic failures—such as lopsided majorities and plurality reversals—are inherent in the functioning of FPTP systems for the reason articulated by Vowles (Chapter 6). The electoral system was never designed to produce the pattern of majoritarian governance associated with it, when it is employed in a parliamentary democracy. That is, while a normative model of single-party governance has been developed around the Westminster systems, the electoral system itself is an inheritance from the pre-democratic era when all it was intended to do was provide local representation. Both lopsided majorities and plurality reversals are bound to result from time to time when the leading parties have skewed geographic distributions of their votes. It is the district-by-district allocation of seats that makes lopsided majorities and plurality reversals possible. It is the normative model of national partisan competition for control of the government that makes such outcomes likely to be viewed as anomalous. It is the possibility that a political party may perceive itself to be 'wronged' by the system, and that voters may agree that normative democratic values have been violated, that makes anomalous outcomes likely to generate the contingent factors for reform. If, on the other hand, party politicians and voters alike perceive politics as more local and regional, FPTP may be sustainable even if national aggregate outcomes appear anomalous to outside observers (such as political scientists).

1.1.2. *Two Types of Contingencies*

No matter how badly an electoral system is performing, it doesn't reform itself. Some actor or actors must take the initiative and propose reform, and any such proposal must clear various institutional and political hurdles before it can be enacted. If the existing system is performing poorly by some 'objective' criteria, yet the party in power prefers to keep the system, there is no reform, unless perhaps new rules can be enacted over the head of the government. Most of the cases covered in this chapter and volume do not have a mechanism for enacting reform over politicians' objections, although in some US states, the potential may exist for reform to come about via citizen-initiated referendum.[4] Some contingency, or series of contingencies, thus must occur before actual reform results, or even before a reform process, as I have defined it here, can begin. The discussion thus far has led us to the possibility that there may be two types of contingency. On the one hand, anomalous outcomes, stemming from the inherent features of the way an electoral system works, may lead the party that perceives the system to be biased against it to seek a change. On the other hand, there may be a public perception that the system is failing to meet normative democratic criteria, and in such a context, one or both major parties may expect to benefit from branding themselves as reformist (or to be punished if seen to be standing in the way of reform).

These two distinct types of contingencies have been noted previously by Reed and Thies (2001) and further elaborated by Shugart and Wattenberg (2001*b*) and Shugart, Moreno, and Fajardo (2007). *Outcome-contingent* factors spur incumbents to vote for reform if they believe they will be better off under new rules; that is, if they prefer the anticipated outcome of the new rules over maintenance of the status quo. *Act-contingent* reasons, on the other hand, are present when politicians expect to benefit from the very act of voting for reform, whether or not they sincerely prefer an alternative electoral system, because the concept of 'reform', albeit perhaps vaguely understood among the public, is itself popular. Both types of contingencies are likely to be present when electoral reforms are enacted, but they may be related to electoral reform in different ways.

If a single opposition party over multiple electoral cycles has been on the receiving end of manifestly anomalous outcomes inherent to the pre-existing electoral system, sentiment may develop within the party to consider electoral reform.[5] If this party comes to power shortly after the anomalies, it may place electoral reform on the government's agenda. A party that has governed frequently in the recent past may be less likely to act on such internal pressures for reform, as its leadership may expect to continue to benefit from seat majorities in the future. A party long out of power, on the other hand, may develop an internal consensus that this coming to power is an opportunity to put in place a less 'biased' electoral system. I do not have the space or inclination here to attempt to model internal party decision-making on reform, but rather my intention is to point out that leaders and activists may have different views of the value of reform (a point also made by Katz 2005). Activists may be more inclined to play the role of 'victim' of a system that has kept them out of power, whereas leaders may be more focused on their short-term enjoyment of 'unbridled power' (as Palmer 1979 put it) that the majoritarian system has at last bestowed upon them.

When might party leaders take the plunge and publicly advocate electoral reform? The short answer is when it is electorally beneficial. This is where both rational strategic interests and act contingencies come in. Party leaders, focused on a campaign, rationally seek to craft campaign messages that will bring more votes to the party and increase their own chances of winning power. Thus, it follows that act contingencies are more likely the more that swing voters might be brought over to the party by its taking on a 'reform' mantle. In this respect, it is probably helpful to the reform cause if there is a generalized sense that democracy is not working as the public expects, which is to say that the normative factors remain in play. It also suggests that voters may not care much about the electoral system, per se, but may respond to a reform message at a more abstract level. It may even be the case, as Katz (2005: 69) suggests, that politicians may find tackling electoral reform as less threatening than

15

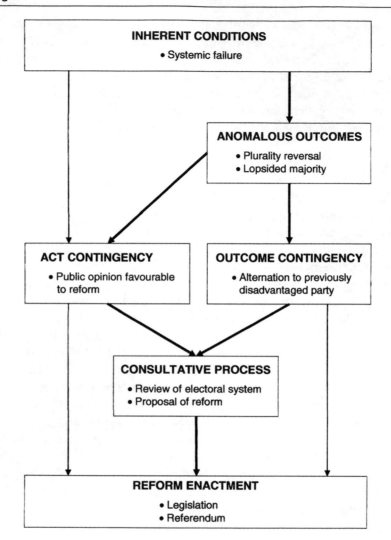

Figure 1.1. A framework for understanding electoral reform

addressing more fundamental political or social problems that have bred the generalized sense of dissatisfaction with politics. Act contingencies are engaged when politicians determine that there is a strategic value in positioning themselves as reformers, whether or not they sincerely favour the reform in question.

Figure 1.1 offers a schematic rendition of the framework. The boxes in the figure depict steps along a path to electoral reform, starting with inherent conditions, passing through anomalous electoral outcomes, and continuing through contingent factors and a consultative process, through to enactment. I am using the concepts of 'consultation' and 'enactment' in much the same way as Blau (Chapter 2) does, although I will not look inside these boxes to the extent that he does. I will focus most of my attention on the upper portion of the figure, on the inherent and contingent factors that precede a decision to initiate a consultative process. A process of (potential) reform could be stopped at any one of these boxes. First, despite the inherent tendencies of the current electoral system to generate anomalous outcomes, they may not occur in practice. Then, having occurred, the previously disadvantaged party may remain disadvantaged by the electoral system, or simply disfavoured by the voters, in which case the outcome contingency does not arrive. Or, voters, perhaps otherwise satisfied with their political process, may not be receptive to a reform message, recent (or even repeated) anomalies notwithstanding, in which case competing parties have no strategic incentive to promote reform (or feel any risk of punishment from cancelling a reform process). Then there is the possibility that a consultative process begins, but that those tasked with review of the electoral system determine that despite the 'anomalies' the FPTP system remains normatively preferred (perhaps with some more minor reforms),[6] and thus no recommendation for major reform is forthcoming. Finally, of course, when a proposed electoral system comes to a decisive vote, the required majority (which may be a super or concurrent majority) may not be reached. Thus there are many obstacles to reform, but the model sketched in Figure 1.1 suggests that the path that leads to (potential) reform enactment runs from inherent conditions, through anomalous outcomes, through both outcome and act contingencies, and then to a consultative process that generates a proposed reform.

In the figure, the dark lines with arrows show the theoretical paths emphasized in this chapter, while the lighter lines indicate potential (but, I argue) less promising paths to electoral reform. For instance, the simplest and most parsimonious explanation of electoral reform would be the step shown on the lower right, with a light arrow connecting the box for 'outcome contingency' with the box at the bottom on 'reform enactment'. In such a scenario, we would have a governing party that perceives itself as disadvantaged by the current system and uses its control of the legislative majority to adopt a new system more to its liking. Such an explanation of reform would be one of pure outcome motivation. The government changes the system because the party in control expects to be better off in future elections under the outcomes expected from an alternative electoral system than from the current system. At least three cases of major electoral reform since 1980 in established democracies fit this pattern: France 1981 and again in 1986, and Italy in 2006. In France 1981 and Italy 2006, governments feared severe electoral losses and adopted a new system intended to minimize those losses. In France 1986, the governing parties expected greater electoral gains under a new (actually, the 'old', pre-1981) system and acted to maximize those gains. However, neither of these electoral-system changes was initiated in a pre-existing FPTP system. More importantly for theoretical purposes, these cases did not involve any process of independent consultation. Why have various governments in various FPTP jurisdictions initiated consultative procedures for possible electoral reform, rather than simply adopt a reform that they perceive as in their own interest? Apparently, the outcome-contingent motivations for electoral-system change are not sufficient for serious consideration of reform to result. They may be necessary—a theme that will be explored below—but they must not be sufficient.

This argument is agnostic about whether governments initiate a process with the several 'hoops' represented by the formation of a consultative process and a subsequent referendum—as opposed to simply using their majority to pass a law changing the electoral system—because they seek to derail a reform that they do not sincerely favour, or because they are seeking 'legitimacy' for a reform they sincerely favour, but fear will be seen as a power grab. Note that in either case, simple outcome motivations are insufficient. In one case, the party is trying to appear 'reformist' while taking steps to minimize the chance that anything actually changes. In the other, the party is using the independent consultation process as a means to get support beyond its own ranks and constituencies, in order to maximize the chance that whatever reform passes will not be reversed if the opposition comes back to power (as, e.g. in France 1981–6 and perhaps Italy 2006). Neither of these explanations—different though they otherwise are—could proceed without popular opinion in favour of reform. Where does such opinion come from? One obvious source is from actual systemic failure that leads to public criticism of the system and a public willingness to consider alternatives. This is where the inherent conditions come in: That is, the presence of systematic flaws in the system makes for tinder brush (an electoral system perceived as failing) that the right spark (an anomaly and/or a formal process of public consultation) can kindle into a fire (replacement of the system). Thus in Figure 1.1, there is a light arrow connecting inherent conditions to the formation of act-contingent motivations for a ruling party to establish a consultative process, but a darker one connecting actual anomalous outcomes to act-contingent factors, suggesting that where there have been actual anomalies, public opinion becomes more receptive to the concept of electoral system to fix a 'broken' system.

If outcome motivations are not sufficient, then there may be an alternative path to reform, via act contingency, whereby the governing party is rewarded by appealing to a pro-reform vote, and hence opens up the process of reform precisely to brand itself as the 'reform' party. It is theoretically possible that this path to reform—depicted by the light arrow from act contingency to enactment—is sufficient, although it is unlikely. That is, while there could be a general public disaffection with the status quo so great that parties tap into the discontent by offering reform options, most likely a governing party also sees a partisan (i.e. outcome-based) advantage from a reformed electoral system. Otherwise, currently enjoying the fruits of electoral victory and the relatively unchecked governance that goes with it under plurality-parliamentary institutions, the party in power would seek to maintain the status quo electoral system (while perhaps steering reformist sentiment in the public down other avenues).[7]

1.2. Case Selection and Reform Processes

Nohlen (1984) observed that major electoral reforms are rare, especially those that shift an electoral system across the competing 'principles' of plurality and proportionality. Yet they do occur. I will leave aside here the many reforms to proportional representation that took place in late nineteenth- and early twentieth-century Europe. Most of those occurred roughly at the same time as suffrage expansions and with the rise of working-class parties (Rokkan 1970; see also Boix 1999). Besides, in very few cases (e.g. Sweden) the starting point was plurality. Rather, in most cases it was a two-round system, which is already more conducive to multiparty (though not proportional) representation than is plurality.

Instead, I shall focus on contemporary democratic jurisdictions, both national and provincial. Perhaps surprisingly, this focus on the contemporary period captures the universe of actual reforms in established democracies from plurality to PR, of which there is one—New Zealand.

Among the 14 cases of 'major electoral reform' that Katz (2005) identifies since 1945, there is no example of reform away from FPTP that my shorter time period misses. Although it is more difficult to be absolutely certain, my case selection also appears to include a large swath (and perhaps the universe) of proposed major reforms in FPTP jurisdictions that have ever had serious official consideration. By focusing on recent decades, my temporal criteria have the further advantage of controlling for cross-era variations in the range of options that are intellectually available[8] and for worldwide trends (economic globalization, rise of 'post-materialism', demise of Communism, etc.) that might increase the likelihood of reform being contemplated in the first place.

The resulting sample of cases includes all cases using the plurality decision rule for the sole or lower house of the legislature, and using this rule in mostly or entirely single-seat districts,[9] provided that there is a jurisdiction-wide party system and that aggregate party vote totals are widely publicized. These criteria do not eliminate very many cases from consideration; however, they do drop the two largest, and thus are worth some further comment. As noted above, the notion that an FPTP system might be perceived as 'failing' when it produces 'anomalous' results rests on there being a jurisdiction-wide political relevance to the aggregate votes totals and their relationship to the partisan distribution of political power in the legislature. Where a very high percentage of votes are cast for regional parties or independents, politics is clearly not about the balance of party strengths across the entire jurisdiction. For instance, in India, in the era since the first electoral defeat of the formerly dominant Congress Party, the electoral process has been characterized by a high number of parties that compete in only one or a few states (Chhibber and Nooruddin 1999; Sridharan 2002). In many elections, these parties collectively have held around half the seats. While India is certainly an important case for the analysis of FPTP more generally, the extent of local and regional politics makes it qualitatively different from all the cases covered in this volume.[10]

The USA, on the other hand, most certainly has a nationwide party system—and it is covered in this volume.[11] However, for US congressional elections, there is no ready reporting of national party vote shares. The percentage of votes obtained by the Democratic and Republican parties is apparently of no political relevance. In fact, there is no single agreed upon source for such data, nor an agreed way to cope with the nontrivial numbers of districts left uncontested by one of the major parties. A quick example will suffice to demonstrate the difficulty of using the US case.

Two governmental sources that produce reports on each congressional election, the Clerk of the House and the Federal Electoral Commission, agree that there was a recent election in which the party with the second most votes won the majority of seats—exactly one of the types of 'anomaly' considered in this chapter. However, they disagree on which election produced this anomaly! One says it was 1996, and the other says it was 2000. In neither case was there any mention of this occurrence in the media to my knowledge. It is hard for an anomaly to be politically relevant—and thus a discussion of possible electoral reform to derive from the experience—if the data are not widely reported, and even harder if two 'official' sources disagree on who won the most votes in the election!

Two other cases have to be excluded for one or both of the reasons that result in the exclusion of India and the USA: Papua New Guinea and the Solomon Islands, neither of which has anything resembling a national party system (see Reilly 2006).[12] Finally, I include only those jurisdictions with over a quarter of a million population, with one exception: Prince Edward Island (PEI). In the interests of coverage of the Canadian case, all that country's provinces are included, even though the smallest has only around 139,000 residents. Thus the cases include Canada and all its provinces, the UK, New Zealand, and the larger Commonwealth Caribbean countries (Bahamas, Barbados, Belize, Jamaica, and Trinidad and Tobago).[13] I also include Botswana, which is generally regarded as having been continuously democratic since independence in 1966.

1.2.1. Tracing Reform Processes

Table 1.1 summarizes the cases included in this analysis. The table also indicates the presence or absence of a consultative process, defined as the establishment of a formal mechanism to review the electoral system and propose an alternative. For those that have had such a process, it indicates the disposition of the process as of mid-2007. The data include 191 elections, 7 of which (3.7%) have been elections that immediately preceded the initiation of a consultative process. The mechanism could be a citizens' assembly, an independent commission, or the creation of a new government agency specifically charged with considering electoral reform. Any of these mechanisms raises the profile of the issue of electoral reform (compared, e.g., to a parliamentary committee or internal party study), thereby suggesting a level of seriousness about, minimally, putting

Table 1.1. Jurisdictions and reform processes

Jurisdiction	Years in data set	Consultative process? (Year, type)	Proposal	Referendum or other action
Alberta	1967–2004	No	—	—
Bahamas	1972–2002	No	—	—
Barbados	1996–2003	No	—	—
British Columbia	1960–2005	Yes (2001, Citizens' Assembly)	STV	57% Yes (defeated; 60% required)
Belize	1979–2003	No	—	—
Botswana	1979–2004	No	—	—
Canada	1957–2006	No	—	—
Jamaica	1959–2002	No	—	—
Manitoba	1973–2003	No	—	—
New Brunswick	1974–2003	Yes (2003, Commission)	MMP	Referendum not currently scheduled
Newfoundland	1975–2003	No	—	—
New Zealand	1960–1993	Yes (1984, Commission)	MMP	54% Yes; MMP in use since 1996
Nova Scotia	1967–2003	No	—	—
Ontario	1963–2003	Yes (2003, Citizens' Assembly)	Pending	Pending
Prince Edward Island	1978–2003	Yes (2003, Commissioner)	MMP	36% Yes (defeated)
Quebec	1960–2003	Yes (2003, government ministry, public consultation)	MMP	Pending
Saskatchewan	1971–2003	No	—	—
Trinidad and Tobago	1966–2002	No	—	—
UK	1959–2005	Yes (1997, Commission)	AV+ (form of MMP)	None

Notes: Proposals and referendum or other action up to date through August 2007. Date for consultative process indicates date of election prior to initiation of the process. For details of the proposed alternative systems, consult Chapter 4 by Massicotte.

Abbreviations: STV: single transferable vote; MMP: mixed-member proportional; AV: alternative vote.

the question on the public agenda. As noted by Blau (Chapter 2), there can be many steps along the path to electoral reform, and governments may at times even use the 'path setting' process to place obstacles to actual reform. Nonetheless, the establishment of a consultative process, as defined here, implies some motivation to signal that alternatives to the status quo are up for debate, whatever obstacles may lie farther down the path.

We see in Table 1.1 that there are six cases of 'reform initiation'; in chronological order (and going by the date at which the government initiating it was elected or re-elected), these are New Zealand (1984), UK (1997), British Columbia (2001), New Brunswick (2003), Ontario (2003), Prince Edward Island (2003), and Quebec (2003). Besides New Zealand, two others have gone as far as a public referendum on reform (British Columbia 2001, Prince Edward Island 2006). Both of these proposals were defeated, although a majority of voters favoured the BC proposal (but short of the mandated 60%). In a third case, New Brunswick, a referendum was scheduled for the spring of 2008, but was cancelled by a new government in 2007 (as discussed later). A second referendum is scheduled in British Columbia (for 2009). The process begun in the UK was aborted: There was an official commission report that recommended an alternative in 1998, but no referendum was scheduled (despite an explicit manifesto commitment in 1997). The other processes have yet to reach the stage of a definitive proposal or the scheduling of a referendum.

The theory sketched above in Figure 1.1 suggests that both outcome and act-contingent motivations must be present for a government in a plurality jurisdiction to initiate a consultative process on the electoral system. The outcome contingency is electoral alternation to a party that has been recently disadvantaged by the electoral system, specifically a party that was on the 'wrong' side of an anomalous outcome in a recent election. The act contingency is the existence of public opinion against the current system to be cultivated by a party that brands itself as 'reformist'.

In order to subject the theory to an empirical test, we need to determine which elections have resulted in anomalous outcomes, whether the disadvantaged party subsequently came to power, and, if so, whether it initiated a consultative process. As noted above, two types of anomalous outcomes are the plurality reversal (when the party with the most seats is different from the party with the most votes) and the lopsided majority (when the opposition is decimated). Let us take up each of these in turn.

Table 1.2 shows the cases of plurality reversals. In the table, these outcomes are shown separately according to whether the party with the most seats had a majority or not. Plurality reversals are likely to be perceived as anomalous, although whether they are in fact is a question that would require analysis of public opinion, newspaper coverage, or other more intensive case analysis than is feasible here. It is possible that those that result in minority situations, rather than a (spurious) majority government,[14] are perceived as non-anomalous in that the party with

Table 1.2. Anomalous outcomes: plurality reversals

Jurisdiction	Year(s)	Alternation in next election?	Terms out of power prior to alternation	Reform initiated?
Majority situations (spurious majorities)				
British Columbia	1996	Yes (2001)	Had not governed	Yes
Belize	1993	Yes (1998)	1	No
New Brunswick	1974	No (re-elected twice)	—	No
Newfoundland	1989	No (re-elected three times)	—	No
New Zealand	1978, 1981	Yes (1984)	3	Yes
Quebec	1966	Yes	1	No
Quebec	1998	Yes (2003)	2	Yes
Saskatchewan	1986	Yes	2	No
Minority situations				
Canada	1957	No	—	No
Canada	1979	Yes (1980)	1 (Less than full term)	No
Nova Scotia	1970	No	—	No
Ontario	1985	No[a]	—	No
Saskatchewan	1999	No	—	No
UK	1974 (February)	No	—	No

[a] Minority government after 1985 election obtained majority in 1987 early election.

the most seats must be cognizant of the preferences of other parties to a degree that a majority government need not be. In some cases, the party with the most seats may be shut out of cabinet anyway, if the party with the most votes forms a coalition or support agreement with a third party. In other cases, the reversal of the vote plurality itself may have resulted from district-level tactical voting, as Blau (2004) suggests for the case of the UK in February 1974. As foreshadowed above, minority situations are unlikely to be seen as symptomatic of systemic failure; even if the votes and seats pluralities are reversed, they are not failures in the sense of placing full cabinet authority in the hands of a majority party that was not the plurality party in votes—the so-called *spurious majorities*.

The table also indicates the result of the next election after the plurality reversal—specifically, whether the disadvantaged party came to power in the next election. Additionally, for cases where this party came to power, the table indicates how many terms it had been out of power. Finally, it indicates whether this party initiated reform. As already indicated, the outcome-based explanation of reform initiation implies that a first step to reform is the alternation to a disadvantaged party. The length of time out of power is a secondary indication of whether a party is likely to perceive itself as disadvantaged. That is, if the party perceives itself to be the 'natural' governing party, it is presumably less likely to see itself as disadvantaged despite having been on the wrong side of a spurious majority in one election. On the other hand, this factor may cut both ways: A party that has never or rarely governed before may interpret its coming to power as evidence that the electoral winds have turned decisively in its favour and it will now become the natural governing party. Thus no firm prediction can be made for the impact of time out of power, so let us proceed to the empirical analysis.

There are nine spurious majorities in the data, as shown in the upper part of Table 1.1.[15] In six of these nine cases, the next election resulted in an alternation to the party that had been on the wrong side of the spurious majority in the previous election. These are the alternation elections in which an outcome-contingent motivation for reform would lead us to expect a reform process to be initiated. As we can see from the table, three of these alternations resulted in a reform process. Obviously, being the party that was previously on the wrong side of a spurious majority is not by itself a strong predictor of whether it will initiate a reform process. We have to look to other factors, as we will do below. In addition, in neither of the two cases in which the 'disadvantaged' party had been out of office for only one term (the term resulting from the spurious outcome) was there reform initiation. One of the two cases with the party having been out of power for two terms and both of the cases of three or more elections out of power resulted in reform initiation.

As for the plurality reversals that resulted in a minority situation, none has led to reform initiation. However, it is not clear whether the absence of reform after these elections is because such situations are inherently less anomalous (as I suggested above), or because the outcome-contingent factor has not been present. In most cases, the next election resulted in a re-election, with a majority, of the minority government that took power after the plurality reversal. In the one exception (Canada in 1979), the alternation that took place was to the party that was the 'natural' governing party, in that the Liberals had been out of office only in the immediate (and shortened) term after plurality reversal. So far, there has been no initiation of a consultative process following a plurality reversal that resulted in a non-majority government (or out of any non-majority government, for that matter); however, we cannot say whether that is because such outcomes are inherently perceived as less anomalous than spurious majorities, or because of the absence of clear outcome-contingent motivations for the 'disadvantaged' party.

The second anomalous outcome that is an inherent possibility under FPTP is the decimation of the opposition—a lopsided majority. Unlike a plurality reversal, this outcome does not lend itself to a clear dichotomy. That is, whether or not an election gives the most seats to the party with the most votes is a binary outcome, but whether the opposition has been 'decimated' or the majority is 'lopsided' is clearly a continuous phenomenon. Nonetheless, we can investigate the cases of most lopsided majorities and determine whether there is any apparent relationship between the decimation of the opposition party and that party's initiation of a reform process if it subsequently comes to power. There are 24 elections in the data set in which the second party obtained less than one eighth of the seats in parliament; in 17 of these, it obtained less than 10%.[16] Looked at in terms of number of seats, rather than percentage, there are 17 cases in which the main opposition party was reduced to five or fewer seats; five of these cases occurred in the six elections in Prince Edward Island from 1989 to 2003.[17] PEI is one of our cases with a reform process. In one case, New Brunswick in 1987, the leading party won every seat; while this province is a case with a reform process, the reform process did not begin until the fourth election after this extreme case of opposition decimation.

Table 1.3 shows all of the cases in the data set in which the main opposition party was left with one eighth of the seats or less. Similar to Table 1.2, it also indicates when (if at all, thus far) this opposition party became the governing party. If alternation to the disadvantaged party occurred, the table also indicates how long the party had been out of power prior to the alternation, just as was done in Table 1.1 for the plurality reversals. Finally, it indicates whether a reform process was initiated or not.

By far the most common occurrence after one of the lopsided majorities shown in Table 1.3 is that the party in power was returned to power in the next election, and usually in the next one after that as well. That is perhaps not surprising, as these outcomes are most likely—and alternations least likely—precisely where one party is electorally dominant. Those lopsided majorities that are of most theoretical interest are those in which there was alternation one or two elections after the decimation of the opposition. The table indicates five cases of alternation within the first two elections after a lopsided majority. Three of these resulted in no reform process, while the other two (New Brunswick and Prince Edward Island, both in 2003) did result in such a process. Another case deserves note: British Columbia initiated a reform process shortly after the 2001

Table 1.3. Lopsided majorities

Jurisdiction	Year	Seat percentage, second party[a]	Alternation followed?	Terms out of power prior to alternation	Reform initiated?
New Brunswick	1987	0.0	No (re-elected twice)	—	No
Alberta	1967, 1975, 1979, 1982, 2001	2.5–9.2	No	—	No
Prince Edward Island	1989, 1993, 2000	3.1–6.3	Yes (1996)	3	Yes, but after party's second re-election (2003)
British Columbia	2001	3.8	No[b]	—	Yes, after this election
Quebec	1970, 1973	5.5–6.5	Yes (1976)	New party (PQ)	No
Botswana	1979, 1984, 1989	6.5–11.8	No	—	No
Barbados	1986, 1999	7.1–11.1	Yes (1994)	2	No
Trinidad and Tobago	1986	8.3	Yes (1991)	1	No
Belize	1998	10.3	No	—	No
New Brunswick	1995	10.9	Yes	3	Yes, but after re-election (2003)
Nova Scotia	1984	11.5	No (re-elected once)	—	No
Jamaica	1993	11.7	No	—	No
Bahamas	1992	12.2	No (re-elected once)	—	No
Saskatchewan	1982	12.5	No[c]	—	No

Notes: Cases of second party having one eighth or less of seats, listed in ascending order of second party seat share.

Abbreviation: PQ: Parti Québécois.

[a] Shown as a range, if multiple elections in same jurisdiction with no electoral reform process.

[b] This was an alternation election, immediately after a plurality reversal (see Table 1.2).

[c] Conservatives were re-elected in 1986, but in a plurality reversal (see Table 1.2).

election. This was the alternation election in which the party that had just been disadvantaged in 1996 by a spurious majority came to power. For that reason, BC is a case that corresponds to the theoretical expectation of reform triggered by alternation to a party that was previously disadvantaged by a plurality reversal, but not to reform triggered by a lopsided majority. Nonetheless, it is likely that the occurrence of these two opposite anomalies in consecutive elections contributed to the BC reform process being carried through to a referendum (see Carty, Blais, and Fournier Chapter 5).[18] As I discuss later in this chapter, any contribution of the 2001 outcome to the reform process would have been in the form of an act contingency, in that now the party in power was one benefiting from an anomalous outcome (and perhaps emerging as a 'natural' governing party), yet following through on a previous commitment to a reform process.

The cases traced in Table 1.3 appear to suggest that lopsided majorities are far less conducive to the initiation of reform than are plurality reversals. Just considering the raw numbers, 3 of 9 spurious majorities have resulted in reform initiation, while only 2 of 25 lopsided majorities have. However, this disparity is largely an artefact of the closeness of electoral competition. Polities that experience lopsided majorities are more likely to have a single party that is electorally dominant, whereas those that experience spurious majorities are almost assured of having close two-party competition. In other words, alternation to the previously disadvantaged party, a factor I have argued is crucial to starting a reform process, is more likely in an election following a spurious majority than in an election following a lopsided majority. When we confine ourselves to those cases of anomaly in which there was alternation within two elections, spurious majorities result in reform initiation in two of six cases, while lopsided majorities in two of five. These frequencies are too low to infer any difference between the reform propensities of alternations following one or the other type of anomaly. Pooling the data from Tables 1.2 and 1.3 gives us a reform frequency of 4 out of 11 (36%) of all alternations within two elections of an anomalous majority. This contrasts to two cases of reform initiation in the other 43 elections (4.7%) in which one (non-anomalous) majority was followed by a different one. There are no cases of reform where either the incumbent or the post-alternation parliament contained no majority party ($n = 14$). In other words, alternations after anomalous majorities are more than seven times as likely to lead to an electoral reform process than are other alternations. Minority situations appear to be not at all conducive to reform initiation, perhaps surprisingly.[19]

Considering the time out of power of the previously disadvantaged party, the results of lopsided majorities are quite similar to those for spurious majorities. There is no reform when the party had been out of power for just one or two terms prior to the alternation, but there was reform in two cases in which the party had been out of power for three years. However, we also have one case in which the party in question had never governed before and did not initiate reform: The Parti Québécois (PQ) in 1976, which is very much the epitome of a new party that would be expected to see its coming to power as a sign of a decisive shift of the political winds in its favour. The case of Quebec is discussed further below.

The discussion so far leaves us with two cases of reform initiation that did not follow an anomalous majority of either type. These cases are UK 1997 and Ontario 2003. Both of these jurisdictions experienced the lesser anomaly of a plurality reversal that led to a minority government; however, in neither case does the trajectory follow the theoretical expectation. In fact, in both cases the incumbent government after the plurality reversal called an early election and was returned to power with a majority.[20] Within the theory advanced here, then, these two cases of reform process are totally unexpected. They will be discussed further in a later section of this chapter.

1.3. The Performance of Plurality Systems: Assessing the Inherent Conditions for Reform

As Figure 1.1 sketched, the framework I am presenting in this chapter suggests that inherent conditions for systemic failure provide two 'assists' to a reform process. On the one hand, they make the occurrence of an anomaly more likely because the system is not providing the normatively expected relationship between votes and seats. On the other hand, the presence of inherent conditions—performance inconsistent with the normative democratic model—may lead to public criticism of the system itself. The occurrence of anomalies is likely to generate within the disadvantaged party an outcome-contingent motivation for reform, as discussed in Section 1.2. The presence of a public perception that the system has failed may create conditions in which one or more parties can benefit electorally from taking up the cause of electoral reform—an act-based motivation.

In this section, I situate the reform cases within a broader comparative context than I have done so far. Up to now our starting point has been the actual occurrence of anomalous majorities (spurious or lopsided), to see what subset of these outcomes has led to the initiation of a reform process. Now it is time to situate these cases of anomaly and reform into a larger sample of the universe of plurality elections. The question to ask here is, can we identify jurisdictions and time periods where the performance of the plurality system is 'extreme' in terms of producing an exaggerated relationship between how people vote and how their representation is distributed across the competing political parties?

In order to identify elections that deviate from a 'norm' we have to identify a norm. At one level, this is impossible to do without detailed jurisdiction-level knowledge of what people actually expect in a given political context. That is, what seems 'odd' and unjustifiable in one country or province might seem 'normal' or at least acceptable in another. Voters might even come to accept some comparatively high degree of distortion in votes-to-seats conversion. Unfortunately, at present, I am not aware of a way to measure normative views of how the plurality system should work across 19 distinct polities.[21] Thus I will adopt a global perspective, based on existing political-science models of how electoral systems are expected to behave.

In previous sections, I have argued that the plurality electoral system is inherently prone to failure to deliver on the basic performance expectations on which the normative argument for the system is based. The normative case for plurality is based on the assumption that the system will generate a clearly identifiable and accountable majority for the plurality party and a strong opposition to monitor that majority and serve as a potential prospective majority at the next election. When the system is parliamentary, this normative expectation from the electoral system further implies a 'majoritarian' pattern of governance with clearly identifiable Government and Opposition. The plurality system has inherent limitations in fulfilling these expectations because its mechanics translate votes into seats not on a jurisdiction-wide basis, but rather in dozens or hundreds of local district contests. When the variance in party votes across districts is either unusually high or unusually low, anomalous outcomes may result, including spurious or lopsided majorities. Such anomalies may focus the attention of both the 'victimized' party and the public on the failure of the system, thereby setting the stage for the contingencies that may result in reform away from plurality.

How, then, do we identify plurality systems that are 'failing'? We need a method of identifying a theoretically expected distribution of seats for the leading parties, for a given jurisdiction-wide votes distribution. That is, we want a mechanism of taking aggregate votes and estimating seats, on the assumption that the popular vote indeed tells us something meaningful about voters' preferences for which party should govern the jurisdiction in question. Of course, to the extent that voters vote on more local considerations, the assumptions underlying such a method break down. Nonetheless, it is hardly practical to collect and analyse district-level votes' data—or, even more meaningfully, district-level voter preference data—across nearly 200 elections in nearly 20 jurisdictions. The method of using aggregate data and a 'politics-blind' estimating technique thus has the advantage of practicality, but it also has the advantage of affording an easy method of identifying elections, or sequences of elections, that deviate from the sort of relationship between votes and seats (and hence political power) that would be typical under plurality rule. Elections thus identified would be cases that are potentially ripe for systemic failure, and for the sort of public-opinion context in which act-based motivations could impel parties to try to brand themselves as 'reformist'. The ability of parties to exploit a reputation for being reformist for electoral gain is greatest if voters hold normative expectations about the relationship of political power to the popular vote—or can be encouraged by a 'disadvantaged' party to develop such expectations.

The method used here, then, is to start with the premise that, barring an extreme degree of local variance of the vote (which could be a sign that electoral politics is not primarily a jurisdiction-wide process),[22] there ought to be a systematic relationship between votes and seats. It has been known for some time that there is indeed a systematic relationship, on average, of the ratio of the two largest parties in seats to their ratio in votes. The earliest articulation of this relationship is the famous *cube law* (see Kendall and Stuart 1950), which posits that cubing the ratio of the votes (v_1/v_2) received by the top two parties yields approximately the ratio of parliamentary seats that they win (s_1/s_2):

$$\frac{s_1}{s_2} = \left(\frac{v_1}{v_2}\right)^3$$

While the cube law expresses an empirical, not normative, relationship, it captures a key aspect of the normative expectation: The largest party will obtain a significant boost in seats relative to its lead in votes, with the resulting effect, in a parliamentary system, of ensuring clarity of governmental responsibility. It has also been known for some time, with respect to British elections, that the empirical relationship was not specifically a cube, but perhaps another, smaller exponent. For instance Laasko and Taagapera (1979) proposed that a two-and-half-power law might be more accurate for the UK. Taagepera and Shugart (1989: 165) generalized this power-exponent law as follows:

$$\left(\frac{s_1}{s_2}\right) = \left(\frac{v_1}{v_2}\right)^n \tag{1.1}$$

and they further suggested that the exponent, n, could be estimated by

$$n = \frac{\log V}{\log E} \tag{1.2}$$

where V is the total number of voters and E is the number of electoral districts in which the plurality rule is applied.[23] For recent UK elections, this equation generates an exponent of 2.6 or 2.7, which is slightly closer to the notion of a 'two-and-a-half-power' law than to a cube law. The use of the Taagepera-Shugart generalized seat–vote equation allows us to incorporate variations across jurisdictions in the voters-to-representatives ratio. Recognizing this variance is important, because many of the jurisdictions that use plurality have assemblies that are rather 'undersized' (e.g. several Canadian provinces and Caribbean island states), while a few are 'oversized' (principally the UK).[24] In addition, the cube law is obviously based on an assumption of a two-party system. However, the reality is that few actual plurality jurisdictions have strict two-party competition. In fact, across all 191 elections in this data set, the mean effective number of electoral parties is 2.57, with a range from 1.67 to 4.09. Thus I use the extended form of the seat–vote equation (Taagepera and Shugart 1989: 188–91), which enters the effective number of parties into the equation.[25] This extended form thus allows us to estimate what the seat share of a given party 'should be' for a given vote's fragmentation (and assembly size and number of votes cast). Thus, while it is 'blind' to the politics of an election with respect to local issues or local-level voter coordination, it takes the party system itself as a given. Close analysis of individual cases (jurisdictions or elections) might reveal actual or potential 'coordination' that affected the effective number of parties (as discussed for New Zealand by Vowles in Chapter 6). However, for aggregate data analysis, we will take the fragmentation of the party system as exogenous.[26] The question thus is, for a given level of vote fragmentation, how closely does the outcome conform to the seat–vote equation's estimate?

Obviously, party leaders and activists—and especially voters—are not aware of the specific exponent or of the role of the size of the assembly and the voting population in producing it. Nonetheless, the inputs into the generalized 'exponent rule' define a baseline for analysis and potentially for normative criticisms of the outcome. Elections that deviate from the baseline—that is, have a much smaller or larger seat ratio (s_1/s_2) than they should have for a given votes' ratio (v_1/v_2), voting population, and number of electoral districts—are relatively more prone to producing anomalous outcomes, particularly in close elections. Such outcomes may trigger outcome-based motivations within the disadvantaged party, and also influence public opinion to be receptive to reform (as depicted in Figure 1.1). Electoral systems that are 'repeat offenders' against baseline expectations may generate criticism from within the under-represented[27] party or from non-partisan advocacy organizations, editorial writers, and others that the electoral system is not working as expected, enhancing the act-based motivations for reform.

Figure 1.2 shows the 191 plurality elections in the data set, with the horizontal axis being the actual ratio of the seats of the two largest parties (s_1/s_2). The vertical axis shows the expected ratio (s_1'/s_2'), based on the seat–vote equation. Elections that produced a single-party parliamentary majority are shown with triangles, while those that returned no party with a majority are shown with daggers. A diagonal line identifies actual two-party seat distributions that are exactly consistent with the estimation of the seat–vote equation[28]:

$$\frac{s_1}{s_2} = \frac{s_1'}{s_2'}$$

The data in Figure 1.2 always take s_1 to be the party with the most *votes*, and to clarify this and because in a subsequent application to individual jurisdictions, we will be concerned with the party with the most seats (given that they are not always the same party), let us add to the subscript an indicator not only of the rank of the party but also v to indicate that it is the rank in votes (or, elsewhere, s to indicate rank in seats). If this party did not obtain the most seats, then the actual

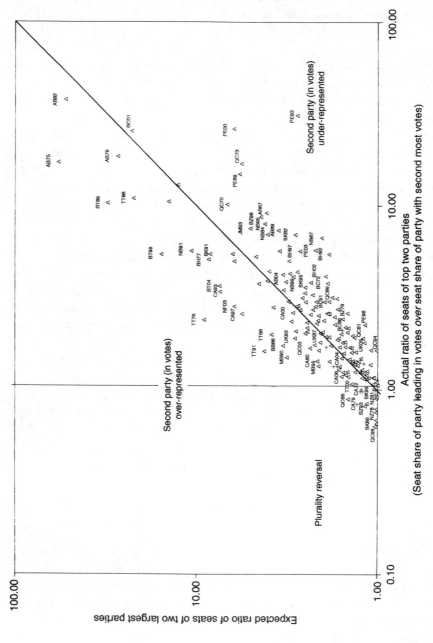

Figure 1.2. Actual and expected seat ratios of two largest parties

ratio (s_{1v}/s_{2v}) will be less than 1.00 notwithstanding that the seat–vote equation, like the normative case for plurality rule itself, always expects a seat ratio of greater than 1.00, such that the party with the most votes is also the party with the most seats. It is obvious at a glance that a large majority of elections are quite close to the diagonal line that indicates an outcome that is quite consistent with the estimation of the seat–vote equation. However, there are several elections with notable deviations.

The graphing of the expected and actual seat ratios allows us to see the interplay of election closeness and the inherent tendency of a given jurisdiction's electoral system to produce anomalies. The closer an election is in votes, the closer will be the expected ratio of the top two parties in seats. Thus elections near the horizontal axis are close elections. As an election with a given *expected* seat ratio deviates from the diagonal (at which $s_{1v}/s_{2v} = s'_{1v}/s'_{2v}$), the party with the second highest vote total is, relative to the equation estimate, over-represented (cases dispersed to the left, including the plurality reversals) or under-represented (cases dispersed to the right).

Only elections that are quite close in votes are likely to result in a plurality reversal: In the data set, there are just two elections that saw the leading parties separated by as many as five percentage points in the vote, yet reversed in their rank in seats (Quebec in 1966 and Canada in 1979). What is now apparent, but was not previously, is that some lopsided majorities occur in relatively close elections, too, when compared to the complete set of lopsided majorities. For instance, whereas the most lop-sided majority depicted on the graph—we can't depict the New Brunswick sweep of 1987—was Alberta 1975, this election was actually a case of the second party being very slightly *over*-represented, relative to what the expectation derived from the seat–vote equation.[29] However, some far closer elections also produced lopsided seat results, and the seat–vote equation, and its graphed results in Figure 1.2, allow us to identify such cases at a glance. For instance, this method allows us to correctly identify the anomaly-prone electoral system of Prince Edward Island. The 1996 election, the first under a major redistricting arrangement, had resulted in a relatively close election by the standards of the province. The leading parties were at 47.4 to 44.8% in votes; however, the seats' result was quite lopsided, at 67 to 30%. This correctly identifies the system as overly responsive, and indeed a 10-point swing in the popular vote in 2000 resulted in an almost 30-point swing in seats, and the near elimination of the second party from parliament (one seat).[30]

The more a case appears off the $(s_{1v}/s_{2v} = s'_{1v}/s'_{2v})$ diagonal, then, but in the lower portion of the graph where elections are closer in votes, the more prone it is to anomalous outcomes. For instance, there are five elections in Quebec since 1966 with an expected seat ratio of 1.8 or lower, but an actual seat ratio that is considerably less or greater than the expected: two to the left side and three to the right side. Note that the 1994 election is one of those on the right side of the diagonal (i.e. for the votes ratio, the result was somewhat lopsided as the party with the second most votes was under-represented) and then the 1998 election appears on the other side (i.e. the party with the second most votes was over-represented—so much that it won a spurious majority).

The graph can also identify jurisdictions that could be vulnerable to future anomalies, if a subsequent election were to be closer, but existing patterns of bias for or against the party with the second most votes remain.[31] For instance, there is a cluster of points representing majority governments just to the right side of the vertical line that indicates an expected seat ratio of 1.00, but well above the diagonal. These are cases in which a hypothetical vote's result considerably closer than these actual elections could easily result in a plurality reversal if the second party (in votes) continued to be over-represented. The cluster includes New Zealand 1966; of course, as we know, a few elections later New Zealand witnessed two consecutive spurious majorities. The cluster also includes the Canadian federal election of 2006, Nova Scotia's election of 2006, and the 2000 election in Trinidad and Tobago. These jurisdiction thus could be said to be on an 'anomaly watch' in that they are failing to give the largest party the large seat bonus that is usually expected in a majoritarian system—a performance that may appear to be a 'failure' only in unusually close elections.

In Section 1.4, the same methodology used here to analyse the votes-to-seats conversion process is applied to sequences of elections in several jurisdictions that have had, or have not had, a reform process.

1.4. Analysis of Trajectories of Inherent Conditions and Reform or Non-Reform

Deriving seat projections from the votes for the leading parties via the seat–vote equation (in its extended form), we can now inspect the performance of individual jurisdictions over time. The data plots in this section depict three variables that have been key to the discussion throughout. The first is an inherent condition: under-representation of the second largest party, relative to what would normally be expected given the ratio of the two largest parties' votes and the other factors that enter into seat–vote equation.[32] The use of this variable, and its calculation based on the second party in *seats*, allows us to place the underlying inherent factor that produces either a lopsided or a spurious majority on a single scale. A lopsided majority results when the second party has a substantially smaller share of seats than it would be expected to have won, based on the vote ratio of the two leading parties. A spurious majority, similarly, results when the second party in parliament has received fewer seats than expected—in this case less than the majority that it was expected to have on the basis of having been the party with the most votes. Second-party seat deficit is thus operationalized as

$$s_{2s} - s'_{2s}$$

As suggested above, the under-representation of the second party is most symptomatic of *systemic* failure (as opposed to simply a single very dominant party) when the election is relatively close, because closeness magnifies the impact of the over- or under-responsiveness of the votes-to-seats conversion. Vote margin is operationalized as

$$v_{1s} - v_{2s}$$

In each jurisdiction's plot the lower part shows $s_{2s} - s'_{2s}$ and the identity of the party with the second most assembly seats, while the upper part shows the closeness of elections. The plots also indicate elections with alternations, because only with an alternation following some anomalous results do we expect electoral reform to be placed on the agenda by the government. A vertical line marks the election, if any, following which the government initiates a consultative process.

The first set of plots, Figure 1.3, shows four jurisdictions in which referenda on electoral reform have been held or scheduled: British Columbia, New Zealand, Prince Edward Island, and New Brunswick. (In the latter case, the referendum was subsequently cancelled, as discussed below.) In the first two cases, an electoral reform process was initiated after an alternation to the party that had been disadvantaged in preceding close elections that had resulted in spurious majorities. The second set represents two cases where initiation of a reform process occurred two or more elections after an alternation, in jurisdictions that had seen periodic lopsided majorities.

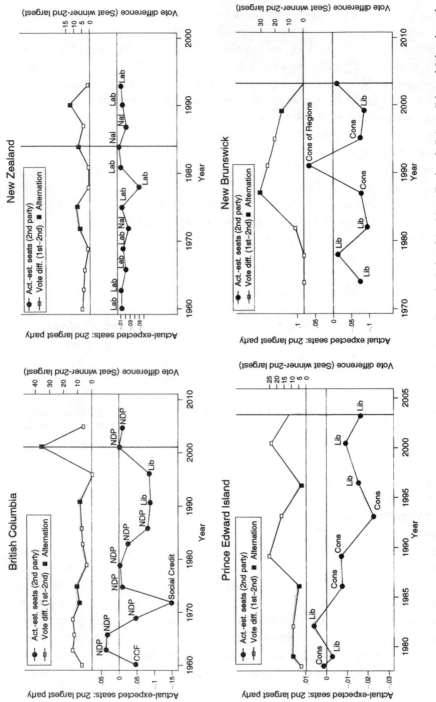

Figure 1.3. Second-party under-representation and election closeness: British Columbia, New Zealand, Prince Edward Island, and New Brunswick

In the case of British Columbia, three straight elections produced a substantial under-representation for the second party, and in the last two of these that was the same party—the Liberals. To make matters worse from the Liberals' point of view, but also for overall systemic performance, the third election of the sequence not only was close but also was one in which the Liberals were on the wrong end of a spurious majority (as revealed by the dipping of the vote-margin trend line visibly below zero). Prior to the 2001 election—in which the Liberal party won control of the provincial government for the first time ever[33]—the Liberals indicated that they would convene a citizens' assembly on the electoral system if elected. As the graph shows, it was not only elected but was elected in a landslide (though not actually over-represented, relative to seat–vote expectations). A referendum on electoral reform was held concurrent with the 2005 provincial election, and while the 'British Columbia–single transferable vote'[34] proposal obtained over 57% of the votes, this was short of the mandated three fifths.

In New Zealand, the Labour party had been out of power for three consecutive elections (and seven of eight) leading up to their winning a majority of seats in 1984. For most of this sequence, the party had been somewhat under-represented. Then suddenly in 1978, its deviation from expectation dropped dramatically in an election in which it obtained the plurality of votes. Then 1981 was an even closer election, and while Labour was not under-represented by much in this election, this election represented the second straight election in which the party found itself on the wrong side of a spurious majority. These two elections thus can be seen as back-to-back examples of a significant bias against the party, implying that even when Labour exceeded National in votes the electoral system could not be counted on to give Labour a majority in parliament. Not surprisingly, then, Labour promised in the 1984 campaign to appoint a Royal Commission to review the electoral system if it won. The New Zealand case, which is so far our only case of actual adoption of PR, is discussed in depth by Vowles (Chapter 6).

The next jurisdiction depicted is Prince Edward Island. The enormous gap between what would be a reasonable expectation for the second party and its actual representation can be seen clearly in the bottom part of the figure, with a substantial decline in the second party's representation relative to expectation between 1982 and 1996. In particular, the electoral system seems to punish the Conservatives after they lost power in the election of 1982. Then the 1996 election saw an alternation that put the Conservative party back in power. It was also a relatively close election, compared to those that had preceded it, and the 1996 election is noteworthy for one other reason: It marked the first election in PEI under significantly revised boundary delimitation. And, compared to previous elections, 1996 saw a lessening of the gap between the second party's actual and expected seat shares. However, as discussed earlier and visible in this graph, PEI remained an ongoing case of considerable under-representation of the second party, even after an alternation changed which party that was. The Conservative government put electoral reform on its agenda for campaign leading up to the 2003 election, in which it was returned to power. However, a referendum on a Commission's recommendation of a mixed-member proportional (MMP) system[35] was soundly defeated in 2005.

In New Brunswick, all but two elections from 1974 to 1999 produced chronic under-representation of the party with the second most seats. The first of these, 1974, resulted in a spurious majority. The Conservatives had benefited from the 1974 reversal of the electoral plurality in a close election, and they retained power through the next two elections, one of which (1978) was also very close. Then the Conservative party split and its splinters lost badly to the Liberals in 1987, when the new governing party wound up with all 58 seats in the provincial legislature. The Conservative party took power again in another election, 1999, that was not close (though it was closer than any election in the province since 1982). In the alternation election of 1999 the second party again was significantly under-represented, thereby suggesting that the bias in the system is genuinely systemic, and not simply a bias against a particular party. The Conservative government made a public commitment to study electoral reform in the run-up to the 2003 election, when it was returned to power. The consultative process resulted in a proposal for a new mixed-member proportional electoral system, and in 2006 the government announced a referendum on this proposal would be held in the spring of 2008. However, in the meantime, the government called an early election, which it lost—in seats; the governing Conservatives won a plurality of votes, but the election produced a spurious majority. The new government announced it would cancel the referendum on the electoral system. This interesting sequence will be discussed below in the context of act contingencies.

The next two cases, in Figure 1.4, are Canada's largest provinces, Quebec and Ontario. The plot for Quebec shows a chronic under-representation of the party with the second most seats over a period beginning with

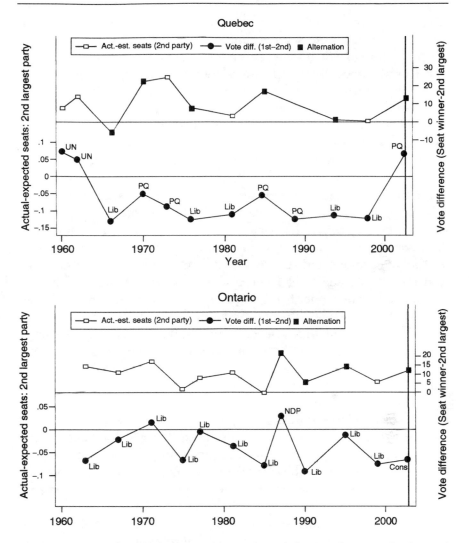

Figure 1.4. Second-party under-representation and election closeness: Quebec and Ontario

the 1966 spurious majority won by the Union National (once a major party that was about to be replaced by the rising Parti Québécois as the main challenger to the Liberals) and culminating in a second spurious majority 32 years later won by the PQ. Both the Liberals and the PQ have been the under-represented party at times, implying the problem is systemic, although the Liberals in particular are harmed by what Massicotte

(Chapter 4) notes is a 'linguistic gerrymander', albeit an unintentional one. The Liberals were severely under-represented in two consecutive elections, both of which were very close in the provincial popular vote.[36] The Liberals proceeded to appoint a ministry in charge of preparing a proposal after winning the 2003 election. (I discuss the 2003 campaign below in Section 1.5.)

In Ontario, the Liberals have been the second largest party in parliament after every election since 1951 (the plot shows elections as far back as 1963), with the exception of 1975 (when they fell to third) and 1987, when they held a one-term majority. In 1985, they had been able to form a minority government despite having the second most seats, which in turn they held in spite of having the plurality of votes. Thus the 1985 election could be considered somewhat anomalous, although for reasons discussed above a plurality reversal that results in a minority situation is clearly less anomalous than one that results in a (spurious) majority. And indeed, the ability of Liberals to form a government resulted in the plurality vote-winner being in power.[37] The Liberal party had been somewhat under-represented in 1985 and 1990, both with respect to their vote share and with respect to seat–vote expectations. The party was under-represented yet again in 1999. It initiated a process leading to a citizens' assembly and eventual referendum on electoral reform after winning a seat majority—for only the second time in 60 years—in 2003. The Ontario case is not one that has any clear example of systemic failure. Thus a reform process in the province is not expected. The Liberal party had been out of power in most preceding elections and consistently punished in the vote-to-seats conversion process, so it could be said to have outcome motivations for undertaking a review and possible reform of the electoral system, but the inherent factors for reform were weak.[38]

The final set of graphs, in Figure 1.5, shows three cases that experienced inherent conditions for potential reform, yet no reform process was initiated. The fourth case shown in the figure is another jurisdiction with a theoretically unanticipated reform process. In the upper left, we see the case of Newfoundland, where the Conservative party was significantly under-represented in four straight elections. The first of these elections was a spurious majority for the Liberal party. However, the Liberals were returned to power and none of the subsequent elections was close. When the Conservatives returned to power in 2003, it was a landslide in votes; they were actually under-represented relative to expectations (suggesting that the bias is partisan-specific rather

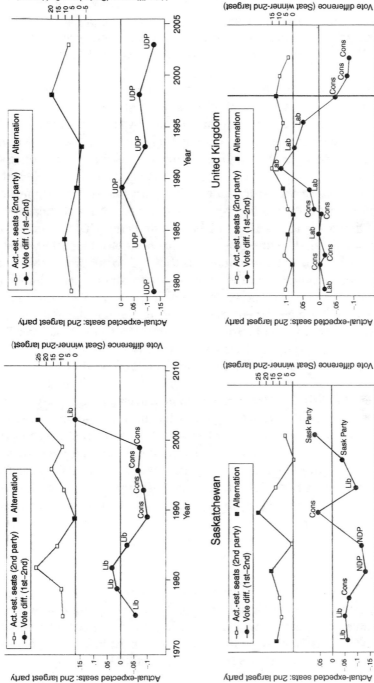

Figure 1.5. Second-party under-representation and election closeness: Newfoundland, Belize, Saskatchewan, and the UK

than systemic), yet the Conservatives still won over 70% of the seats. The absence of alternation soon after the reversed plurality of 1989 means the reform-promoting contingent factors were not present in Newfoundland. No reform process would be expected, and none has resulted.

In Belize, there is a systemic tendency to under-represent the second largest party, evident in every election since 1979, with the exception of 1989, in spite of frequent alternation in power. It is worth noting that this tendency to exaggerate vote swings in the less close elections is not simply a result of the small assembly size, as the number of seats available is taken into account by the seat–vote equation.[39] In 1993, the second party was on the wrong side of a remarkable spurious majority: The People's United Party (PUP) won a majority of votes, yet there was a spurious alternation to the United Democratic Party (UDP), which won a majority of seats. The close loss in the previous election, 1989, would not have been much of an incentive for the UDP to advocate reform, as its 49% of the vote indicated that it would have an excellent chance at a majority government of its own in the near future, and when it finally did win a majority government despite losing the popular vote by 2.5 percentage points, it was enjoying the benefits of a systemic failure. The PUP expanded its already existing votes' majority in 1998 and retained a smaller one in 2003, thus apparently keeping reform off the agenda.

In Saskatchewan, there have been significant swings from election to election in the deviation from the second party's expected seat share. Twice (1991 and 2003) the second party has been over-represented relative to expectation, but in most elections there has been a significant bias against the second party. The identity of that party has varied over time, suggesting the flaw is systemic, not a party-specific bias. The New Democratic Party (NDP), which has been the governing party in all but two elections in the province since 1971, was on the wrong side of a spurious majority in 1986. This could be seen as a case that would generate interest in reform, but for the NDP this was an aberrant election—a rare close election and only its second election out of power. It returned to power comfortably in the 1991 landslide. When another reversed plurality occurred in 1999—this time resulting in a minority situation, rather than a majority—the party on the losing side was the new Saskatchewan Party,[40] which proceeded to lose the next election. Thus the NDP in Saskatchewan has had little interest in electoral reform, and the Saskatchewan Party has had no opportunity to promote it even if it wanted to.[41] Whether it would have outcome-based reasons to initiate reform were it to come to power is ambiguous. It was on the wrong side of a plurality reversal in 1999, but as the graph shows, in 2003, it was actually over-represented, and might have been a few percentage points of the vote short of being on the winning side of a plurality reversal.[42]

Finally, the last plot shows the UK. The Labour party contested the 1997 election with a manifesto commitment to consider electoral reform, and upon winning power it appointed a panel popularly known as the Jenkins Commission. However, as the plot shows, there was no systemic failure in the UK prior to 1997, although there was the brief parliamentary term after the February 1974 election in which Labour ruled in a minority government despite being second in votes. After 1979, the Labour party found itself in opposition to the Conservatives of Margaret Thatcher and then John Major over four straight elections, but the party was actually over-represented relative to the estimates of the seat–vote equation. Nor were these close elections. Thus the British electoral reform upon Labour's return to power is not expected by the theory. The Labour party had been out of power for some time, but not because of any systemic bias against it. Perhaps it is not surprising that the reform proposal was tepid (i.e. minimally proportional by design) and the Prime Minister's reaction was to shelve it. Nonetheless, the theory I have advanced here does not say that tepid proposals should result in the absence of either inherent conditions or electoral-system-derived disadvantages to the party initiating consultation. It says instead that consultative processes that may result in fundamental electoral reform should happen only in the presence of such factors. The theory does, however, suggest that the absence of systemic bias (an inherent condition) would imply little public pressure for reform—this is an act-based contingency, which I return to in Section 1.5.

If there is a bias in the UK system, it appears not to be systemic, but rather partisan, as detailed by Blau (Chapter 2). As can be seen in the plot, the second largest party was under-represented only after the Conservatives became that party. The 2005 election shows the second party well below expectations, in a relatively lopsided majority, given the vote ratio (note the presence of the 'UK05' point in Figure 1.2: expected seat ratio of 1.19, but actual ratio of 1.80). As a result, the UK may be on a 'watch list' now for a bias that could lead the Conservatives to come around to the idea of electoral reform—especially if they lead in votes in a future election, but Labour retains the seat plurality, or majority. The inherent conditions for a plurality reversal are present, if the election is close enough to produce such an outcome.

1.5. Sustaining a Commitment to the Reform Process: Act Contingencies

The bulk of my analysis thus far has focused on the underlying conditions for the initiation of a consultative process that might lead to replacement of FPTP with some form of proportional representation. As I have noted, there may be many obstacles on the path between initiation of consultation on reform and the holding of a referendum or other final decision point at which reform might be enacted; moreover, the very path itself may be chosen by the governing party in a manner that either facilitates or makes less likely an ultimate change to the electoral system (see Chapter 2 by Blau). One of the elements of the theory I have advanced here is that a governing party under FPTP is almost by its very nature likely to be equivocal (perhaps as a result of internal disagreements) over the prospect of the enactment of a proportional system. On the one hand, it may have been disadvantaged by the FPTP system when in the opposition in the recent past (providing it outcome-contingent motivation). On the other hand, it is now in power, and enjoying the seat bonus and (in a parliamentary system) unchecked executive power, thanks to the existing electoral system. Why would a party that is suddenly advantaged follow through on a stated interest in reform and actually risk that it may never again be in such a strong position over other parties in parliament? A premise of the theory is that a governing party under FPTP is more likely to continue the process if there is favourable public opinion such that a commitment to reform—the very act of promoting it—is electorally beneficial, or perhaps more to the point, if back-pedalling on reform might be electorally detrimental. This section will attempt to probe the plausibility of this act-contingent explanation of when a reform process moves forward to a final decision, and when it does not. In doing so, it focuses on the period after the previously disadvantaged party has come to power, but before a referendum has been voted on. This is the period in which the now-ruling party might be able to drop the issue of reform if it thought it could get away with doing so, now that it is the advantaged party. It is also the period before we have evidence from actual voter behaviour as to whether the electorate favours a specific reform proposal. If parties act to a significant degree out of interest, and not out of normative commitments with respect to the issue of electoral reform, this is the most perilous period for electoral reform.

To address the notion that following through on a reform commit-ment is more likely when act-based factors are present than when they are absent, ideally we would undertake an extensive analysis of public-opinion data, party manifestos, and newspaper and other media atten-tion to the issue of electoral reform. However, given current space and resource limitations, it is not feasible to do so in depth for all the cases covered here. However, the chapters of this volume provide evidence of the presence (or absence) of act-contingent factors in four cases: New Zealand (Chapter 6), British Columbia (Chapter 5), Quebec (Chapter 4), and the UK (Chapter 2). I will review the evidence from these case stud-ies. In addition, for these and other cases, I will offer some (necessarily incomplete) original research into campaigns for which the previously disadvantaged party came to power and any other elections that came thereafter, but before an electoral reform referendum. While I do not have any direct evidence of the degree to which act-based factors were present, I do have evidence of parties acting (or not) as if they *believe* such factors are present. That is, if parties place electoral reform in election manifestos, and especially if both major parties do so, then it suggests that they are seeking to cultivate a pro-reform vote or to avoid being branded as anti-reform. If, on the other hand, they fail to go to the electorate advertising their reformist credentials, they may believe there is no pro-reform vote to be cultivated or no danger of electoral retribution from backing down from any previous commitments they have made to advance the cause of electoral reform.

New Zealand is the one jurisdiction to have enacted electoral reform (and to have held several subsequent elections under a PR system). The record in New Zealand is clear that act-contingent factors were present: The two leading parties found themselves competing over which one was more sincere about reforming the electoral system, even though there were various indicators that the real answer was that neither of them wanted such a sweeping reform as the Royal Commission had recommended. An initial contingency of the assumption of power by a previously disadvantaged party was necessary for the Royal Commission to be appointed in 1985. But it was not until 1993 that the referendum on adopting a mixed-member proportional system was finally held. I will not extensively review the history of the reform here (see Chapter 6 by Vowles; I also draw on Denemark 2001 and Nagel 1998). The Commission made an unexpected but resounding recommendation for MMP, after which both parties seemed more determined to delay than enact the proposal. Had it not been for the unpopularity of the radical economic reforms begun by the same Labour government and continued by its National successors after 1990, the issue might have died. But the issue of the electoral system, which was clearly tied up with the degree of unchecked power with which these parties implemented drastic economic policy change, became a campaign wedge. In the run-up to the 1987 election, the Labour PM David Lange committed what was either a gaffe or a crafty attempt to catch his opponent off guard (depending on whose version one buys) by promising a referendum, which it never held, giving National an issue to use against it in 1990. With both parties now having committed—apparently reluctantly—to allow a vote on reform, the issue had taken on a momentum of its own. As Vowles (Chapter 6) notes, during this period in which voters felt their single-party governments had begun to violate an 'implicit social contract' not to deviate from their own pre-election manifestos, New Zealanders' democratic norms appear to have shifted: A model of democracy involving coalitions and consensus was now appealing. When given the chance, voters directed the government to enact the Royal Commission recommendation. The New Zealand case thus offers a perfect illustration of act-contingent factors at work, as both parties showed little serious interest in allowing a definitive referendum, yet circumstances following the publication of a formal recommendation for reform offered the major parties electoral advantages to be gained from furthering the reform process—and potential retribution from standing in the way.

The lesson of the New Zealand events is that act contingencies, in the form of political points to be scored by appearing to be 'reformist' in a context of popular discontent with the status quo, may be necessary to impel the process forward. Outcome-contingencies in the form of a previously disadvantaged party seeking reform to improve its position are not sufficient. The contrasting case of the UK suggests why. There, too, a Labour party initiated a consultative process on the electoral system. The possibility of reforms had been placed on the internal party agenda as a result of the long shutout at the hands of an opposing party that never came close to a majority of votes, yet pursued a dramatic neoliberal economic agenda. The concept of reform also appealed to some party leaders who looked forward to potential 'Lib–Lab' cooperation in the future (Chapter 2 by Blau; see also Farrell 2001b: 526–7). The incoming Labour government in 1997 followed through on its commitment to initiate a consultative process. However, the Jenkins Commission recommendations, issued in 1998, languished, despite a previous Joint Consultative

Committee report in 1996 in which the Labour and Liberal parties said that they believed there should be a referendum before the end of the life of the parliament elected in 1997. The large Labour majorities elected in 1997 and re-elected in 2001 (on barely 40% of the vote) thus offer a prime example of a party that toys with reform when long out of power, but finds a renewed enjoyment in having large and generally unfettered parliamentary majorities once back in power.[43] I have suggested that significant anomalies or under-representation of the second party (an inherent condition) would tend to make the ground fertile for public disapproval of the existing system and receptive to the idea of PR. In the UK, these factors were not present. Thus, the outcome-contingent motivation for the Labour party to initiate a reform process is ambiguous: even though the party had been out of power for some time despite the combined centre-left vote having been greater than that of the Conservatives, there had not been an anomaly since the brief minority government based on a plurality reversal in 1974. Nor was there any unusual degree of bias against Labour, as the second party, in votes-to-seats translation. If the outcome contingencies are ambiguous, the act-contingent factors are quite unambiguous: Without any obvious systemic failure to engage public attention on electoral reform, there was no cost to the Labour party of dropping the idea when it no longer looked to be in the interests of the party—even though that very idea might have had some role in the party's coming to power (for instance by promoting tactical voting by Liberal voters, as suggested by Blau in Chapter 2).

Two other jurisdictions that have moved a reform process all the way to a referendum (though not to reform enactment) are British Columbia and Prince Edward Island. Thus, these two cases are critical cases to probing the impact of act-contingent factors on the process. In the BC case, the parties' positions on electoral reform have evolved, with evident correlation with the changing fates of parties under the FPTP system, and consistent with the presence of act-based factors. For instance, the day before the 1996 election, which would result in a spurious NDP majority, the party leaders were asked if they supported PR.[44] The NDP leader Glen Clark said, 'No. Our parliamentary democracy has worked very well for British Columbians, providing real choice every election.' Given that his party was seeking re-election, and had just enjoyed five years of executive control despite just 41% of the vote in 1991, the position is not surprising. Liberal leader (and, after 2001, Premier) Gordon Campbell likewise said, 'No ... Liberals believe that every constituency should have the right to select the candidate of its choice.' Then, as Carty, Blais, and Fournier (Chapter 5) note, the Liberal party entered the next campaign with a proposal for a citizens' assembly on the electoral system as a part of its manifesto, and Campbell himself reminded his caucus of the commitment as the proposal came up for legislative debate. The authors also note that the lopsided majority the party received in that 2001 election 'may only have confirmed their view that the electoral system was unable to meet the minimum requirements for effective Westminster-style parliamentary governance'. It also presumably was behind the remarks by the leader of the NDP—whose party had been decimated in 2001—to back the bill to set up a citizens' assembly. The recognition of both major parties that the electoral system was one source of what Carty, Blais, and Fournier refer to as a 'general democratic malaise' among the public was borne out in the result of the referendum, which was concurrent with the 2005 legislative election. Despite the general low visibility of the issue—with both major parties officially neutral—over 57% of the public voted in favour of changing the electoral system. Because the result was both a strong demonstration of public interest in reform, yet short of the legally mandated 60% threshold,[45] the government shortly thereafter announced a second referendum, this time with publicly funded campaigns (both for and against).

The other jurisdiction to have had a referendum, as of mid-2007, since the initiation of a consultative process is Prince Edward Island. In April, 2002, about a year and a half before a provincial election, Premier Pat Binns responded to a report from a special Election Act committee of the legislature, in which his Conservative Party held 96% of the seats, by noting that 'Given the wild swings we have had in the election results, there's a need to examine this more closely.' The committee did not endorse any specific system, but it did list several options, including proportional representation.[46] Binns' government appointed a retired judge to head a PEI Commission on Electoral Reform, which began public hearings in 2003, as elections approached. The government was re-elected in September 2003, and the Commission proposed a new MMP system. A referendum was scheduled for October 2005. As the referendum approached, the premier signalled hesitation, suggesting a simple majority in favour would not be enough for his government to proceed to enactment and even cutting the number of polling places. Quite different from the BC situation, virtually all MLAs from both parties opposed the referendum, as noted by Massicotte (Chapter 4). While the holding of hearings on electoral reform during the run-up to an election suggests that the governing party expected that promoting reform would have electoral benefits (or at least entail no costs to its re-election bid), consistent with the act-contingent expectations, the premier's late attempt to change the rules for approval in the referendum likewise suggests no fear of electoral retribution from betraying 'cold feet' at the idea of electoral reform. In any event, the proposal was defeated soundly, and with a small turnout. There was thus little evidence that the major parties perceived significant act-based reasons to favour reform, and indeed reform was defeated.

In Quebec, as Massicotte (Chapter 4) notes, the Parti Québécois has flirted with electoral reform in the past, though its own caucus has shown less interest in the issue than its first premier, Rene Levesque, once did. After the party came to be a periodic governing party, despite never winning the majority of votes, there was no sustained commitment to reform. In fact, it was the Liberals who later initiated a reform process, albeit one without either an independent commission or a citizens' assembly. As noted previously in this chapter, the Liberals initiated a reform process after coming to power in the election following one in which they had been disadvantaged by spurious PQ majority. That election campaign, in 2003, featured a process that suggests an effort to appeal to popular sentiment for electoral reform, only in this case initiated by the government that had been advantaged by the spurious outcome in the preceding election. The PQ government initiated an Estates General that indicated support for PR, and it appears to have done so in response to electoral competition. However, the case of the Estates General actually reveals what could be an inherent obstacle to act-based factors for reform in Quebec: The PQ was more concerned about competition with the Action Démocratique du Québec (ADQ), a rival for the Francophone vote, than about competition with the Liberals. Moreover, the Estates General, as Massicotte describes it, was a 'preliminary brainstorming exercise' for a potential constitution for an independent Quebec, rather than an effort to head off Liberal competition for a reformist (but federalist) vote. Then in the 2007 election, the Liberals were reduced to minority status as the ADQ surged significantly in seats and the PQ fell to third place. It does not appear that electoral reform—and in particular, the existing Liberal government's proposal—was a factor in the 2007 campaign. If a process for electoral reform proceeds in the current parliament, it will be the first such example among elections that resulted in a minority or coalition cabinet. In fact, the relatively proportional translation of the three parties' votes into seat shares and the closeness of the overall result probably make each party—including the formerly distant third ADQ—optimistic that FPTP will benefit it in the near future.

Finally, the case of New Brunswick is instructive, as it is the only case other than New Zealand and the UK to have held a general election after the publication of a reform proposal arising out of a consultative process, but before a referendum on that proposal. We have already seen how the existence of the reform proposal in New Zealand ultimately led the two major parties to compete electorally over the issue of reform—suggesting both parties believed it was risky to appear anti-reform—while in the UK the Labour party has won two additional elections in spite of reneging on a commitment to bring the Jenkins Commission proposal to a referendum. In New Brunswick, the Conservative government of Premier Bernard Lord committed in its 2003 campaign platform to initiate a consultative process. However, the premier himself made a remark in May 2003, that, if taken at face value, imply he did not see an outcome-based reason for going ahead now that his party had ceased to be the disadvantaged party: 'I like the system we have now, and you can probably understand why'[47]—a clear allusion to the very large majority he enjoyed at the time. The Commission on Legislative Democracy, appointed after the Conservative's very narrow re-election victory, recommended a series of political reforms, including MMP. Some months later the government responded favourably, with a promise to hold a referendum in the spring of 2008. However, in the meantime, the Conservative government was about to lose its precarious parliamentary majority (due to a member's retirement), and so it called a snap election. An election campaign months after the government's formal response to the MMP proposal and about a year before a planned referendum would seem to be the ideal time for the two parties to indicate their commitment to reform. That is, it would be an ideal time if they (or at least one of them) believed that there were votes to be won by appealing to pro-reform sentiment in what was a close campaign. However, neither party even mentioned the idea of electoral reform (or political reform more generally) in its campaign manifestos for the September 2006 election.[48] To thicken the plot further, the outcome of that election was anomalous: The Conservative party retained its vote plurality, but the Liberals won a spurious majority of seats. If this outcome was perceived by New Brunswick voters as anomalous, it could spark public support for the scheduled referendum. However, it is instructive that press coverage immediately following the election appears not to have focused on the plurality reversal, suggesting that it may not be politically relevant.[49] By June 2007, the new government had issued a formal position paper on the Commission's report; in this report the government called for making 'improvements' in the way FPTP works, but indicated it would not proceed with the previously scheduled referendum on replacing FPTP.[50]

Thus we can summarize this overview of act-contingent factors as follows. There is clear evidence that such factors were present in New Zealand and a strong indication of their presence in British Columbia. There is no evidence of their presence in the UK, Prince Edward Island, or New Brunswick, while the case of Quebec is somewhat ambiguous. While it is impossible to draw any firm conclusions from so few cases and with only an indirect method of investigating the presence of act-based motivations, it may be no coincidence that the only two jurisdictions thus far to have had referenda in which majorities favoured a change to proportional representation were precisely the two in which there was evidence from party behaviour—after the post-anomaly alternation but before the holding of a referendum—that parties saw the cause of reform as potentially popular.

1.6. Conclusions

In this chapter, we have seen that consultative processes to consider the possibility of replacing a first past the post electoral system with some variant of proportional representation happen only rarely. In a data set consisting of 191 elections, there are 7 (3.7%) that have been followed immediately by the appointment of a commission, citizens' assembly, or other formal review mechanism that was not directly under the control of the governing party. While the establishment of such consultative bodies is rare, it tends to follow patterns predictable by the theory advanced here. The plurality electoral system is inherently prone to produce outcomes from time to time that appear to violate its own norms, either by putting the 'wrong' party in power (the party with only the second highest vote total) or by decimating the opposition. Anomalous election outcomes in the form of either spurious or lopsided majorities preceded five of the seven instances in which consultative processes were initiated. Anomalous majorities are much more common, however, than are consultative processes on the electoral systems that produced them. In order for reform to be initiated after one of these anomalies, there must have been alternation to the party that had been disadvantaged by the previous anomalous outcomes. When a previously disadvantaged party comes to power, it may perceive an outcome-contingent benefit to electoral reform, in that it perceives the current system as having been biased against it.

Of course, a paradox of reform in parliamentary FPTP systems is that it must be initiated by the very party that was advantaged by the existing system at the most recent election—the party with the most seats in parliament. Once it is in power, the previously disadvantaged party may be less enthusiastic about following through on a commitment to review the electoral system. If, on the other hand, it perceives an electoral advantage from branding itself as reformist or fears retribution from voters for backtracking on a commitment to consult with the public on the electoral system, it is more likely to follow through. This is the act-contingent motivation, and indeed, the only two cases (as of mid-2007) in which referenda have resulted in majorities of the electorate voting for an alternative electoral system are precisely those in which we saw both parties making public commitments to the consultative process even after the alternation to the previously disadvantaged party, but before the referendum itself. These two cases are New Zealand and British Columbia, where sequences of elections had produced outcomes that could be seen to be violations of the underlying normative principles of the FPTP system, and thus may have contributed to a generalized public dissatisfaction with the existing democratic model itself, or even to shifting public norms in favour of the more consensual style of politics expected to result if PR were adopted.

By analysing the patterns of votes-to-seats conversion, it was possible to identify systems exhibiting poor performance even in the absence of a visible anomaly. Most of the cases to have had a consultative process experienced outcomes in which the party with the second highest seat total was significantly under-represented, even before an actual anomaly. The UK leading up to the 1998 reform proposal is the only case in which a consultative process was initiated without any such history of under-representation. The (subsequently aborted) British process is, therefore, totally unexpected. Ontario is the only other case not to have had the expected anomalous majority prior to the initiation of a consultative process; it did, however, have several elections in which the party that initiated the process had been under-represented, relative to the estimates from the seat–vote equation. Other jurisdictions have experienced similar periods, but no reform process to date. In some cases, these jurisdictions have not had anomalies in part because elections have not been very close; however, were the patterns of bias against the second party to remain in a close election, their inherent tendency towards anomaly could become manifest. The theory advanced here would predict that should the party disadvantaged by such an anomaly return to power soon thereafter, it would be highly likely to initiate a consultative process on the electoral system. Thus, the analysis of vote–seat patterns allowed us to develop a 'watch list' of potentially anomaly-prone systems that could be ripe for reform processes in the near future, including Saskatchewan, Trinidad and Tobago, and the UK.

Electoral reform—and even its formal consideration—is a rare event, but its being rare does not mean that we cannot generalize from the actual experience of FPTP systems with and without reform. This chapter has suggested that the appearance on the public agenda of serious consideration of alternative electoral systems tends to follow systematic patterns of inherent conditions (the tendency of FPTP systems to generate normatively unacceptable outcomes) and contingent factors based on both a disadvantaged party's outcome-oriented interest in reform and the establishment of a public-opinion context in which the very act of promoting (or being seen to block) reform has electoral consequences.

The plurality system is by no means in danger of dying out, but the number of jurisdictions using it may dwindle, as the convergence of inherent and contingent factors puts reform under serious consideration. Nonetheless, it is worth remembering that, to date, only one jurisdiction, New Zealand, has actually made the leap into proportionality for general elections. As Nohlen (1984) observed over two decades ago, fundamental change across the competing principles of representation in established electoral systems is indeed rare and difficult.

Notes

1. The other two are the UK (sixth largest democracy) and Canada (eighth). If we look at countries democratic since only the mid-1980s, there would be one other large country worthy of mention: the Philippines. While mostly FPTP for its lower house, it has a very small tier of seats allocated to minor parties via party list. After Canada, no other FPTP countries are found among the world's 100 largest democracies, even when we consider all countries that have been democratic since the mid-1980s.
2. That is, the focus here will be exclusively on legislative electoral systems, and not on election of executives.

55

3. The concept of systemic failure, as defined here, could be applied to any other category of electoral system, including PR. For instance, a PR system could be said to have failed if a set of parties closely allied with one another obtained a majority of votes, but not the seats to form a government (perhaps due to fragmentation, failure of some allied parties to cross the threshold, etc.). However, a PR system would not be said to have failed on its own normative criteria on account of frequent coalition governments or their breakdown between scheduled elections. The latter are occurrences that are expected under PR, and even considered advantages by the system's advocates. The concept of systemic failure in systems other than FPTP deserves further treatment, but the present work will be confined only to FPTP.

4. In the majoritarian parliamentary democracies, citizen-initiated referenda are essentially unknown. In fact, such a process is contrary to the very idea of majoritarianism, as Lijphart (1999) has noted. A partial exception is British Columbia, but the initiative process in that province played no direct role in the reform process (aside from an earlier failed effort by a minority party to promote electoral reform). See Bowler and Donovan (Chapter 3) for a consideration of the impact of the initiative process in US states.

5. I will not attempt to theorize about these intraparty discussions, and thus will generally speak of parties as if they were unitary actors. Of course they are not, and there may be internal disagreements about such a fundamental decision as to take up the matter of proportional representation. Nonetheless, the decision to establish a reform process is taken by the party leadership, acting on behalf of the party as a whole, whatever the internal disagreements may be. The chapters in this volume by Blau (Chapter 2) and Vowles (Chapter 6) discuss intraparty dynamics with respect to the British and New Zealand cases, respectively.

6. Examples of more minor reforms might be changes in the boundary-delimitation criteria or in what institution is responsible for drawing boundaries.

7. Many potential political reforms, short of adopting proportional representation, could have the potential to mollify discontent with the status quo. Many of them might even be more popular, given general shortage of public knowledge about electoral systems. Examples might include tighter campaign-finance regulation, more 'free votes' in parliament, or fixed-term parliaments (to eliminate the perceived manipulation of governments' timing their own re-election bids to maximum advantage). Each of these indeed has featured in several of the reform processes discussed in this chapter, but given the focus of this volume on the electoral system, I shall not pursue these alternative varieties of reform further here.

8. For example, the single transferable vote and party-list PR were known by 1900, but the currently widely favoured mixed-member models did not really appear until after the Second World War when Germany adopted such a system.

9. If more than 10% of the seats at any election were elected in multi-seat districts, I exclude it. I am grateful to Kashi Tanaka for supplying data on the incidence of multi-seat ridings in Canadian provinces. The case of Prince Edward Island deserves mention. Through 1996 districts elected two members, but in a way that was essentially two single-seat races occurring simultaneously. From 2000, the rules have been conventional single-seat plurality.

10. While many of the other plurality systems have some region-specific parties that confound easy estimates of votes-to-seats conversion (e.g. the Bloc Quebecois or the Scottish and Welsh nationalist parties), no case in the present data set has such parties forming almost half the votes cast nationally, as has India since 1989.

11. Bowler and Donovan (Chapter 3) note that there is considerable experimentation at the local level in the USA with electoral rules other than FPTP. However, there is no evidence of a movement towards any proportional representation methods at the national level, and only a few infant reform movements towards PR for state legislative bodies in a few states.

12. As Reilly notes, Papua New Guinea has become a case of electoral reform in an FPTP jurisdiction, having changed to the alternative vote.

13. The only country larger than Prince Edward Island but having a population less than 250,000 that uses FPTP is St Lucia, where the 17-seat national parliament makes huge partisan seat swings almost inevitable. Even PEI, by contrast, has 27 seats. The importance of assembly size will be more apparent below.

14. I borrow the term, spurious majority, for these outcomes from Siaroff (2003).

15. The data series end before the New Brunswick election of 2006, which resulted in a spurious majority (and is discussed briefly below).

16. These also represent about 13% and just over 10%, respectively, of the total number of observations. Elections in which the leading opposition boycotted the election (Jamaica 1983 and Trinidad and Tobago 1971) are excluded.

17. Because of the small size of the PEI assembly, one case of fewer than five seats actually represents nearly 15% of the seats for the second party.

18. Saskatchewan in 1982 and 1986 likewise experienced consecutive elections with each of the two opposite types of anomaly. However, the second anomaly in this case was a plurality reversal that kept in power the very same party that had been the winner of the lopsided majority in the previous election. Thus, while the parties alternated in votes' ranking, they did not alternate in power, and hence no reform initiation is expected; none has occurred to date.

19. Compare the suggestion by Blau (2004), which he has softened in his chapter in this volume (Chapter 2).

20. In the case of Ontario following the 1985 plurality reversal, the incumbent party at the new election actually was the party with the plurality of votes, as the party with the seat plurality had been unable to obtain confidence from parliament.

21. Counting each of Canada's polities as 'distinct' from Canada as a whole.

22. Local factors that affect the vote could be any of several decisions by voters to vote on district-level concerns, e.g. a preference for constituent services, a belief that their district has unique local interests that matter more than national issues, or tactical considerations of the potential impact of the local race on the national outcome. Whatever factors go into the aggregate jurisdiction-wide partisan votes distribution are taken as exogenous to the model.

23. In the case of single-seat districts, obviously, E is equivalent to the overall size of the assembly.

24. On assembly size in the Caribbean and its consequences, see Lijphart (1990). On assembly size more generally, and its relation to population size, see Taagepera and Shugart (1989).

25. The extended form estimates the seat share of any given party, s_k, based on its vote share, v_k, the effective number of parties, N, and the exponent, n (derived from equation 1.2):

$$s_k = \frac{v_k^n}{v_k^n + (N-1)^{1-n}(1-v_k)^n}.$$

26. The effective number of parties, as entered into the equation, is thus that from each given election, rather than an average over a longer period. Taagepera and Shugart suggest using an average over several elections; however, for present purposes we want to know if specific elections deviate from an expected pattern. Thus, any sudden fragmentation or consolidation of the party system at a given election is valuable data that should not be subsumed beneath longer trends.

27. Unless otherwise noted, throughout this chapter when I say 'under-represented' I mean relative to expectations based on the 'exponent rule' and not the more conventional sense of under-represented relative to actual vote share. Plurality systems are expected to under-represent parties other than the largest in the conversion of votes into seats.

28. While only the two largest parties' votes and (expected) seats are graphed, the estimates themselves are, as noted above, based on an extended form that includes the presence of other parties through the incorporation of a term for the effective number of parties.

29. This was a very lopsided voting result, with the leading party having 62.3% and the second party having 18.2%. The seat–vote equation suggests the second party could have had only one seat, when it actually won four.

30. PEI in 2000 saw the two leading parties getting 58 and 34% of the votes. The seat–vote equation suggests these parties should have divided the seats, 69 to 31%, but in reality it was far more lopsided: 96 to 4%.

31. As Blau (Chapter 2) notes, in any given case, if the current second party does better in votes (especially if it takes over the leading vote position), the bias

may not remain. Whether it does or not depends, of course, on whether the swing is uniform or sufficiently variable as to make a significant change in seat bonuses.

32. Overall fragmentation (indicated by the effective number of parties), and the exponent derived from assembly size and voting population.

33. Not counting wartime coalitions with the Conservative party.

34. Single transferable vote; see Chapter 5 by Carty, Blais, and Fournier for details.

35. Important details of this proposed system may be found in Chapter 4 by Massicotte.

36. Massicotte (Chapter 4) focuses on the consistent tendency of the electoral system to under-represent the Liberals in Quebec. However, the graph in Figure 1.4 shows that, when defining under-representation as relative to 'normal' seat–vote translation expectations, as I do, the Quebec FPTP system has tended to represent *whichever party came in second* in votes, although most of the data points in the figure for deviation from the seat–vote expectation are indeed lower for the Liberals than for the PQ.

37. It should be noted that the 1987 election thus is not an alternation: while the Liberal party went from second most to most votes, the election was called early *by a Liberal government*, which was seeking (and won) a majority of seats on its own. Thus 1987 does not represent a coming to power by a party that had been on the wrong side of a plurality reversal in the previous election.

38. Whatever the motivation, a campaign document produced for the 2003 election by the Liberal party was also quite explicit in promising 'a full open public debate on voting reform', potentially including PR, 'engaging citizens', and holding a referendum ('Government that works for you', Liberal Party of Ontario, accessed 14 November 2006 at http://leonarddomino.com/reference/platform-ontarioliberal.pdf.).

39. The exponent in Belize since the expansion of the assembly to 28 (later 29) seats in 1984 has been around 3.4. This exponent results in an estimation of a large bonus for the largest party, but the actual bonus has tended to exceed the expectation, especially in elections that are not close.

40. The Saskatchewan Party combines remnants of the provincial Conservative Party, which was battered by scandal, and some defectors from the Liberal Party.

41. The party indicates a commitment to reviewing the electoral system in its policy guidelines, though it is vague on what that might mean (http://www.saskparty.com/index.cfm?page=290, accessed 16 February 2006).

42. The party won 48.3% of the seats in 2003 on 39.4% of the vote. It was two seats short of a majority, while the NDP obtained a one-seat majority on 44.7% of the vote.

43. As Blau (Chapter 2) notes, part of the interest within the Labour party in reform was driven by expectations of the more ideologically moderate leaders

that the majority would be small and hence subject to possible defections by leftist members of the caucus. In such a scenario, cooperation with the Liberal Democrats would have assisted the policy agenda. With a large majority, these concerns vanished.

44. 'NDP, Liberals reject electoral reforms', *The Vancouver Sun*, 27 May 1996, Final Edition, p. B2.

45. In addition to 60% province-wide, the proposal also needed to pass in 60% of the provincial electoral districts to be binding. It easily cleared the latter hurdle.

46. 'Sweeping electoral reforms possible for Island', *The Guardian* (Charlottetown), 17 April 2002, p. A1.

47. 'Lord said he'll consider new voting system for N.B.', *Fort McMurray Today*, 26 May 2003.

48. I reviewed the manifestos published at the websites of the New Brunswick Conservative, Liberal, and New Democratic Parties; only the small third party, the NDP, mentioned the scheduled referendum or the question of electoral reform in any way.

49. There was a revision of the electoral boundaries before the election. As Vowles notes (Chapter 6) for the New Zealand case, it is thus possible for the outcome to be 'reasoned away', rather than used as an argument for fundamental electoral reform. See Hyson (1995) on the boundary-adjustment process in eastern Canada more generally.

50. *An Accountable and Responsible Government: The Government's Response to the Final Report of the Commission on Legislative Democracy*, June 2007 (available at http://www.gnb.ca/0012/PDF/ResponseFinalReport-CLD-June2007-e.pdf, accessed 7 August 2007).

2

Electoral Reform in the UK: A Veto Player Analysis*

Adrian Blau

2.1. Introduction

This chapter examines the prospects for electoral reform in the UK. Multiparty competition can increase the pressure for reform in plurality systems, and minor parties took one in three votes and one in seven seats at the 2005 British general election. But pressure for reform has been resisted before and the obstacles remain significant.

To assess the likelihood of reform, I combine electoral and political analysis—to see when preferences overlap with power. Reform requires that those who think a different electoral system will benefit them, or who think it is simply right, also have the resources to get the change onto the agenda and into law.

This approach helps to explain why, as Shugart (Chapter 1 in this volume) shows, the UK had a 'totally unexpected' reform process—the Jenkins Commission in 1997–8. After briefly outlining some developments in the British electoral and party systems (Section 2.2), I explain why the UK is a partial exception to Shugart's model, by supplementing his analysis with further exploration of the incentives for reform. This implies a broader model: interests and attitudes determine when political

* For comments and criticisms on earlier versions of this chapter, I thank Tim Bale, Giacomo Benedetto, André Blais, Shaun Bowler, Ken Carty, Malcolm Clark, David Farrell, Indriði Indriðason, Csaba Nikolenyi, Meg Russell, Matt Shugart, Mary Southcott, participants at the Plurality and Multiround Elections conference, Université de Montréal, 17–18 June 2006, participants at the Elections, Public Opinion and Parties annual conference, University of Nottingham, 8–10 September 2006, and participants at the Constitutional Futures 2 meetings in Bristol and London.

actors advocate reform, and these motivations are not fully captured by Shugart's list of systemic failures (Section 2.3).

I consider four reasons why Labour or the Conservatives might initiate a reform process in the UK: because prominent party figures think that reform is simply right; to get temporary minor-party backing in a hung parliament; to improve the party's vote-share by proposing a popular reform; or because the effects of the electoral system would benefit the party in votes, seats, policy, or office. The second reason is the most likely way for a reform process to start, but for this to end in actual reform, the fourth condition is probably needed too (Section 2.4).

Even here, significant political obstacles remain. I thus use veto player theory. The power to say no is a significant power and can affect what gets onto the agenda. An instrumentally rational agenda setter should propose a policy which is within the 'winset', the set of policies that could defeat the status quo (plurality elections). I add a further idea to standard veto player theory—the idea of 'path-setting', by which the agenda setter chooses not only what goes onto the agenda but also the legislative path along which the reform proposal passes. For example, the likelihood of reform depends on whether a referendum is held before the parliamentary stage, after it, or not at all (Section 2.4).

Many people who discuss electoral reform implicitly use veto player theory when they suggest that self-interested MPs would reject an electoral system which threatens their seats. For example, Tony Benn airs the common view that 'turkeys do not vote for Christmas' such that the Jenkins Commission's reform proposal did not have 'a cat in hell's chance of succeeding' (House of Commons debate, 5 November 1998). I show that turkeys could in fact vote for Christmas: a careful government can overcome MPs' opposition to reform. Nonetheless, this could be costly and risky. Pre-emptive reform, in particular acting before a hung parliament, may be needed (Section 2.5).

This chapter does not reach any unexpected conclusions. Electoral reform remains possible but unlikely, mainly because it is probably not in Conservative or Labour interests. I thus water down my earlier suggestions that reform may be hard to resist after one or more hung parliaments (Blau 2004: 445–7). The gradual decline of the British electoral system makes reform more likely but significant barriers remain. Nonetheless, this chapter advances a conceptual framework which allows for more rigorous analysis and (potentially) for modelling and empirical testing of reform choices in the UK and elsewhere. The veto player framework, in particular, highlights the UK government's unusual flexibility in helping or hindering reform through its path-setting powers.

I will briefly expand on the conceptual distinctions which I use in this chapter. First, I talk of preferences being based not only on *interests* but also on *attitudes*. Many scholars imply that politicians' preferences about electoral systems reflect interests alone (e.g. Reed and Thies 2001). This assumption is easier to test and may well be the dominant explanation in practice (see, e.g. Benoit and Schiemann 2001). But electoral system choices are sometimes influenced by normative beliefs about legitimacy and other collective goods, even when these do not entirely match interest-based preferences (Birch et al. 2002: 171–2, 178–9, 183–5; Carty, Blais, and Fournier Chapter 5). And reform is likeliest when there is an 'intersection' between normative attitudes and self-interest, as Shugart (Chapter 1) puts it.

So, we need not restrict instrumental rationality to interest-based preferences alone: someone can be instrumentally rational on the basis of attitudinal preferences about the common good, say. One of the tragedies of twentieth-century political science was the way that so many defenders and critics of 'rational choice' conflated two different ideas of rationality: instrumental rationality, which involves finding good means to ends, and rationality as self-interest, which involves a particular end.

I thus characterize an attitudinal preference as a preference based on what an individual believes is good, independently of how she thinks the policy affects her interests, and an interest-based preference as a preference based on how she thinks the policy affects her interests, independently of her attitudes. Two types of interest are especially important here: self-interest and party-interest. A self-interested preference is based on what an individual thinks would benefit her, a party-based preference is based on what she thinks would benefit her party. Later, I briefly consider class-interest, and I occasionally touch on *dispositions* like risk-aversion and willingness to compromise (Hamlin 2006). Attitudes, interests, and dispositions may be difficult to untangle in practice, of course.

A further distinction is whether interests involve *votes*, *seats*, *policy*, or *office*. An MP or party leader may want an electoral system which gives her or her party a greater share of votes, a greater prospect of turning votes into seats, more policy influence, or more executive office. These four interests may or may not pull in the same direction. *Uncertainty* in these areas also matters: a party leader may avoid reform because of uncertainty about its effect on votes, say, or might advocate reform because the new system would at least be more predictable in translating votes to seats. We may also distinguish between *positive* and *negative* outlooks: some politicians want to maximize their advantage when they do well; others want to minimize the damage when they do badly.

The most important distinction is between *act-based* and *outcome-based* reasons for supporting or opposing reform. Act-based motivations involve the very act of supporting or opposing reform. Outcome-based motivations involve the perceived effects of the electoral system. Again, both are usually relevant, and they may or may not pull in the same way. This is very important in the UK: we will see that even those who are opposed to reform for outcome-based reasons can be induced to accept it for act-based reasons. The act/outcome distinction follows Reed and Thies (2001), but I have dropped their reference to contingency as I use that term differently elsewhere (Blau 2004), and I have altered their implication that only interests are relevant. Six types of act-based and outcome-based motivations are shown in Table 2.1. Note that I am not endorsing the claims in the examples in the two right-hand columns.

Next, although 'electoral reform' is usually considered to include more proportional changes only, the most likely reform in twentieth-century British politics was the Alternative Vote (AV), a majoritarian system which remains a plausible reform. For this chapter, then, electoral reform includes any change in the electoral formula (Lijphart 1994: 13). (I do not address reforms to other electoral rules.) We may thus distinguish between reforms which are strongly proportional, moderately proportional, or majoritarian.

Finally, I distinguish between three aspects of the reform process: *consultation, legislation,* and *enactment.* I call the start of any reform process *reform initiation,* whether this involves consultation or legislation. Reform consultation means asking a body to examine alternative electoral systems and make a recommendation. But this may not lead to reform legislation (which involves a referendum, bill, or executive order to change the system) or to reform enactment (where the referendum, bill, or executive order becomes law). In short, many things can stop pressure for reform turning into reform consultation, or consultation turning into legislation, or legislation turning into enactment.

Table 2.1. Different motivations for and against electoral reform

Type of motivation	Explanation	Example (for reform)	Example (against reform)
Act-based self-interest	The very act of supporting/opposing reform is in an individual's interest.	Opposing reform would be punished by party leaders.	Supporting reform would lead to loss of votes in constituency.
Act-based party-interest	The very act of supporting/opposing reform is in a party's interest.	Proposing reform would make the party look more modern and increase its vote-share.	Supporting reform would lead to core supporters switching parties.
Act-based attitude	The very act of supporting/opposing reform is good.	Opposing a reform bill that one's party leader wants is wrong.	A referendum has already backed reform; opposing this would be undemocratic.
Outcome-based self-interest	The effect of the new electoral system would benefit the individual.	An MP is more likely to have ministerial office after reform.	The new electoral system would lose the MP her seat.
Outcome-based party-interest	The effect of the new electoral system would benefit the party.	The new electoral system would increase a party's seat-share.	The new electoral system would see a party lose votes to new minor parties.
Outcome-based attitude	The effect of the new electoral system is good/right.	The new electoral system would be more equitable.	The new electoral system may have unforeseen problems.

2.2. A Very Brief History of the UK Electoral and Party Systems

Until 1885, most UK constituencies elected two members using the block vote, with a few three-member and four-member districts. From 1885, all constituencies were single-member districts except for a few two-member and three-member university seats using the Single Transferable Vote (STV). These were removed in 1948. Aside from these changes to the electoral formula, many other electoral rules have changed (Curtice 2003: 483–95), as in the USA (Chapter 3 by Bowler and Donovan).

Two-party 'Westminster' politics has been the exception rather than the rule. Even after Irish independence in 1921, removing Irish MPs who did not fit into the mainland mainstream, the party system fluctuated while Labour replaced the Liberals as the chief alternative to the Conservatives. Only from 1945 to 1970 has the UK fitted classic images of Westminster two-partyism (Dunleavy 1999: 214–17)—depending, of course, on how we define 'two-party politics' (Blau 2008).

Electoral reform has been advocated throughout this period. The inter-war period saw several attempts to change the system, discussed below. Electoral reform became a less prominent issue after the war; indeed there was little disquiet in 1951 when the Conservatives won a majority of seats despite coming second in votes. Things changed with two unsatisfactory elections in the mid-1970s. In February 1974, not only was there a hung parliament with no overall majority, but Labour also came second in votes and first in seats. Nine months later, Labour scraped a majority in a second election, but lost it in 1976, leading to a pact with the Liberals, before minority government again in 1978; the government finally fell after losing a vote of confidence in 1979. This weakened claims that single-member plurality (SMP) fostered stable, secure government.

The treatment of minor parties has been a second cause of discontent with SMP. There has been a gradual increase in third-party votes and seats, alongside significant under-representation, as in New Zealand (Chapter 6 by Vowles). In 1983, the Social Democratic Party (SDP)/Liberal Alliance won 26% of the votes and 4% of the seats. At the 2005 election, minor parties won one in three votes and one in seven seats.

Calls for reform come mainly from outside of the major-party duopoly. As John Curtice notes, 'Labour and the Conservatives only wavered in their support for the current system when their prospects for power appeared to be in question,' as when the Conservatives lost four out of five elections from 1964 to 1974, and Labour lost four successive elections from 1979 to 1992. 'In both cases, however, eventual restoration to office unsurprisingly helped restore faith in the current system' (Curtice 2003: 509). In effect, the two main parties collude in retaining SMP: each party stomachs losses, even big ones, because it expects to hold sole power in the future. So, 'electoral reform cannot happen unless a government breaks its historic (if implicit) pact with its main rival...to resist all pleas...for electoral reform' (Mitchell 2005: 174).

Conservative MPs remain predominantly opposed to reform. This has many roots: dislike of constitutional change in general, scepticism about the ideal of political equality which drives many reformers, and the fear that more proportional systems would disadvantage the Conservatives.

By contrast, more Labour MPs are open to reform, although the bulk remain unconverted. While in opposition, Labour leader Neil Kinnock, who allegedly favoured proportional representation (PR) (see Section 2.3), set up a commission to examine electoral systems in 1990; but the final report (Plant 1992) was a political cop-out. Nonetheless, Labour's election-winning manifestos of 1997, 2001, and 2005 all had commitments to a referendum on electoral reform. But unlike the British Columbia situation (Carty, Blais, and Fournier Chapter 5), Tony Blair did not act on these commitments. Nor did he implement the minor electoral reform which, it is alleged, he had agreed with the Liberal Democrats (see Section 2.6). He instead set up the Jenkins Commission to consider electoral reform, but he ignored its proposal for a mildly proportional MMP (Mixed-Member Proportional) electoral system (Jenkins 1998). Gordon Brown has thus far maintained Blair's stance on electoral reform: Brown's opening salvo on constitutional reform only included a commitment to review the recent experience of other electoral reforms introduced since 1997 (Justice Department 2007: 46).

These other electoral reforms do deserve attention, though. Since 1997, Labour has introduced closed-list PR for elections to the European parliament, MMP elections to the Scottish Parliament and the Welsh and London assemblies, STV in the Northern Ireland assembly and Scottish local government, and the Supplementary Vote in London mayoral elections. These reforms are not my focus in this chapter, but as Section 2.4 notes, they alter the debate about electoral reform at Westminster.

Interestingly, several reform processes have started in the UK. In three cases, reform consultation led to reform legislation but not reform enactment. First, the 1916–17 cross-party Speaker's Conference proposed PR in about a third of the seats and AV elsewhere, but the Commons rejected PR and the Lords rejected AV. To avoid losing the whole bill, the only change was to have STV in a few two-member and three-member university seats (Hart 1992: 181–6). Second, the minority Labour government introducing a bill for AV in 1931, to win Liberal support and to fend off a Liberal/Conservative alliance. With Liberal backing, the bill passed the Commons, but the Conservative-dominated Lords weakened it significantly, and the 1931 financial crisis soon toppled the Labour government (Hart 1992: 239–44). Third, in 1998 the Jenkins Commission recommended MMP, but no legislation resulted because key Labour figures did not see reform as being in Labour's short-term interests (Dunleavy and Margetts 2001: 303–4). Note that reform legislation need not have a separate consultation phase. The 1920s saw several failed attempts at electoral reform via Private Member's Bills or similar techniques (Hart 1992: 213–31).

Importantly, in several of the above cases, reform initiation started without systemic failure, to which I now turn.

2.3. Systemic Failure in the UK?

Shugart (Chapter 1) discusses three types of systemic failure in plurality elections: (a) lopsided majorities, where the winning party has an unduly large seat-share; (b) reverse winners, where the party which won most seats only came second in votes; and (c) minority governments, where no party has a majority of seats. If one or more systemic failures occur, an electoral reform process may start under the following two contingent conditions: (a) an expected change in government to a previously disadvantaged party, which may favour reform, along with (b) close elections, which the second-placed party may have lost due to partisan bias benefiting the winning party, or which the second-placed party might hope to win in the future if a commitment to PR brings extra votes.

Shugart's model accounts for the reform process in most cases but not the UK, where in 1997 the incoming Labour government upheld its manifesto commitment and created the Jenkins Commission to examine alternative electoral systems. But Labour shelved the 1998 report and broke its manifesto commitment to hold a referendum on the commission's proposed reform. So, reform did not happen, as Shugart's model predicts, but even the consultation process was unexpected on Shugart's model. To explain the UK's partial anomaly, we must ask whether systemic failure covers all reasons for reform.

Shugart is right that systemic failure is not *necessary* for reform initiation. As he states, without systemic failure no reform is 'likely' (Chapter 1). Certainly, reform processes can start without systemic failure. In the UK, cross-party Speaker's Conferences were set up in 1916, 1944, and 1965 to tackle electoral issues like registration; electoral reform got onto the agenda each time and, in the 1916 case, even onto a parliamentary bill, though this failed (Hart 1992: 178–99, 258–63, 278). A more interesting example is France in 1985, where François Mitterrand's Socialists replaced the two-round single-member-district majority system with a form of PR. They expected such a loss of votes that they might be decimated in seats, whereas PR would safeguard their seat-share and improve their coalition potential (Tsebelis 1990: 226–8).

The French example in particular implies a broader model of reform initiation: interests and attitudes determine when political actors, especially party leaders, advocate or initiate reform. This captures a wider range of cases, although of course it is hard to operationalize and has less predictive value than Shugart's model. Shugart's list of systemic failures frequently underlies such situations, as when lopsided majorities or reverse winners reflect a strong partisan bias. Shugart's model presumably accounts for most cases of reform initiation because his three types of systemic failure tap into the interests and attitudes which motivate reform. But inevitably, some reform initiations will not be captured by Shugart's list of systemic failures.

As Shugart explains (Chapter 1), the UK's 1997 reform process is one such case. Indeed, the wrong party initiated reform according to the seats–votes equation. The seats–votes equation predicts each major party's seat-share; if a major party actually does much worse than expected, according to the odds-ratio of the two parties' predicted seat-shares to their actual seat-shares, then the disadvantaged party may have an interest in reform. The seats–votes equation does not include partisan biases between the major parties (Taagepera 1986: 490), and applying the equation to British general elections shows that Labour does far better than the equation predicts from 1979, while the Conservatives do far worse from 1992. This partly reflects pro-Labour partisan bias: Labour's vote is distributed more efficiently, its seats are smaller on average, and minor parties win more seats off the Conservatives than Labour (Blau 2004: 440–3). Shugart's criteria for lopsided majorities are met or almost met in 1983, 2001, and 2005.

So, the seats–votes equation rightly shows that Labour has been strongly advantaged in seats over the Conservatives. Yet, few Conservatives seek electoral reform, Labour initiated reform in 1997, and prominent Labour MPs still advocate reform. What explains this?

One possibility is that Labour's actions and the Conservatives' inactions have been instrumentally irrational, due to incomplete information or incorrect understanding of the effects of reform. This would not weaken Shugart's model, which shows what instrumentally rational politicians should do given their interests; it does not pretend that politicians always see these interests accurately or act appropriately. But another possibility is that the model does not capture all of the interests or attitudes favouring reform. Both explanations appear to be relevant, as shown by the following discussion of the interest-based and attitudinal sources of Labour reformism.

The twentieth century was the 'Conservative century': a divided left, many argued, gave the Conservatives power for two-thirds of the period. Tony Blair, who took the Labour leadership in 1994, wanted the twenty-first century to be a progressive century, realigning the left through PR (Ashdown 2000: 386–7, 452, 508). Many Labour figures felt that in the 1980s, plurality elections with a divided left had let the Thatcher governments win large parliamentary majorities on just 42–44% of the vote (Kinnock 2005). The ensuing policies, on this view, seriously harmed working-class people. According to John Denham, a Labour MP and advocate of reform, 'Britain has a built-in centre-left majority of voters on most issues' (quoted in Grice 2006), such that plurality elections damage both party-interest and what we might call 'class-interest'.

Moreover, in the mid-1990s Labour leaders expected a majority of no more than 50 seats; an oversized coalition with the centrist Liberal Democrats, in exchange for electoral reform, might give a centre-leaning Labour leadership the extra MPs to sidestep left-wing Labour rebels and could keep the Conservatives out of office if Labour lost seats in the future (Ashdown 2000: 283, 286–7, 310–14, 413). What changed many Labour minds was that in 1997 Labour won 418 seats and the Conservatives just 165, producing a Commons' majority of 179. This was partly through the anti-Conservative parties learning to play the system against the Conservatives, with tactical campaigning and tactical voting in marginal seats giving Labour a further boost in seats (Curtice and Steed 1997: 309–18). Having suffered from the Conservatives' divide-and-rule electoral politics in the 1980s, Labour now enjoyed an advantage.

Even so, Blair was right to implement the pledge to review the electoral system. This avoided an early breach of a manifesto commitment and appeased the Liberal Democrats without leading to actual reform. Keeping the Liberal Democrats close to Labour continued to foster the tactical campaigning and tactical voting that so damaged the Conservatives in 1997; this probably explains Labour's 2001 manifesto commitment to review the electoral system (Dunleavy and Margetts 2001: 304), and doubtless the 2005 commitment too.

Many Labour figures still seek reform. For some, the centrist incentives of plurality elections mean that Labour's majorities have come 'at a cost to some of our radical aspirations' (John Denham, quoted in Grice 2006). For such reformists, PR might reunite Labour with its core working-class supporters. Some reformists believe that the 2005 election showed how plurality elections are 'driving the progressive parties to fight each other harder' (Cook 2005; Denham 2005). A repeat of the 1980s is feared. Plurality elections may maximize seats when Labour does well in votes but the same would be true when the Conservatives do well in votes; according to these reformists, electoral reform makes Conservative rule harder. From the 1980s to the present day, Labour reformism has often been negative—focusing on what happens when Labour is unpopular.

Some of these claims rest on questionable data or inferences. For example, it may be wishful thinking to assume that PR would reunite Labour with its core support: plurality elections are not the only incentives pushing Labour to the centre, and PR systems can have centrist incentives too. So, Labour support for electoral reform is not always as instrumentally rational as it sounds. But *if* there is a progressive majority and *if* it would remain cohesive after reform, then reform could benefit Labour in policy-seeking and office-seeking terms. So, Shugart's list of systemic failures and contingent forces do not exhaust the situations where a party has an interest in reform. Nor are attitudinal sources of reform addressed, although these are harder to prove and may best be left out of testable models. Shugart's model does appear to account for most cases of reform initiation in the plurality systems examined, but at least for the UK other explanations are needed.

2.4. Party-Interest: Votes, Seats, Policy, and Office

I now examine future prospects for reform. This allows me to correct an overstatement in an earlier publication (Blau 2004). I showed that four developments had weakened the British electoral system: the cube law's decline, the rise of minor-party seats, increased government backbench rebelliousness, and the rise of pro-Labour bias. The first two developments make hung parliaments and small government majorities more likely, as estimated according to the equation

$$\text{Probability of failure} = \frac{8\left(\left(\frac{\text{Required number of seats}}{\text{Total number of seats} - \text{Number of minor party seats}}\right) - 0.5\right)}{\text{Responsiveness index}}$$

With a responsiveness index of around 2, the chance of a hung parliament at a given election is very roughly one in three. Meanwhile, increased backbench rebelliousness makes small majorities harder to control, and pro-Labour bias makes it more likely that the Conservatives could beat Labour in votes but still finish second in seats. I concluded that in a hung parliament, especially one with a reverse winner and/or one following a government weakened by its small majority, pressure for electoral reform 'might . . . be hard to resist' (Blau 2004: 445–6).

Notwithstanding the word 'might', this now seems to me to overstate the ease with which a hung parliament could prompt electoral reform, for four reasons. First, minor-party pressure can be deflected. True, the Liberals would probably have achieved electoral reform if the financial crisis had not toppled the minority Labour government in 1931 (Butler 1963: 83), but they could not enforce reform in February 1974 and they failed again when they held the balance of power from 1976 to 1979.[1]

Second, minor-party pressure can be diverted—bought off with other reforms. In particular, the Liberal Democrats might drop their request for electoral reform in the Commons if offered House of Lords reform, probably including PR in the Lords.[2] This would solidify the Liberal Democrats' influence in the upper house (Russell and Sciara 2006), without preventing Commons electoral reform in the longer term. So, minor parties might not insist on electoral reform in a hung parliament. As Richard Katz (2005: 62) notes, 'both proponents and opponents of electoral reform may be prepared to trade their preferences or interests [about electoral reform] for support on other questions.'

Third, governments can call another election when the time is right. Control of time is a key agenda-setting power, as we will see. Therefore, a single hung parliament may not be enough—although two in a row might be more problematic.[3] Even reverse-win hung parliaments can be shrugged off, as in February 1974.

Fourth, while pro-Labour bias is a problem for the British electoral system, I did not address the other side of bias: it gives Labour further reasons against reform, even in hung parliaments. Bias may thus make reform less not more likely, at least under certain conditions.

Overall, then, I was too quick to suggest that the British electoral system's problems may well lead to reform. My analysis, in short, was overly electoral, and based on a misreading of some of these electoral incentives; here and over Sections 2.5 and 2.6, I seek to correct this misreading and to add political considerations.

There are four main reasons why a major party's leadership might sanction reform consultation, legislation, or enactment. The first reason is if the leaders believe, attitudinally, that reform is simply right on outcome-based grounds, for example that a different system is more equitable or leads to better governance. While this helps to explain the British Columbia and New Zealand reform processes (Carty, Blais, and Fournier Chapter 5; Vowles Chapter 6), it does not seem to have been a significant motivation in twentieth-century British history. We should not discount it in the future, nonetheless. For example, a reformed House of Lords elected partly by PR could make the Commons look increasingly dated, and the generally positive experience of PR in Scotland and Wales should gradually weaken some of the more spurious attitudinal criticisms of PR, attune British politicians to coalitions, and may influence new generations of MPs to accept PR on attitudinal grounds. Nor should we preclude cross-party acceptance that electoral reform is needed, for example if government is weakened by successive hung parliaments and/or small, unmanageable parliamentary majorities—undermining a common defence of plurality elections in the UK (Blau 2004).

The second reason is act-based: a major party may initiate reform to get minor-party backing in a hung parliament. This is distinctly possible. If the Conservatives or Labour fell short of a majority in a hung parliament, they might start a reform process to get minor-party support, probably from the Liberal Democrats, the largest minor party. Initiating reform might simply buy one or two years of time while a prime minister waits for an opportune moment to call another election and hopefully win a parliamentary majority.

The third and fourth reasons why a major party might support reform are, respectively, the act-based reason that initiating reform might help the party in votes, and the outcome-based reason that the new electoral system might help it in votes or seats. I will first consider this with respect to the Conservatives, then Labour.

Tim Bale (2006) uses both reasons to argue that the Conservatives should change the electoral system. In terms of act-based party-interest, proposing electoral reform would present the Conservatives as a modern, democratic party. This is a plausible argument. But Bale is less convincing when he draws on outcome-based party-interest to argue that electoral reform would benefit the Conservatives in seats. In the 2005 general election, it took about 44,000 votes to elect each Conservative MP compared to only 27,000 for Labour. 'Best guesses', he writes, 'suggest that, even if the Tories had drawn level with Labour in terms of vote share...Labour would still have won 336 [seats] to the Conservatives' 220.' Bale thus concludes that a more proportional system 'would...increase the chance of converting Conservative votes into Conservative seats' (Bale 2006: 28–30).

This conflates two aspects of seats–votes relationships which should be kept apart if we are to understand the incentives for major parties concerning reform. It took fewer votes to win Labour seats than Conservative seats partly because of the 'responsiveness' effect, by which a mere plurality of votes can be exaggerated into a majority of seats (Blau 2004: 432–5). This 'winner's bonus' is larger in plurality systems than under more proportional systems. Labour benefited in 2005 but the Conservatives would profit if they win in votes. So, part of the Conservatives' apparent disadvantage in 2005 was simply because they came second in votes.

Partisan bias is something different. Whereas the winner's bonus favours the winning party, whether that party is Labour or the Conservatives, bias favours one party over the other, whether that party is the winner or not. Bias has favoured Labour over the Conservatives at the last 7 elections and at 9 of the 10 elections between 1970 and 2005, through such factors as a more efficient Labour vote distribution, smaller Labour seats, and minor parties winning more seats off the Conservatives than off Labour (Blau 2004). Bias is the main reason why the Conservatives' 7.5-percentage point lead in votes in 1992 only gave them a 21-seat Commons majority, while Labour's 9-point lead in 2001 produced a 167-seat majority. In 2005, the Conservatives were 3 points behind Labour in votes but 24 points behind in seats; in English constituencies, which amount to five-sixths of the UK total, the Conservatives led by 54,000 votes but won 93 fewer seats. Large biases have arisen elsewhere, including Quebec (Massicotte Chapter 4) and have led to reform initiation in several cases (Shugart Chapter 1).

But would this bias necessarily be as large if the Conservatives won? Bale's estimate of bias—a 116-seat Labour lead if the two parties had been level in votes—implicitly assumes uniform swing: the same swing in votes is applied from Labour to the Conservatives in every seat until the two parties have the same vote. But uniform swing is not the 'best guess' which Bale implies. It was once a useful predictor of election results but no longer works as well. Some bias reflects *non*-uniform swing, and further non-uniform swings might plausibly reduce this bias if the Conservatives recover in votes (Blau 2004: 441–5). We cannot say how electoral geography, electoral behaviour, or the party system will change over the next 20 years, but while the Conservatives will probably face a sizeable bias in the near future, it is less obvious that this bias would out-weigh the other advantages that the Conservatives should enjoy if their vote recovers. I cannot fully examine this issue here, but remember that the Conservatives were only mildly under-represented in 2005, winning 32.4% of the UK vote and 30.7% of the seats. It is entirely possible that at least in terms of translating their votes into seats, even a biased plurality system will often benefit them more than a less biased or unbiased PR system—especially when they have a large enough lead in votes. Note too that some PR systems might see the Conservatives' vote-share reduced by right-wing parties like the anti-Europe UK Independence Party and the far-right British National Party.

In short, we should be careful when making inferences from the Conser-vatives' current problems to the future. If the Conservatives are far enough ahead in votes, the magnifying effects of plurality elections should out-weigh anti-Conservative partisan bias, even if the resulting majority is smaller than might have been expected. If the Conservatives only have a small lead in votes, a different electoral system would probably not give them many more seats. Realistically, advocating PR would be an admission that they could not win power by themselves and that PR was the price to pay for a secure coalition with another party. The Con-servatives remain sceptical about reform (Cameron 2006), which seems sensible.

I now turn to Labour. A more proportional system would almost cer-tainly reduce the magnifying effect of plurality elections and reduce or remove pro-Labour bias. As with the Conservatives, Labour should not seek reform on act-based grounds: even if this gained Labour a few points in votes, the effect on seats would significantly outweigh this, unless Labour was already doing very badly in votes.

A more likely Labour reason for reform, discussed in Section 2.3, is the fear of another long period of Conservative rule. A Labour gov-ernment struggling in the opinion polls and facing defeat at a forth-coming election might thus seek reform. Labour leaders could also con-sider reform on policy-seeking grounds: an oversized Labour–LibDem coalition could give Labour leaders more policy influence than would a small Labour majority with Labour rebels causing problems, as under all Labour governments since 1964. Indeed in Scotland since devolution in 1999, the Labour–LibDem coalitions have mainly enacted Labour leg-islation, with exceptions like university fees in the first coalition and STV for local government in the second. This latter example is espe-cially pertinent: the Liberal Democrats appear to have dropped much of their policy agenda in return for electoral reform in local government. The same could well apply to an initial Labour–LibDem coalition at Westminster.

More likely, Labour might simply seek electoral reform on office-maximizing grounds: a minimal winning Labour–LibDem coalition could let Labour stay in office if it lost or expected to lose its overall majority. Individual factors might be relevant here, such as a Labour politician having waited many years to be prime minister, then facing the likelihood of losing that post very quickly—or a Labour leader willing to wait and hence rejecting a coalition deal.

Nonetheless, in either situation reform initiation may depend on the Liberal Democrats' bargaining strength. Consider a parliament where the Liberal Democrats hold the balance of power and only Labour has enough seats to form a minimal winning coalition with them. Ideally, the Liberal Democrats want a coalition with PR, Labour wants one without PR. If Labour sticks to this position, the Liberal Democrats must either accept a coalition without PR, or stay out of government, also without PR. If Labour does not fear temporary minority government, Liberal Democrat requests for PR could thus be rejected.

Now consider a parliament where the Liberal Democrats hold the balance of power and *both* Labour and the Conservatives have enough seats to form a minimal winning coalition with them. (e.g. in the 1929–31 parliament, Labour, the Conservatives, and the Liberals had 47, 42, and 10% of the seats, respectively.) The Liberal Democrats' bargaining power then depends also on their ideological position. If they could not reasonably join a Conservative coalition then the situation would be equivalent to that described in the previous paragraph. But if they could form a coalition with either party, their bargaining power is correspondingly increased. By refusing a coalition deal with PR, Labour might thus end up not as a minority government but in *opposition*. This fear of the third party supporting the Conservatives was one reason why Labour legislated for AV in 1931 (Hart 1992: 238–9). Of course the bargaining game is still asymmetrical if the Conservatives could not accept electoral reform, or could not accept a reform as proportional as Labour would accept: Labour would have some bargaining advantage in such cases. That is one reason why the Conservatives should be ready to start reform consultation, to get minor-party support.

So, electoral reform is more likely if the Liberal Democrats could form a coalition with either major party. I will discuss the Liberal Democrats' electoral incentives in Section 2.6, but for here the political incentives are clear: an instrumentally rational Liberal Democrat leader should recognize that PR is likelier if the LibDems can deal with either major party. Two hung parliaments in a row would also give the Liberal Democrats a stronger bargaining position, especially if a major party had stopped a reform process in the first hung parliament by calling an election in a failed attempt to win a majority by itself. The Liberal Democrats have been important to the long-term decline of the British electoral system (Blau 2004: 443–7) and now we see that their ability to form coalitions with either major party could initiate a knockout blow.

2.5. Electoral Reform as a Veto Game

Section 2.4 showed that it is possible (though unlikely) that Labour or the Conservatives might initiate reform, even if only by grudgingly creating a commission to placate a minor party in a hung parliament. But could electoral reform move from the agenda to the statute book? To answer this question I use veto player theory (Tsebelis 2002; Cox and McCubbins 2005).

Electoral reform can be interpreted as a veto game. A veto game has one or more veto players and one or more agenda setters. A veto player has negative power, the power to say no—here, the power to stop an electoral reform bill from becoming law. An agenda setter is a veto player who also has the positive power to push a proposal to a final vote on the floor of the legislature. Here, the agenda setter is the leadership of the largest Commons party, which controls the legislative agenda; below this is usually assumed to be the leadership of Labour, the major party most likely to initiate reform.

Instrumentally, rational agenda setters should keep other veto players in mind. This may mean non–decision-making: the agenda setter may not even propose a policy which she expects to fail. Veto power can also turn into positive influence: the agenda setter may propose a compromise if her ideal policy is unacceptable to a veto player. This involves backwards induction: the agenda setter reasons from what a veto player would accept to what should thus be proposed. Backwards induction means that the power to say no can shape the agenda even before proposals are made. (For instrumentally rational and non-rational reasons, agenda setters may not act like this.) Veto player theory makes explicit what every politician knows: the people with the power to say no often get at least part of what they want.

In the UK, the most likely veto points are the Commons, the Lords, and a referendum. A Lords' veto is unlikely. This is partly because in Tsebelis's (2002: 26–30) terms the Lords could be 'absorbed' as a veto player if the Commons and the Lords overlap sufficiently in partisan terms. Furthermore, the Commons usually wins bicameral disagreements, although peers' veto power increases in the last year of a parliament when the temporary veto becomes absolute—and when an unpopular government might be most tempted to change electoral systems. The Lords might also veto a highly partisan reform proposal which offends the democratic attitudes of enough peers. An instrumentally rational agenda setter should recognize this and act accordingly unless the upper house can be overridden. The upper house's challenge should be taken seriously: it has defeated the Commons nearly 300 times between reform in 1999 and 2005, sometimes leading to changes in government policy (Russell and Sciara 2006).

A referendum could easily fail, although focus-group analysis suggests that support for moderately proportional reforms may increase once citizens are more informed about electoral systems (Farrell and Gallagher 1999). Like the Lords, a referendum might well reject a highly partisan reform proposal (as in Ireland in 1959 and 1969 when Fianna Fáil tried to change STV to SMP), especially if the party/parties favoured were currently unpopular. A referendum could also veto an electoral reform bill foisted onto an unwilling major party by a minor party in a hung parliament. That would give opponents of electoral reform much ammunition about minor parties having excessive influence.[4]

Instrumentally, rational actors should avoid the above proposals or avoid a referendum. But three successive Labour manifestos have pledged to hold a referendum before changing the electoral system, and the government reiterated this position after the 2005 election (Baroness Ashton, House of Lords debate, 26 May 2005). This in effect adds a veto point, which increases the likelihood of the reform being blocked—unless the extra veto point affects the behaviour of other veto players.

That proviso is very significant. The veto players chosen, and their sequence, can affect the behaviour of other veto players and of the agenda setter. This highlights an important agenda-setting power which has not, to my knowledge, been adequately addressed by veto player theorists: the agenda setter may have what I will call 'path-setting' powers. The agenda setter can choose not only what proposals to place on or off the agenda and in what order proposals should be addressed (Cox and

McCubbins 2005) but also what *political/legislative path* these proposals should take. Here, the agenda setter can pick between several routes for an electoral reform proposal, as well as the sequence of the actors; the precise route and sequence may affect the likelihood of veto. This makes electoral reform path-dependent in the sense that its success may depend on the political path taken. As far as I know, path-setting is not explicit in the veto player literature, although it is implicit in places (e.g. Cox and McCubbins 2005: 76, 88, 144), it is to some extent recognized by Schattschneider (1960), and it could be interpreted partly in terms of heresthetics (Riker 1986).

The probability of veto interacts with the likelihood of the particular path being taken and the type of electoral reform proposed. The path affects the likelihood of veto and the type of electoral system that may be accepted. If a veto is likely on one path, a different electoral reform may be proposed or a different path taken. And the type of electoral system proposed affects the likelihood of veto and influences the path to be taken.

In the UK, there are nine likely paths—nine likely veto games:

(1) *Parliament then Referendum.* An electoral reform bill is placed before Parliament and then, if successful, put to a referendum. I discuss two-stage referendums below.

(2) *Parliament only.* Given the possibility of a referendum veto, the government might not call a referendum at all, although for Labour this would be difficult given its manifesto commitments.

(3) *Referendum then Parliament.* The government could effectively side-step the Commons by calling a referendum first, as in New Zealand. This is not a complete sidestep, however: British referendums need prior parliamentary legislation. But blocking such a bill would probably be unpopular. So, this particular path might help to pass an electoral reform that backbenchers disliked. Note that this veto game differs from Tsebelis's (2002; Chapter 5) account of legally binding referendums: British referendums are indicative, not binding. In effect, a negative referendum would stop a proposal, but a positive referendum would pressure parliamentarians to enact it.[5]

(4) *Citizens' Assembly then Parliament then Referendum.* A government could also sidestep partisan controversy by setting up a Citizens' Assembly. The democratic credentials of citizens' assemblies should make a Commons veto less probable, especially if the Citizens'

Assembly had cross-party parliamentary backing, as in British Columbia (Carty, Blais, and Fournier Chapter 5). But Citizens' Assemblies may propose reforms which the government dislikes: the British Columbia choice of STV is more anti-party than UK governments would like, for example.

(5) *Citizens' Assembly then Referendum then Parliament.* This reverses the last two stages of option 4 and thus makes a Commons veto even less likely.

(6) *Citizens' Assembly then Parliament.* This is the same as options 4 and 5 but without a referendum.

(7) *Commission then Parliament then Referendum.* This is the same as option 4 but replaces the Citizens' Assembly with a commission, as in a Royal Commission, Independent Commission, or Speaker's Conference. The latter two are easier for the government to influence, as reportedly happened with the Jenkins Commission in 1998 (Dunleavy and Margetts 2001: 303). Commissions make the ensuing bill look more independent than a proposal emanating from a government department, but sensible commissioners are likely to choose something that the government could accept.

(8) *Commission then Referendum then Parliament.* This reverses the last two stages of option 7 and makes a Commons veto even less likely.

(9) *Commission then Parliament.* This is the same as options 7 and 8 but without a referendum.

The agenda setter's choice may of course be constrained: for example a minor party might insist on a Citizens' Assembly, to depoliticize a situation and dampen claims that reform was being forced on an unwilling major party. Note also that I do not assume fixed views: for example a referendum campaign might see many citizens change their minds about reform. And note, finally, that different veto player theorists count veto players in different ways (Ganghof 2003: 3–4); my approach is looser than Tsebelis's, who sees only the governing party/parties as veto players in the UK (Tsebelis 2002: 78–9).

The wide range of paths gives the government greater flexibility than standard accounts of electoral reform imply. For example, the Commons is in effect treated as the only veto game in town by the one study which, to my knowledge, explicitly discusses UK electoral reform in veto player terms (Dunleavy and Margetts 1995: 17–23). Recently, however, the Citizens' Assembly model has changed the structure of the game and could prove useful in a partisan deadlock.

Importantly, the agenda setter's path-setting powers can both help and hinder reform. For example, if the agenda setter wants reform and expects a Commons majority, a referendum is unnecessary and increases the probability of failure; if a Commons majority is unlikely then a successful referendum increases the probability of success, as Section 2.6 shows. (Probability of success is not the only influence on path-setting, of course. A government might think that a referendum is just right, say.) As in Canada, then, the agenda setter can partly sidestep legislators (Massicotte Chapter 4).

The agenda setter's path-setting powers can also help it to *block* a reform which it does not want. Consider a major party in a hung parliament which starts reform consultation or reform legislation in exchange for minor-party support. If the major party does not want reform, it can play for time by picking a path where the issue will fade away, or it can pick a path which increases the likelihood of veto. For example, it could choose (*a*) a referendum on whether to keep or change the system, then (*b*) a Citizens' Assembly to pick an alternative system, then (*c*) a second referendum stage, voting on the Citizens' Assembly's model, and then (*d*) Parliament, voting to enact the referendum. This could take two or three years, and either referendum could fail. A particularly shameless agenda setter could even set a referendum question that privileges the status quo. For example, a three-way choice between plurality, MMP, and STV could split the reformist vote, potentially letting the plurality system win by plurality vote (see also Riker 1986: 78–88).

So, the UK government's considerable path-setting and agenda-setting powers can help or hinder reform. Nonetheless, the nine veto games all involve Parliament because parliamentary statutes are required for electoral reform, even for referendums. And the primary veto point in Parliament is the Commons. Or, in Tsebelis's terms, the Commons is an institutional veto player but the real, partisan veto player is the pivotal party or median MP in the Commons (2002: 19). If a Commons veto is likely, the government may not propose a bill or may take a path with less chance of a Commons veto, as in paths 3 to 6 or 8. So, the agenda setter must decide whether an alternative electoral system could win majority support in the Commons, and then whether the path or sequence chosen could alter this.

2.6. MPs' Attitudes and Self-Interest

To enact electoral reform, a major party must not only start a reform process but must also get majority support for any ensuing legislation. But even if a reform is in the major party's interest, it may clash with its MPs' self-interested and attitudinal preferences.

The key problem is incumbency, which involves outcome-based self-interest: most electoral reforms would threaten the seats of incumbent MPs. This is often seen as an insuperable obstacle to reform. In fact, two types of electoral system can overcome this obstacle. First, we can keep existing seats and introduce preferential voting, probably AV. Under AV, also called Instant Runoff, citizens rank each candidate in order of preference. If no candidate has a majority of first preferences, the bottom-ranked candidate is eliminated and her preferences are reallocated. This continues until one candidate has a majority.

In three-party contests, AV tends to disadvantage the Condorcet loser, the party that would lose to the other two parties in pairwise contests. In recent elections the Conservatives have been the Condorcet loser in many marginal seats, losing some of these through tactical voting between Labour and Liberal Democrat supporters. AV would have extended this: in 2005 Labour's majority might have been 20–30 seats larger (Baston 2005: 42). AV's anti-Conservative potential and the likelihood that it would not have threatened the incumbency of most Labour and Liberal Democrat MPs means that Labour should still have won a Commons majority between 1997 and 2005. This reflects the incentives keeping the Liberal Democrats closer to Labour in recent years: both parties have benefited from anti-Conservative tactical voting, which itself reflects a perception by many citizens who dislike the Conservatives that Labour and the Liberal Democrats are ideologically close (Fisher and Curtice 2006: 57).

Things could be changing, though. The Liberal Democrats have been distancing themselves from Labour in Commons and Lords votes (Cowley and Stuart 2004; Russell and Sciara 2006) and are in coalition with the Conservatives in some local councils. If Labour becomes very unpopular in the polls, the benefits of aligning with them decrease. Voting behaviour is also starting to change. The 2005 general election saw some 'unwind' in Labour/Liberal Democrat tactical voting in certain areas (Russell, Cutts, and Fieldhouse 2007). More importantly, the 2006 local elections saw anti-Labour tactical voting (Baston 2006: 58). AV could seriously disadvantage Labour if it becomes the Condorcet loser. Although at least one senior Labour figure recommended AV before the 2005 election (Hain 2004), the leadership did not budge and the opportunity may have passed.

The second kind of electoral system which would not threaten incumbency is an unusual form of MMP system. (In the UK, MMP is often called the Additional Member System or AMS.) Under MMP, part of the legislature is elected in single-member districts and part is elected in a second, more proportional tier with higher district magnitude. MMP systems have previously been thought to fit into the turkeys-voting-for-Christmas category. Even replacing 150 plurality seats with a second tier of the same size would disrupt all other MPs since each remaining plurality seat would have to be made bigger. One solution is the New Zealand option, adding the extra tier on top of existing MPs *without reducing the number of MPs elected in single-member districts*. Thus, one could keep the existing 650 plurality seats and add, say, 50, 100, or 150 top-up seats, constituting 7, 13, or 19% of a chamber with 700, 750, or 800 MPs, respectively. No incumbent need lose her seat. We can call this 'super-sized MMP'. The additional seats could be allocated in several ways (Massicotte and Blais 1999) but proportionality between votes and seats may not be markedly improved with these low levels of top-up seats (Dunleavy and Margetts 2005: 864–6). Indeed, its limited proportionality makes it *more* palatable to a major party, which would not lose out much in seats. It is alleged that in 1996 Tony Blair agreed to a 50-seat second tier but saw a 150-seat second tier as too large for the public to stomach (Ashdown 2000: 426, 528).

That highlights the obvious defect of super-sized MMP—more MPs in a chamber which is already unusually large (Taagepera and Shugart 1989: 175). Meanwhile many onlookers want to cut MPs: the 2005 Conservative manifesto pledged to reduce the Commons by a fifth. (That would be even harder to get through the Commons than an electoral reform bill, of course.) Opponents of reform, and sceptical journalists and citizens, would certainly attack moves to expand the house. Anticipating derision, potential reformers would either (*a*) avoid a referendum and pick a path involving Parliament only, (*b*) pick a 50-seat second tier, though that might not be proportional enough for the Liberal Democrats, or (*c*) reject this option out of hand, for fear of losing votes and seats. This last option is most likely.

Super-sized MMP is thus very unlikely: the mere act of attempting to introduce it might lead to a significant loss of votes. Nonetheless, a government could decide that the chance of continued office was worth risking vote losses since, as we will see, any reform that challenges incumbency would be costly in other ways. Reformers could defend themselves by pledging to cut seats in the future, for example removing 40 single-member-district seats whenever boundaries are redrawn every 10–15 years—a rate of change that should not worry incumbents overly. A bill could explicitly aim for an eventual 450-seat legislature with a third of MPs elected in second-tier seats, say. Reformers could also present positive arguments such as more MPs enabling better representation, both in principal–agent terms and as regards proportionality between votes and seats; for example, this would improve representation for citizens in 'electoral deserts', such as the Labour-dominated inner cities and Conservative-dominated countryside. Even so, for act-based reasons super-sized MMP is unlikely to be proposed.

So, there are two electoral reforms which would not threaten incumbency, and both could be introduced quickly—which could be important if a party needs reform in a hurry. But each reform has problems. AV may not be in Labour's outcome-based party-interest and could threaten the self-interest of many Labour MPs in marginal seats. Super-sized MMP is probably not in any party's act-based interest: the very way in which it meets MPs' self-interest makes it politically unpalatable.

Attitudes are also worth emphasizing. Many Labour MPs want greater proportionality and might reject AV as it can be less proportional than plurality elections. Meanwhile, other Labour MPs might oppose *any* electoral reform. It was estimated that between 1997 and 2005, Labour MPs were split roughly into a third who supported a more proportional system, a third who opposed it, and a third who were undecided or would not say. (We do not know to what extent these views reflect attitudes and/or interests.) The 2005 election saw many pro-reform MPs lose their marginal seats, ironically often to Liberal Democrats, such that the current Labour party probably contains somewhat more opponents than proponents of reform.[6] Even if Labour leaders wanted reform, there may be opposition not only from those worried about losing their seats but also from those with attitudinal opposition to reform.

Unless their views could be changed through discussion, how might MPs who oppose reform on interest-based or attitudinal grounds be induced to vote for reform? A manifesto commitment to reform (rather than merely to a referendum) would require pre-emptive action, before a hung parliament, and could well be insufficient anyway: an election result that left the governing party without a majority of seats might be interpreted as showing insufficient support for that manifesto commitment to bind MPs.

A second option is a referendum before the parliamentary stage. If the referendum passes, unwilling MPs might feel impelled to support it. This might be through act-based attitudes, if opposing a positive referendum result were seen as undemocratic or act-based self-interest, if opposing a positive referendum result might see these MPs lose their seats. Thus Dunleavy and Margetts (2001: 317) view a referendum as the most likely way to get electoral reform: the public could 'bind reluctant MPs to accept a radical change of Westminster elections'.

A third option is simply to whip hard and rely on party cohesion. This would motivate a reluctant MP through act-based attitudes, whereby she feels a duty to support her party leaders, and act-based self-interest, whereby she would be punished if she voted against instructions. In the Scottish Parliament in 2004, Labour members eventually supported STV in local government as the price of a coalition with the Liberal Democrats. But that involved turkeys voting for other turkeys' Christmases. It is difficult to say whether such whipping would suffice if MPs were being asked to remove their own seats. To maximize the chances of reform, a government should announce the bill as a confidence motion; losing this would lead to another election. Most or all reluctant MPs would fall into line.[7]

Each option would be costly. Government MPs might attack other legislation if they felt that they had been coerced or manipulated to back a reform that would remove their seats. Averting such anger by pork-barrel politics would involve further costs. Relying on a positive referendum result is also risky unless popular support for electoral reform rises to the levels found in New Zealand in the early 1990s (Vowles Chapter 6). But at the moment, electoral reform is not a major issue for most citizens, as in Canada (Massicotte Chapter 4). Referendums are more likely to fail if they look like a partisan fix or are proposed from positions of weakness.

So, incumbency-based self-interest endangers electoral reform; tackling it would be costly or risky. But I disagree with the common claim that electoral reform is impossible because it would involve turkeys voting for Christmas. Reluctant MPs can be induced to back reform, both on attitudinal and interest-based grounds.

Note the importance of *timing*. Veto player theory is usually static (e.g. Tsebelis 2002), but the temporal dimension is relevant. If a party's decline is sudden or unexpected it may not have time to reform the electoral system. The British Liberals did not reform the system when they had the chance in 1917–18; by 1924 they were a minor party with just 40 seats (Bogdanor 1981: 128–37). Neil Kinnock has stated that when he was Labour leader, from 1983 to 1992, he could not campaign for electoral reform, despite his preference for it: this would have looked like an admission that Labour could not win by itself. Reform remains in Labour's interests, he argues, so Labour should introduce it while in government, before the opportunity passes (Kinnock 2005).

Timing also affects the choice of electoral system. As discussed above, it may already be too late for Labour to adopt AV. More generally, simple legislative mathematics suggests that a party may need to initiate reform *pre-emptively*. As the number of a party's MPs falls, the greater the proportion that would be needed to vote for reform. Let us assume 80 minor-party MPs backing reform, 5 Sinn Féin MPs who do not take their seats, and full turnout in a Commons vote. Three hundred and twenty-one MPs would be needed for a majority. (Some of these assumptions are obviously unrealistic but the general point is valid.) Let us also assume that Labour MPs are split into a third who favour reform, a third who oppose it, and a third who are undecided. Under these assumptions, a reform bill would need the backing of 242 Labour MPs—two-thirds of the current 353 MPs. If Labour lost 32 MPs, creating a hung parliament, three-quarters of the remaining party would need to vote for reform. If Labour lost 95 seats and could just form a minimal winning coalition with the Liberal Democrats, 9 out of every 10 Labour MPs would have to back reform. Worse, Labour MPs who oppose reform are more likely to be in safe seats; indeed as noted above, several reformists already lost their marginal seats in 2005.

So, the more a party needs reform, in a hung parliament where it wants minor-party support in exchange for electoral reform, the harder reform becomes. This reflects both legislative mathematics and, in Labour's case, the current relationship between attitudes and marginality. An instrumentally rational party leader must thus look ahead, estimate whether reform is in the party's interests in the next parliament, weigh up the costs of forcing the reform over unwilling MPs, and consider whether pre-emptive action would make things easier.

In short, the winset of opportunity is narrow. In veto player theory, the 'winset' is the set of policies that can defeat the status quo, and as we have seen the winset is often closed or contains only a few options. But the size of the winset changes over time, so if the median MP is more likely to back reform before rather than after a hung parliament, then an instrumentally rational party leader should consider pre-emptive actions. This is risky, however, and many politicians have optimistic dispositions: they often think that they can regain enough votes and seats to escape situations like hung parliaments. So, while uncertainty can help reform, for example if a party introduces PR to avoid risking a decade in opposition, uncertainty can also hinder reform: by the time a hung parliament arises, the opportunity for reform may have gone.

2.7. Conclusion

Like all political institutions, plurality electoral systems contain the seeds of their own destruction. Plurality elections usually give the largest party a seat bonus but can disadvantage parties which do badly in votes, whose geography of votes is inefficient, or whose opponents coordinate better. This gives incentives for a governing party to reform electoral institutions if it expects to be disadvantaged in one of these ways. But the winset of opportunity is narrow, in terms of interests, attitudes, and timing.

This chapter has combined an understanding of the electoral and political incentives for and against change with a veto player analysis of the many paths to reform. In effect, this shows the need to argue both forwards and backwards—forwards, from the interests and attitudes of those who set the agenda and can make proposals for institutional change, and backwards, from the interests and attitudes of those with the power to block these changes. Veto player theory tells us to expect some accommodation between what the agenda setter and the veto players want. But politicians work in multiple arenas and even those with interests or attitudes opposed to reform could be induced to back it if the agenda setter finds the right strategy. In the UK, however, such strategies may be costly and risky.

So, reform could easily get onto the agenda, especially in a hung parliament, but reform is less likely to get off the agenda and onto the statute book. Most reforms challenge the incumbency-based self-interest of many MPs and face further attitudinal opposition. But the veto point in the Commons can be hurdled, for example by holding a referendum first. I have thus rejected the common claim that reform is impossible because turkeys will not vote for Christmas.

The bigger problem is that reform is not obviously in either major party's interests. Reform would not avert the Conservatives' current disadvantage. Labour's case for reform is stronger, although Labour reformists sometimes indulge in wishful thinking. Overall, those who expect hung parliaments to usher in electoral reform should not be overly optimistic.

These conclusions are largely unsurprising. They are also uncertain: I have described reform as 'possible but unlikely', which is obviously vague. This uncertainty reflects the multiple perspectives that politicians take, which is why I have combined veto player theory with other conceptual frameworks, especially the distinction between act-based and outcome-based motivations; the question of whether parties focus on votes, seats, policy, and/or office; and the dilemma of whether they aim to maximize their position when they do well or minimize the damage when they do badly. These considerations make accurate prediction difficult, because different politicians have different interests, attitudes, motivations, perspectives, dispositions, information, and understanding. For example, a Labour leader might focus on the divided progressive forces or on Labour more narrowly, she might be a risk-taker or more cautious, she might have a good understanding of the effects of reform or not. These will not always point in the same direction and it is difficult to guess how any given individual will weigh up these different considerations.

Ultimately, the benefits of veto player theory will come with more formal modelling of the conditions for electoral reform, and more empirical testing of these hypotheses in reality, in plurality systems and elsewhere. But even this chapter's relatively informal and abstract application of veto player theory has clarified the issues. Two further advantages of the particular veto player perspective used here are the idea of what I have called 'path-setting', and the emphasis on timing. The agenda setter chooses not only what goes onto the agenda but also the legislative path by which it travels. The flexibility to choose between various veto points and the sequence in which they act can help or hinder electoral reform, depending on the agenda setter's preferences. Timing also matters: the agenda setter must look ahead to consider whether reform should be started sooner rather than later.

In short, the winset of opportunity for electoral reform in the UK is narrow. The British electoral system's weaknesses mean that electoral reform could well become a prominent issue but the prospects for change are slimmer than is sometimes implied. Even if a hung parliament arises, electoral reform may not be initiated; even if electoral reform is initiated, it may not be implemented; even if electoral reform is implemented, it may not be a radical change.

Notes

1. I thank Kevin Morgan for advising me to consider these historical parallels.
2. I thank Meg Russell for pointing out this scenario.
3. I thank Alan Ware for criticizing my earlier arguments on this point.
4. I thank Lewis Baston for pointing out this scenario.
5. I thank Robert Hazell and Alan Trench for advice on referendums.
6. I thank Mary Southcott for these data on Labour MPs.
7. I thank Ken Ritchie for pointing out this scenario.

3

Election Reform and (the Lack of) Electoral System Change in the USA

Shaun Bowler and Todd Donovan

As other chapters in this volume show, many of the long established examples of single-member district (SMD) elections have been under review in recent years. New Zealand's change in 1993 was the most dramatic but continuing debates within both Canada and UK—at least at the sub-national level—point to the end for SMD. In the USA, however, there seems to be a relative lack of interest in election reform and electoral system change. In this chapter, we seek to advance an understanding of the reasons for the lack of change of electoral system in the US case. Along the way we make three points.

First, explaining the lack of system change is difficult. While there are several possible explanations for the lack of system change it is not entirely clear which (if any) apply. Second, the lack of system change should not be equated to a lack of electoral reform; and certainly not when we consider attempts at the state and local level. Perhaps more than any other example the US case shows that a great deal of electoral reform takes place even as the system of translating votes into seats remains the same. Third, the lack of electoral system change coupled with the frequent reform of electoral laws raises a series of other questions about how one should measure electoral institutions and electoral change. 'American exceptionalism' may be problematic for broader theories of electoral change. We illustrate this point by using as an example debates over reapportionment in the USA in the 1920s and 1930s.

3.1. The Lack of Electoral System Change in the USA

There seems to be no moment of conscious choice of SMD at the founding of electoral institutions in the USA. Colonial and then American elections followed the English practice of plurality elections. These were, in any event, the basis of the only popular elections held during the seventeenth century and so provided the only model for how to conduct elections. Sometimes with multi-member districts but generally conducted according to plurality rules (see Morgan 1989 for an account of colonial electoral institutions), but this practice gradually died out.[1]

But while there may have been few alternative electoral systems at the start of the American republic there are certainly many alternatives to choose from today, and other nations with a heritage of plurality elections have begun to reconsider the standing choice of plurality. The chapters in this volume on New Zealand by Jack Vowles (Chapter 6), on Canada by Massicotte (Chapter 4), and on the UK by Blau (Chapter 2) all show the range and vibrancy of reform debates: SMD may have had its day. In the USA, however, no serious consideration is being given to changing the system of elections away from SMD to one of the very many alternatives on offer.

Despite the examples of change worldwide, the general theoretical expectation is that electoral systems should not change at all. The 'stickiness' of institutions is one of the leading stylized facts about institutions and (the lack of) institutional change. Indeed, given the strength of factors that drive stickiness, one major concern seems to be accounting for the fact that institutions change at all. The essential problem of electoral system change remains that it asks winners to change the rules that made them winners and this is not an easy thing to ask; not least because even new winners with fresh memories of being losers soon realize the advantages of the institutions that have just made them winners. There are many arguments, then, that stress the difficulty of change in general. Andrews and Jackman (2005) for example stress factors such as risk adversity and uncertainty and the role of unintended consequences as ones that put brakes on electoral reform (see also Shvetsova 2003). Blau (Chapter 2) notes that both the major parties in the UK have reasons to be reluctant supporters of change. But these kinds of factors presumably operate everywhere—what is it about the USA in particular that is unusual? Of course, having said that, we should note that given the very strong expectation of 'no change' in some ways it is the UK,

New Zealand, and others who are exceptions since they have introduced changes. A more precise statement about the US case is, then: what is it about the USA in particular that makes the resistance to change unusually strong?

Explaining the absence of an event is difficult at the best of times; and understanding the lack of electoral system change in the USA is no exception to this rule. As is often the case the observation (no change) is overdetermined by the range of different theories and explanations that may be brought to bear.

One way in which we may begin to understand the absence of change is by considering arguments that seek to explain change. What we can then do is set out some of the theoretical arguments that seek to explain change in electoral systems and then examine the US case. Presumably, in the US case, we should see the absence of factors that are held to produce electoral system change.

Generally speaking, explanations of change take some form of an argument that emphasizes the strategic choices of winners and losers (Anderson et al. 2005). An emphasis upon the calculations and expectations of winners and losers is largely informed by a rational choice framework and, also, conforms with our general expectation that incumbent politicians will not want to change an electoral system if it means committing electoral suicide. One version of this argument is that losers under current arrangements will want to change the system. If and when these losers become winners they will then introduce changes. A second version of the winner/loser argument is that current winners will want to change the system to reinforce or preserve their status. Either way, the emphasis is upon winning and losing within a framework that presupposes self-interested politicians.

The literature to date contains a number of examples of these arguments. Shugart (Chapter 1) for example argues the case for a variant of the first of these arguments. Change in SMD is more likely after an election which has produced an 'upside down' result. When a party that wins the popular vote loses the election then this party becomes a powerful voice for change. That is, when bitter losers under SMD become winners the stage is ripe for change. An example of this would be the move to electoral reform in British Columbia (BC) discussed in Chapter 5. One of the difficulties here is that it seems that elected members from winning parties tend to realize the hitherto hidden benefits of the system that made them winners. Blau (Chapter 2) discusses this effect in the British context where an example is provided by the British Labour government's waning ardour for changing the system of elections for Parliament—the elections that matter.

An example of the second version of the argument is found in Boix's account of the switch to proportional representation (PR) from plurality systems in mainland Europe in the early part of the twentieth century (Boix 1999). Boix's account has come under some criticism (Andrews and Jackman 2005) but does represent a version of the winner/loser argument that locates the demand for change among winners (not, as in Shugart's argument, among losers): when winning parties expect to lose (and lose badly) under plurality because of new entrants into the political system they will support a change to PR as a way to minimize their losses. In the modern period, Australia provides examples of this kind of argument. Farrell and McAllister, for example, note the package of changes introduced in New South Wales to reinforce the position of bigger parties (Farrell and McAllister 2006a: 68–9). Another example is the Australian Labor party's decision to adopt PR elections for the Australian Senate in 1948 (Uhr 1999) in order to avoid electoral defeat. France's shift to PR for National Assembly elections in 1986 would provide another example of this kind of change. It is important to note, however, that Boix's argument in relation to the specific historical cases he studies does require a component of social change. For him it is the entry of new parties that represent new groups of voters that has the potential to threaten and disrupt the old arrangements and so pushes the winners under current rules to propose changes that limit future losses.

To the extent that these versions of the 'winners and losers' argument hold as explanations for change then the absence of the preconditions identified by both Shugart and Boix in the US context would go some way to explain the absence of electoral system change.

The kinds of argument relating to expansion of the franchise and social change identified by Boix do not seem to readily apply in the US case. By contrast to European experience the franchise was—for white voters—relatively inclusive. The main expansion of the franchise to embrace previously excluded social groups which may be seen as broadly similar to the kinds of expansions covered by Boix's account, grounded in the work of Rokkan and others, was the inclusion of African-Americans from the 1960s onwards. African-American participation was channelled into existing party structures rather than resulting in the setting up of new and separate political parties. But the American example does leave some questions unanswered: it is not entirely clear why minorities have not sought to develop ethnically based political parties. There is something that is perhaps specific to the racial dimension of American politics that means the Rokkan style argument of Boix has limited application outside the specific historical examples of European politics during the early twentieth century.

In general, new party entrants to the system have largely been kept out of politics by the dominance of the two main parties.[2] Through the use of restrictive ballot-access laws and flexible policy stances (that allows, e.g., the co-optation of nascent third party issues and considerable sensitivity to local variation in ideology) the two main parties have managed to maintain their duopoly position in ways in which European counterparts were unable or unwilling to copy. If anything, then, the US case would seem to suggest that such changes as we do see fits the broad argument of 'winners introducing changes to preserve their status'. None of these changes, however, have required altering the electoral system.

At first blush, Shugart's argument—which is less historically specific than Boix's—does seem to apply to the US case. At the national level— for Congress—it does generally seem to be the case that overall there is relatively little evidence of the kinds of distorted result that provoked, for example, the BC reform or any of the other cases noted by Shugart. Hence the trigger for reform is missing. We can illustrate the 'absence of cause' by looking at the relationship between seats and votes in the USA.

Table 3.1 takes data from the Center for Voting and Democracy (CVD), the main US lobby group in favour of electoral reform. For the past seven elections the party that won the most votes took the majority in the House.[3] At the national level, then, Shugart's argument would seem to give us some insight. Congress has not seen 'upside down' results and so there are few sustained calls to reform the electoral system.

But nationwide results can give a misleading sense of how successful US elections are at turning votes into seats. Table 3.2, also taken from CVD, presents state-to-state variations in the disproportionality of the system by reporting a measure of electoral distortion (defined in the table). The figure in the last row of the table shows the low level of distortion nationally, but this figure masks considerable distortion at the state level.

The point raised by Table 3.2 is that while there may be no reason or impetus for reform nationwide there surely must be such an impetus at

Table 3.1. Votes–seats relationship for US Congress 1992–2000 (in %)

	GOP	DEM	Other
1992			
Votes	45.4	50.8	3.8
Seats	40.5	59.3	0.2
1994			
Votes	52.4	45.4	2.2
Seats	52.9	46.9	0.2
1996			
Votes	48.9	48.6	2.5
Seats	52.2	47.6	0.2
1998			
Votes	49.1	47.9	3
Seats	51.3	48.5	0.2
2000			
Votes	48.2	47.9	3.9
Seats	50.8	48.7	0.4
2002			
Votes	50.9	46	3.1
Seats	52.6	47.1	0.2
2004			
Votes	50.1	47.5	2.4
Seats	53.3	46.4	0.2

Source: The Center for Voting and Democracy website.
Abbreviations: GOP: Republican Party; DEM: Democratic Party.

the state level—just as in British Columbia in Canada. Yet there is no such argument at the state level.

The extent of the problem at the state level can be shown by some more specific examples from the state level. Table 3.3 shows such an example using state-level electoral data from the State of Georgia that shows the kind of 'upside down' result in both 2000 and 2002 that should lead the losing party to demand changing the electoral system entirely—but has not happened.

Thus while Shugart's argument may be seen to fit national patterns it does not seem to fit state patterns, yet presumably should do so. At least part of the explanation for the lack of a demand for change is that the existing parties rely on redistricting—rather than electoral system change—for redress. The Georgia redistricting meant that the 2004 results were not as distorted as earlier ones. And often court-mandated redistricting—as in the case of Pennsylvania[4]—operates as a corrective mechanism to produce broadly proportional outcomes through periodic redistricting. The two main parties would, then, seem to prefer to wage

Table 3.2. Seats to votes 'distortion'

Ranking	State	Seats-to-votes (%)	Ranking	State	Seats-to-votes (%)
1	New Jersey	0.7	26	Oklahoma	12.3
2	Missouri	1.1	27	Mississippi	14.5
3	Wisconsin	1.3	28	Ohio	15.4
4	Illinois	1.4	29	Connecticut	15.5
5	South Carolina	1.7	30	Maryland	15.8
6	North Carolina	2.8	31	New Mexico	18.5
7	Minnesota	3.0	32	Massachusetts	18.5
8	Texas	6.3	33	Indiana	19.9
9	California	7.1	34	Kentucky	20.6
10	Colorado	7.2	35	Arkansas	20.7
11	Washington	7.3	36	Iowa	23.2
12	Georgia	7.6	37	Oregon	24.6
13	Utah	7.9	38	Alaska	25.6
14	Tennessee	8.5	39	Vermont	28.2
15	West Virginia	8.6	40	Rhode Island	29.3
16	New York	9.1	41	Idaho	29.9
17	Louisiana	9.4	42	Delaware	30.3
18	Michigan	9.5	43	Nebraska	31.4
19	Virginia	9.5	44	Montana	34.2
20	Kansas	10.4	45	Hawaii	36.4
21	Arizona	10.8	46	New Hampshire	38.3
22	Alabama	11.1	47	North Dakota	40.4
23	Nevada	11.2	48	Maine	40.5
24	Florida	12.2	49	Wyoming	43.3
25	Pennsylvania	12.3	50	South Dakota	46.3
				USA	2.3

Notes: The seats-to-votes distortion measures the extent to which one party wins a greater percentage of seats than votes and the other party wins a smaller percentage of seats than votes. It is determined by adding the percentage distortion for each party and dividing by two. For example, if Democrats won 10% more seats than votes and Republicans 6% fewer seats than votes, the distortion would be 8%.

Source: The Center for Voting and Democracy website.

their battles by using some combination of redistricting and legal action rather than altering the electoral system.

For both variants of the argument of electoral system change grounded in the expectations and preferences of winners and losers, the American case provides only partial support. The arguments—and specifically the arguments of Boix and Shugart—can be adapted to apply to the US case but do seem to require some subsidiary or additional argument in order to make them work. An additional argument could be about the actions of the parties themselves or the special impact of race in the USA or something else. Whatever it is, however, that argument would seem to have to be made.

Table 3.3. Seats–votes shares for Democratic Party in
Georgia state elections (in %)

	House		Senate	
	Seats	Votes	Seats	Votes
2000	57	45	58	47
2002	54	46	59	51
2004	38	42	47	44

Source: Georgia Secretary of State; authors.

A more concrete example may help fix the point: an argument
grounded in the incentives of winners and losers does get us some way
towards understanding change (or the lack of change) in the USA—but it
does not get us all the way. We take as our example how US politicians
treated reapportionment, that is the distribution of seats between states.

At first blush this could be seen to be a case of moving the goalposts
of the argument. After all, this volume is about electoral system change
in first past the post systems, not about reapportionment. But the difference in talking about the theoretical understanding of reapportionment
as opposed to a theoretical understanding of electoral reform is more
apparent than real. True, reapportionment is not the same as an electoral
system; but they are both components of the same set of rules and regulations that govern the conduct of elections (see Bowler, Carter, and Farrell
2003; Massicotte, Blais, and Yoshinaka 2004). Moreover, reapportionment
(the allocation of seats to population) and redistricting (the drawing of
boundaries) are at the forefront of factors that shape the results in first past
the post systems. Perhaps more than most places the USA illustrates the
point that electoral systems are but the tip of the electoral iceberg and it
is a tip that is tightly connected to the vast bundle of laws and regulations
submerged below view. Because of the close relationship between electoral
laws and electoral systems, electoral laws should be open to theoretical
explanation by the same kinds of theoretical arguments that are applied
to understanding electoral systems. This should be especially true when
we look to such features as reapportionment and redistricting where there
are real possibilities of shifting a party balance. That is, it would seem
to be plausible to suppose that changes both in electoral law and also
electoral system should be explained by the same theoretical framework,
and it is especially plausible to believe that theories grounded in a win-
ner/loser framework would hold for both types of changes. Thus, while
a look at reapportionment is not quite the change as a look at electoral
systems the two should be very closely related, hence our understanding

of apportionment should help inform an understanding of the applicability of theories electoral system change (or lack of change) in the USA.

3.2. Explaining Changes in US Electoral Laws: Winners, Losers, and the 1920s Reapportionment

All districted systems including first past the post require the drawing of district boundaries. Periodically, these boundaries are redrawn in order to accommodate changing populations. Shifts in these boundaries can be hugely consequential in terms of who gets represented. Part of the consequence of Britain's 1832 Reform Act, for example, involved a shift in seats from the Southern to the Northern part of the country and a shift in who was being represented. In the USA in addition to redistricting (which occurs within each state) there is an additional process of reapportionment. That is the number of seats allocated to each state is—in principle—renegotiated after every census. While the reapportionment was supposed to occur after every census it did not occur after the 1920 census until late in the decade.

The debates and discussion over reapportionment in the 1920s are important in that they present an illustration of a moment where changes in important rules governing elections were decided. Furthermore, the consequences of the change were not at all uncertain. Here, then, we should see an example of one of the family of winners/losers arguments to hold.

The 1920s saw a series of debates over how to reapportion. Part of this was due to a debate over competing methods of reapportionment that involved the National Academy of Sciences, to arrive at a means of apportionment. One of the issues was that one method, the 'method of equal proportions', gave small states more seats than did the 'method of major fractions'—at least on the basis of the 1920 census (see Schmeckebier 1941: 64).[5] To some extent, too, debates over method masked continuing disagreement between rural and urban interests since the 1920 census results implied that the rural interests would lose out to the urban ones. The debates dragged on through the 1920s with much parliamentary manoeuvring. A 1921 bill was killed in Senate committee, as was one in February 1929. Schmeckebier counted 42 bills introduced in the House between 1920 and 1927 (Schmeckebier 1941: 121; see also Sweeting 1956: 440). In 1929, an act was passed that did permit reapportionment on the

Table 3.4. Roll call vote on 1929 Reapportionment Act (Probit model; dependent variable 1 = support for Act)

	House	House	Senate	Senate
State	**1.37*****	**1.47*****	**.61****	**.72****
(1 = state gains seats; −1 = state loses seats; 0 = stays same)	(.17)	(.17)	(.27)	(.29)
Party	**−.89*****	−.27	**−1.04****	−.01
(1 = Republican, 0 = Democrat)	(.16)	(.47)	(.005)	(.42)
DW-nominate	—	.86	—	**1.80****
(from Poole)		(.63)		(.42)
Constant	1.07	.63	1.14	.72
Pseudo R^2	.27	.28	.16	.27
N	361	361	93	93
Probability of voting for measure				
If from a state losing seats	.25	.24	.53	.57
If from a state gaining seats	.98	.98	.90	.95

Notes: If paired votes are included the N increases slightly and the results still hold (although there are missing data).

Figures in **bold** significant at .10 level or better.

Source: Poole DW-nominate data; *Congressional Record*.

basis of the 1930 census and allowed for automatic reapportionment in subsequent years. That roll call is notable for two points.

First, the roll call vote shows the strong and clear relevance of winner and loser effects. The leading theoretical argument informing our understanding of how change should come about is thus supported. Expectations of winning and losing plainly strongly influenced the Congressional roll call on the act. Table 3.4 presents a very simple model of the roll call vote in which vote to support the proposed change in reapportionment is modelled as a function of the home state of the Member of Congress (whether the member's state gained seats under reapportionment, whether they stayed the same, or whether they lost seats) as well as two measures of 'ideology': one a simple party dummy, the other the first dimension of the DW-nominate score. As can be seen from the predicted probabilities listed in the table, the effect of state identity is very large indeed. Furthermore, as one might expect, the effect is much larger for the House than the Senate.

The results of Table 3.4 then suggest that a winner/loser argument has much to tell us about the politics of changing rules governing elections. We can pursue this point further by looking at those members of Congress who voted 'wrong': that is, those Congressmen from states that would gain seats who voted against the proposal and those from states

Table 3.5. Tracking those who voted 'wrong' in 1929

	In 1929	Ran in 1930	Won in 1930	Ran in 1932	Won in 1932
All candidates					
Voted for measure in state that would lose	14	13	11	10	5
Voted against measure in state that would gain	20	18	14	9	5
Republicans only					
Voted for measure in state that would lose	12	12	10	8	3
Voted against measure in state that would gain	19	17	13	9	5

that would lose seats who voted for the proposal. Such Congressmen would be violating the assumption of self-interest and so deserve closer attention.

One pattern, consistent with an argument about expectations, is that those who supported the reform (but 'should not have') will be electorally safer than those who opposed the reform (but who 'should have' supported it). That is, expectations of personal electoral success and failure may well drive 'mistakes'. Some Congressmen in states that would lose from reapportionment might support it if they, personally, were safe, while some of those in states that would gain seats might not like it if they, personally, were at risk of being defeated. To some extent that expectation is borne out. By 1932—when the redistricting first took effect—there would seem to be a somewhat higher retention rate and a lower retirement rate among those who 'mistakenly' supported the measure than those who opposed it. In 1932, 5 of the 14 who supported the measure in 1929 were re-elected (36%), while 5 of the 20 (25%) of those who had opposed the measure were still in Congress.

The pattern is a little less clear when we consider Republicans alone but the general point of Tables 3.4 and 3.5 would seem to be that expectations of electoral success or failure can drive change, that is that a suitably defined version of winner and loser effects can be shown to influence American attitudes to changing the electoral system.

Second, and more importantly, while the results of this model do provide strong evidence for the existence of winner and loser effects, we should note that they only tell us part of the story. In particular, they do not tell us why the reform happened when it did. Some reform would seem to have been likely for a number of years prior to 1929 if only because reapportionment was demanded by the Constitution itself. Furthermore, the supporters of reform had a slight edge in the House, at least, where the states that lost seats had—combined—67 seats (i.e. votes), while the gainers had between them 93 seats from 1920 onwards. This means that winner/loser concerns shaded towards support for change from 1920 onwards.[6] These factors would seem to push towards some kind of reapportionment; the repeated delays throughout the 1920s showed that change was far from automatic: that is winner/loser expectations may provide a necessary but not a sufficient explanation of change in apportionment policy.

One of the main reasons for the reform comes down to an individual. A key policy entrepreneur was John Tilson of Connecticut who engaged in parliamentary tactics to ensure the passage of the reform. In particular, he managed to defeat two killer amendments. Both amendments considered whom to count for purposes of apportionment.[7]

Hoch of Kansas sought an amendment to remove aliens and non-citizens from the count. This would clearly hurt the claim of north-eastern states that contained large numbers of non-native residents. In retaliation to that proposal Tinkham of Massachusetts offered an amendment to exclude disenfranchised persons (i.e. African-Americans) from any count relating to reapportionment: while Southerners may not have wanted African-Americans to vote, they certainly wanted them to be counted as voters for purposes of reapportionment. Essentially, the impact of both proposals for the north-eastern and Southern states was very similar. For example, the 1920 census lists the foreign born percentage of population of New York as ~27% and for Connecticut as ~28%. Meanwhile the black population comprised roughly 39% of Alabama's total population, 27% of Arkansas', and 50% of Mississippi's 1920 population. The extent to which people were disenfranchised in the Southern states is illustrated by Schmeckebier's tables (1941: 98–106) listing turnout by Congressional district for the years 1936 and 1938.[8] The numbers are, quite simply, astonishing. While the North-east, West, and Midwest saw turnout as a percentage of population around the 40–50% level, turnout in the Southern states hovered around—and often under—10% even in Presidential years. While some of this low turnout may well have been due to uncontested elections in the 'one party South', these figures illustrate the truly staggering level of black disenfranchisement in Southern elections. The Tinkham amendment would have, therefore, taken many seats away from the South while Hoch's amendment would have reduced the North-east's delegation by about a quarter and redistributed those seats to the South and Midwest.

Both these amendments passed and were included in the bill. If they remained part of any bill then neither Southerners nor north-easterners would support that bill. Tilson then moved an amendment of his own. In his own words,

My task was to have eliminated both amendments. The method used was the simple one of offering in Committee of the Whole an amendment to strike out the entire section relating to reapportionment and insert substantially the original Senate provision in somewhat different phraseology. To secure votes enough to adopt such an amendment it was necessary to combine the two groups opposing each of the offending amendments thus using each of these amendments to kill off the other. It was like mixing an acid with an alkali to neutralize both.

(comments of Rep Tilson 11 June 1929 at 2676 *Congressional Record*)

Having moved his amendment, and successfully staving off renewed efforts by Hoch to reinstate the alien amendment, the Act was passed.

In short, and notwithstanding the demands of the Constitution and the push given by winner and loser effects, success of the reapportionment measure depended at least in part on the efforts of a specific entrepreneur to move the reform along. This example of a fight that is now long forgotten illustrates a point that was seen in both the New Zealand and also the British Columbia cases: yet another reason why electoral reform is hard to see is the lack of skilled entrepreneurs with an interest in reform. There is an important difference between necessary and sufficient conditions for change. That is, the kinds of factors outlined in Tables 3.4 and 3.5 show necessary conditions for electoral reform, but they may not be sufficient. Not surprisingly, the default prediction for any episode of electoral change is that there will be no change.

3.3. The USA: An Unchanging Electoral System but Constant Change in Electoral Law

There have been a few, sporadic attempts at change. Congresswoman McKinney of Georgia introduced the Voter Choice Act of 2005 HR 2690 109th CONGRESS to 'provide that a State may use a proportional voting system for multiseat congressional districts, to require the use of instant

Table 3.6. Roll call voting data 83rd–108th Congress: 1953–2004

	Total votes by topic	Of which final passage/adoption of a bill	Of which passed	Passage/adoption of a bill under suspension of rules	Of which passed
Campaign finance	127	12	11	19	7
Election procedures	23	3	3	2	2
Federal Election Commission	18	2	2	1	1
Equal time/fairness	14	2	2	0	0
Voter registration	26	4	4	1	1
Redistricting	9	2	2	1	1
Congressional term limits	16	0	—	0	0
Miscellaneous	31	3	3	5	3
Total	264	28	27	29	15
Total in data set	20,597	3,224	3,138	2,016	1,912

Notes: Excludes 35 votes on the VRA.

Source: Rohde, David W., *Roll Call Voting Data for the United States House of Representatives, 1953–2004.* Compiled by the Political Institutions and Public Choice Program, Michigan State University, East Lansing, MI (2004), http://www.msu.edu/~pipc/pipcdata.htm.

Abbreviation: VRA: Voting Rights Act.

runoff voting (IRV) in certain elections for Federal office, and for other purposes'. The proposal was not co-sponsored and went to the Judiciary committee's Subcommittee on the Constitution in July 2005 where it remains. In 1997, she introduced HR 3068 to allow multi-member districts. The proposal had 13 co-sponsors but it was referred to the same Subcommittee in December 1997. Prior to that in 1995, she had introduced HR 2545 to 'provide that a State that uses a system of limited voting, cumulative voting, or preference voting may establish multi-member congressional districts'. The proposal had six co-sponsors and was referred to the Judiciary Committee's sub-committee on the Constitution where it remains.

The lack of electoral *system* change should not be conflated with the lack of electoral law change. In fact, the USA does seem to experience a considerable amount of change—especially at the sub-national level. Even at the national level, however, Congress has considered a number of reforms of the electoral process. Although questions of electoral reform are a tiny share of the total number of roll calls and, in particular, of the bills voted on (see Table 3.6), it would seem that electoral reform efforts of various kinds are voted on in Congress—and pass—once every couple of years.

Of course, in the unicameral, majoritarian, and unitary government of New Zealand, the barriers to introducing changes by a reform-minded government were probably at their lowest. In near-unicameral, majoritarian, and unitary case of the UK, barriers were almost as low. For both these countries at least there are few veto players to consider and so it is more likely we will see reform in those places. Unlike the UK or New Zealand, politics at the national level in the USA is quite circumscribed by checks and balances, divided government, and a series of veto players. This may imply yet another reason for the lack of change in the USA at the national level—considering the number of veto players, it is very hard to pass any change in the rules of the game (Tsebelis 2002). It means that electoral success by former losers is hard to translate into the kinds of quick enactment of reform efforts seen in British Columbia. On the other hand, at least at the state and local level, some of the other components of government are often a source of change. Two in particular deserve mention. First, the court system is able to insist on local communities following federal law. Indeed, the massive body of electoral law as a form of jurisprudence to itself seems to mark the USA as different from other democratic societies in and of itself. Sometimes, this may mean something as straightforward as redistricting but can also lead to the adoption of non-SMD alternatives. Roughly 100 communities have experimented with a range of systems including cumulative voting as a redress for minority rights (Bowler, Donovan, and Brockington 2003). The courts, however, have not been interested in compelling this solution for federal elections.

A second source of change at the sub-national level is that of the initiative process, as shown in Table 3.7. In many ways, the presence of the initiative offers an all too easy explanation for institutional change. After all, institutional changes produced by the initiative process are examples more of political murder than of political suicide since they are instances where voters impose changes on politicians rather than seeing politicians change the rules themselves. Direct democracy thus provides one mechanism by which an exogenous change to electoral laws may occur. Examples of these kinds of changes to election procedures include the introduction of term limits, the introduction of campaign finance reform, or changes to the primary system such as California's blanket primary proposal (Proposition 198). One measure of the seriousness of these proposals is the extent to which they have been subject to legal challenge by the parties themselves. Proposition 198, for example, was struck down by the courts, and several term limit proposals have been subject to challenge by both courts and legislature. Still, relatively few of these proposals, however, have concerned electoral system change.

Table 3.7. Electoral reform via initiative 1911–2001

	Number	Pass rate (%)	Example (year, state, number/identifier, topic)
All propositions of all types	2033	41	—
Of which			
Campaign finance	46	70	1994, OR, 6, Candidates may only use contributions from district 1996, ME, 3, Voluntary spending limits and public funding
Term limits	62	79	1994, UT, A, Term limit on state legislature and Congress 1996, ND, 5, Term limits on state legislature
Election reform	79	62	1904, OR, 2, Direct Primary Nominating convention 1982, AZ, 202, Voter registration by driver's licence
Apportionment	39	39	1982, OK, 556, Creation of new congressional districts 1981, OH, 2, General Assembly and Congressional redistricting

Source: I & RI website.

A handful of communities have adopted Instant Runoff Voting (more generally known as the Alternative Vote) via the ballot box.[9] While they are few in number, they do add to the overall total number of examples of electoral system practice that move away from first past the post.

At the state and local level considerable variation in institutional reform takes place including a considerable body of reform and experimentation that exists at the local level in the USA. Over and above the experiment with cumulative voting elections many cities employ a wide range of techniques in state and local elections. Many cities, including major ones such as Los Angeles, use runoff elections for city offices while other examples of more exotic practice are the use of single transferable vote (STV) in Cambridge, MA, and the use of 'Instant Runoff Voting' (the alternative vote) in San Francisco.[10] Ohio cities had long experience with STV (Barber 1995). Similarly, several states use different methods of electing the state house. A number of states have multi-member elections for the state legislature including the lower house of Arizona, New Jersey, and North and South Dakota and both of Vermont's (Richardson and Cooper 2003). Most of these examples have two members elected from the same district although West Virginia's House of Delegates is divided into 58 districts that elect between one and seven members.[11] For most of the twentieth century, Illinois used cumulative voting to elect its state house.

To be sure, for the most part these electoral experiments seem to operate as at-large elections and so tend to operate as simple plurality elections but in multi-member districts. Nevertheless, there do exist many deviations from the 'norm' of SMD Congressional elections in US practice.

To some extent these deviations were the result of exogenous shocks to the local political system—either the courts or the initiative process were the source of the change. These exogenous forces of change offer a different kind of explanation than one grounded in winners and losers. And this may well make sense: changes in the UK to the Scottish, Welsh, and London Assemblies and to the European Parliament were simply presented to local politicians as a *fait accompli*. The process of change in localities, then, is likely to differ from change at the national level because of this difference in legal status and is, perhaps, likely to be more common because of that difference.[12] In the US case, it certainly seems to be true that the lack of change at the national level is not matched at the state and local levels. The set of laws, rules, and regulations that govern elections seems to be in near constant revision and change.

Earlier we noted that there is a relationship between electoral systems and electoral laws and that sometimes the analytical line between electoral systems and electoral laws may be too sharply drawn. We generally consider electoral system change to involve changing the algorithm that translates votes into seats. But there are many different attributes of elections and election law. In principle, for example, such attributes as term limits, redistricting, or campaign finance all have an impact, and possibly an important and sizable impact, on elections (Massicotte, Blais, and Yoskinaka 2004). So, for example, the National Conference of State Legislatures (NCSL) reports show that similar patterns of change displayed in Table 3.1 for the Congress exist at the state level, but with greater frequency. In 2001, for example, 2,088 bills were introduced on election law into state houses, 321 of which passed. In 2002, 1,555 bills were introduced (171 passed) and in 2003, 1,735 bills were introduced (324 passed).[13]

Many of these reforms seem innocuous. One example of an innocuous reform might be the requirement to pay poll workers federal minimum wage (Montana HB 151 2003); another relatively innocuous reform required voters to produce ID (Alabama HB 113 2003). But other changes concern potentially more serious matters such as absentee voting procedures, recount procedures, or registration, for example granting felons the right to register and vote (Alabama HB 3 2003) or Connecticut's (vetoed) HB 6370 (2003) that would have allowed election day registration.

These examples raise the question of what constitutes a meaningful change in electoral practices. There are big changes in electoral practices and there are small ones: rules on paying poll workers are simply not likely to be as consequential as allowing same day registration or moving towards a runoff system of elections. Reforming the rules on participation do constitute electoral reform but not in the same sense as a 'big' change in electoral system from an SMD to a PR system. But there seems little a priori theory as to which is which or, at least, where the boundary is between a big change and a small one. For example, after the fact, the move to 'above the line' voting in Australia made little difference to the actual conduct of STV elections in the Australian Senate since voters were already following the guides issued by parties. Yet, on paper, the reform transformed what was—at least in principle—a preferential system into something close to list PR. Perhaps a little more controversially, we might point to the lack of deep change in either Japan or Italy as a consequence of their reforms: the Liberal Democratic Party is still entrenched in power in Japan and in the latter the reforms have done little to alter coalitional logjams. All these are examples of ways in which a seemingly important change turned out not to be so important after all. Conversely, changes in candidate access to the ballot may seem very minor compared to a change in electoral system but can have enormous consequences for the number of parties running in an election as third party candidates in the USA find each election cycle.[14]

The difficulty in theorizing about changing electoral laws and systems lies not so much in determining the impact (or lack of impact) of a change after it has occurred but in predicting the likely consequence of reforms a priori. We do not always know with precision the consequences of reform, nor do we always know the triggers for reform. One advantage in looking at the 'upside down' result as a trigger to reform as Shugart does (Chapter 1) is that it does allow prediction in a set of cases. One disadvantage is that it does not always work (see the example of Georgia in Table 3.3) and is not clear how the trigger translates into other systems to help provide a generic model of electoral system change. Uncertainty about the consequences of reform can clearly put a brake on reform attempts. As the account of the Congressional vote over apportionment showed, it is possible to construct quite successful hypotheses grounded in variants of the winner and loser argument when the consequences of a change in electoral law are well understood and uncertainty is low. But this is rare. Even then, the change itself did seem to require an entrepreneur willing to help the change come about. It can be quite hard to find entrepreneurs of that kind. Moreover, even when one finds an entrepreneur, he or she may have a hard time collecting allies. Take the example of Congresswoman McKinney's unsuccessful efforts to change the electoral system. Her efforts were in part related to the question of minority representation—McKinney herself is African-American and so would seem more consistent with a Boix-type explanation than a Shugart one.[15] As some evidence of this we can note that all six co-sponsors of the 1995 proposal were minority (African-American or Latino) as were 10 of the 13 co-sponsors in 1997.[16] But it is notable that not all members of the minority caucuses signed on. There were roughly 40 members of the Congressional Black Caucus during this period yet the proposal did not attract support from a majority of this group. It is not clear why they did not sign on, nor why McKinney proved to be an unsuccessful entrepreneur.

As André Blais and Matthew Søberg Shugart note in the Conclusion to this volume, there is a surprisingly large role for randomness in explanations of change: the presence or absence of skilled entrepreneurs would be one component of that randomness.

3.4. Discussion

As a discipline political science has a very strong and very clear theoretical presumption: politicians will not vote to commit suicide and so changes in electoral systems and electoral laws will not take place. As the Conclusion by André Blais and Matthew Søberg Shugart notes, that theoretical presumption appears clearer on paper than it is in practice.

There is little trouble in advancing an argument for why there is no change. For example, the absence of a franchise expansion to new social groups and the absence of upside down results for Congressional elections imply the absence of some triggers for change in the theories of Boix and Shugart. In that sense the US case does not raise problems for the theories. In addition a string of arguments, some general—some specific to the USA, can be brought to bear. The uncertainty of electoral change, the lack of entrepreneurs, the number of veto players, and the entrenched self-interest of the two major parties can all be plausibly brought to bear to explain the lack of change. The difficulty here lies not so much in thinking up explanations for why nothing is happening but in sorting out which one is the correct explanation.

But the US experience presents some puzzles in part because many of the conditions for change (in particular massive expansions of the franchise and, also, upside down results) exist at the state level, yet change does not occur. It seems, then, as though additional assumptions or arguments are needed to make the USA 'fit' the theories of change based. It seems necessary to refer to some exogenous agent (such as the courts or the initiative process) or some feature (the number of elections) that is specific to the US case to make the theory 'work'. Perhaps more importantly, the pattern of very frequent change in electoral laws is at odds with the more glacial changes that are seen elsewhere. The US case does, then, illustrate a number of questions for the literature on electoral system change. There are, for example, some nagging questions that relate to issues of measurement. It is no surprise, then, that electoral institutions are 'sticky'. What is less clear is just how sticky are electoral institutions—and whether we should expect them to be 'stickier' than other kinds of institutions and so, perhaps, expect changes in electoral system to be stickier than changes in electoral laws. Just how 'sticky', in other words, are electoral institutions? Relatedly, we may not see changes in electoral system but we see dozens—hundreds—of changes in electoral law. When is a change an example of reform as opposed to just a change—are some kinds of changes inherently more innocuous than others? But rather than end on a rhetorical question we should, perhaps, try to phrase things a little more positively. If there is one thing that the US example seems to show it is that the literature as a whole seems to be pretty good at identifying necessary conditions for electoral system/rule change, just not quite so good at identifying sufficient conditions for change.

Notes

1. The 1967 Single District Mandate finally removed the few remaining multi-member districts for Congress.
2. A point that is consistent with one made in the chapter by Blau (Chapter 2).

3. Work by Charles Franklin (2006) does, however, seem to suggest that the responsiveness of seat share to vote share has flattened in recent years.

4. In Pennsylvania in 2003 Republicans held 12 of 19 Congressional seats despite the Democrats having 445,000 more votes statewide [Vieth v Jubelirer (02-1580) 541 U.S. 267 (2004)].

5. The debate is broadly analogous to the debate over largest remainder or highest average in formulas of proportionality.

6. The remaining 275 votes were from states that neither gained nor lost seats under the reapportionment plan.

7. The following account is taken from Sweeting (1956).

8. These are a little after the period under view but there is little reason to believe they altered much over the preceding 5–10 years.

9. Instant Runoff is essentially a version of the Alternative Vote system. Voters are allowed to express three preferences for candidates. So, a little less restrictive than the version in London where voters are allowed two preferences. At the time of writing only a few communities have adopted IRV. Although some of these communities are very large: San Francisco, Minneapolis, Oakland, and Davis have all adopted IRV as has Pierce County, WA. Although to date, of these communities, only SF has used IRV.

10. For an example of the SF ballot see http://www.sfgov.org/site/uploadedfiles/election/Elections_Pages/demonstration_ballot(1).PDF.

One feature of US elections that makes preferential approaches hard to adopt wholesale is the sheer number of elections that goes on. As Stalin is once supposed to have remarked 'quantity has a quality all of its own', and this would seem to apply to US elections as well as the Red Army. In the 2002 election California voters cast a vote for Governor, Lt Governor, Secretary of State, Controller, Treasurer, Attorney General, Insurance Commissioner, Board of Equalization, US Representative (Congress), member of the Assembly, Supreme and Appellate Court Judges, the Superintendent of Public Instruction as well as seven statewide ballot measures. In addition half of the state's voters had the opportunity to vote on State Senator and for other voters many cities and counties had their own elections, too, for school district, water district, city, mayor, or county council, and of course any local measures on the ballot. There is, one would think, a physical limit to both ballot design and voter tolerance for systems such as STV in the face of such a ballot.

11. http://www.wvsos.com/elections/history/results/allgeneral04.pdf WV does seem to allow for ticket voting equivalent to Australia's 'above the line' voting.

12. One additional reason why change may be more common at the local level than at the national level may simply be that there are more units and so more opportunities to change.

13. http://www.ncsl.org/programs/legman/elect/electlaws.htm.
14. US ballot-access laws vary both by state and by office. So the laws may differ—even within a state—depending on which office is being sought and whether the actor is a party or candidate. Persistent lobbying and judicial action by minor parties has loosened up some of these rules in some jurisdictions (http://www.ballot-access.org/) and for examples of state-specific rules see http://www.ballot-access.org/2006/080106.html#14.
15. In line with some of the experiences in BC, Canada, her interest in electoral reform may also have a personal basis. In 1995 the Supreme Court ruled in *Miller v Johnson* her district as an unconstitutional gerrymander and so the district boundaries were redrawn forcing her to run in a 'new' district.
16. The other three were Bernie Sanders (Independent), Barney Frank and George Brown (from California's heavily Latino 42nd district).

4

Electoral Reform in Canada

Louis Massicotte

Electoral system reform has been haunting discreetly the Canadian political scenes, both federal and provincial, since the turn of the millennium. This is admittedly not a first in the country's history, as the issue achieved some prominence twice in the past. The purpose of this chapter is to analyse this ongoing wave of debates on electoral reform, and to point out to what extent it differs from earlier waves.

In theory, Canada had much potential for innovation, having 10 provinces endowed with full autonomy, within the limits set by the Charter, when it comes to determining their own electoral arrangements, plus thousands of municipalities whose electoral systems are decided by their respective provincial legislatures. Actually, the plurality system has been almost always used. Multi-member constituencies, once widespread, have given way everywhere to single-member districts. This has not precluded discussions from taking place, and reforms from being implemented sometimes.

4.1. First Wave

The first wave of debates on electoral system reform unfolded during the years that followed the end of the First World War (Pilon 1997, 1999). It coincided with the end of the two-party system due to the irruption of the Progressives in the House of Commons, in the legislative assemblies of provinces located West of the Ottawa river, and sometimes in their governments as well. This still is the most important wave so far, because it led to actual changes.

The standard reform package advocated at that time was a combination of the Single Transferable Vote (STV) in urban areas and alternative voting (AV) in rural single-member districts. In Manitoba, this formula was established in two stages, not necessarily by design. STV was introduced in 1920, under a Liberal administration, for electing Winnipeg provincial legislators, while AV was adopted in 1924 for the other (mainly rural) constituencies by a Progressive administration (Jansen 1998, 2004). In Alberta, both STV (in Calgary and Edmonton) and AV (everywhere else) were introduced in 1924 under a Progressive government. Between 1916 and 1928, 18 municipalities, all located in the Western provinces, adopted STV for municipal elections (Johnston and Koene 2000).[1]

These were the only successful attempts that were made. Ontario's Progressive-Labour coalition government tried in 1923 in the dying days of its term, to introduce the same formula that later prevailed in Manitoba and Alberta, but failed due to Conservative obstruction in the legislature. In Quebec, voters of the city of Montreal rejected STV for municipal elections in 1921, while the next year an opposition motion calling for the creation of a parliamentary committee to study this topic was talked out in the Assembly. In 1933, a motion in the Saskatchewan Legislative Assembly by a Progressive Member supporting the use of AV in single-member constituencies where more than two candidates had been nominated, and proportional representation (PR) in plural-member constituencies was passed 26 to 21, against the wishes of Premier Anderson.[2] Although former Premier Gardiner supported the motion, as did all but one of his fellow Liberals, nothing was heard from it after Gardiner was returned to office the next year.

Well before the end of the 1920s, the wave had abated. On the federal scene, the Progressives were being gently swallowed by the Liberals, though they remained in power in some provinces. During the decades that followed, PR became quite unpopular in leading political and academic circles. In a standard post-war textbook, PR, together with occupational representation, the initiative and the referendum, was dismissed as 'plans for improving democratic government that time has laid to rest'. They had been advocated and tried in various parts of the world, but 'as a result of their failure, faith in them has almost entirely disappeared and thus they need not be discussed in detail' (Corry and Hodgetts 1959: 266). Indeed, the 1950s saw both Manitoba and Alberta undoing the reforms of the 1920s and reverting to plurality in single-member districts. In the former, only the Communists opposed the move, while in Alberta only the ruling Social Credit supported it. The only attempt made to replace the plurality rule in these days was the introduction in British Columbia (BC) of AV province-wide in 1951. This move can be interpreted as a rather crude, maybe Australian-inspired, and ultimately unsuccessful, attempt to preserve the position of both traditional parties against the socialist threat. Passed after the break-up of the Liberal–Conservative coalition in 1951, against the opposition of the Cooperative Commonwealth Federation (CCF), AV purported to allow both parties to field distinct slates of candidates and to incite their respective supporters to exchange their second preferences, so as to defeat CCF candidates wherever they failed to secure a majority of the vote. The trick was effective: the CCF was leading in 21 constituencies on first count (seven seats ahead of their main challenger), but was reduced to 18 (one seat behind their main challenger) after ballots had been transferred. Preferences helped the new Social Credit party to reach office in 1952. The defeat of Liberal incumbent Premier Byron Johnson in his own constituency, due to the counting of preferences (he was leading on first count), should stand as a warning for prospective electoral system manipulators. One of the first measures passed by W.A.C. Bennett's Social Credit government after it reached majority status in 1953 was to restore first past the post.

4.2. Second Wave

The second period when electoral system reform was widely discussed, at least for the federal Parliament and in Quebec, was the 1970s and 1980s. Not a single change was ever passed, but unusual interest was shown for electoral systems and new remedies were envisaged.

On the federal scene, the perspective that dominated thinking on this issue originated from an influential paper by Alan Cairns, which indicted the plurality system for hampering the working of Canadian federalism. Plurality had the effect of exacerbating regional cleavages, leading federal parties to write-off in advance the regions where they were weaker. It was difficult to find out cabinet ministers from some provinces. PR would not eliminate regionalism, but could soften regional cleavages (Cairns 1968). The Pépin-Roberts Task Force on Canadian Unity (1979) adopted that view and put forward a German-inspired mixed system as an alternative. Actually, this was a mild proposal, as it envisaged adding only 60 seats to the House of Commons, to be distributed among parties on the basis of their popular vote (a parallel or superposition system). As list seats obtained by each party went in priority to the provinces where they were the most under-represented, this had the effect of moderating regional cleavages, but also had the effect of altering the representation from each province, thus generating possible constitutional challenges. During the brief period that elapsed between his resignation and his comeback as Liberal leader in late 1979, Pierre Trudeau expressed sympathy for the idea.

Scores of proposals on these lines were aired at that time (Irvine 1979, 1980–1; Elton and Gibbins 1980; Dobell 1981), and federal electoral politics of 1979–80 dramatized the issue, with successive Progressive Conservative and Liberal administrations relying on only a handful of elected Members in Quebec or in the West respectively. It came to nothing. Despite the preferences of the Prime Minister, the Liberal caucus fiercely resisted any attempt first to introduce some PR for elections to the House of Commons (1980) and even for a directly elected Senate (1984). Further, Brian Mulroney's resounding success in 1984, with his party leading in every province and territory, suggested that regional cleavages were less solidly entrenched than most academics had assumed.

Electoral system reform also became an issue in Quebec in 1970, but for entirely different reasons (Massicotte and Bernard 1985). The province was undergoing a major electoral realignment, with the once powerful Union Nationale being weakened decisively (1970), disappearing temporarily (1973) and later definitively (1981) from the Assembly, and two new parties, the secessionist Parti Québécois (PQ) and the Ralliement Créditiste, reaping the spoils. While the Créditistes did well in 1970 thanks to the concentration of their vote, the PQ got only 7 seats out of 108 even if 23% of the voters had supported them. Being second in the popular vote, they were downgraded to the fourth and last rank in the Assembly. Defeated party leader René Lévesque was speaking, as he put it, 'on behalf of one quarter of the voters, dangerously reduced to one-fifteenth of legislators'. A mixed system providing for the election of one-third of Members by PR was advocated as a solution, and the German example was cited. The Liberal government chose to focus instead on malapportionment and eliminated the so-called 'protected ridings', whose boundaries under the Canadian Constitution could be altered only with the consent of a majority of their Members. At the 1973 election, the PQ lost one seat despite increasing its vote to 30%, but won official opposition status, and from then on the issue lost salience for a while.

When the PQ came to office, PR or some dose of it was aired twice. It appears that the driving force was Premier Lévesque's conviction that his party ought to be true to its commitment. In 1978, Minister Burns was unable to convince his cabinet colleagues to implement the reform envisaged in the party's permanent programme. He was allowed to publish in April 1979 a green paper outlining three options (mixed-member proportional a parallel system, and a regional list PR system) as a basis for a public debate that was never held. In 1982, government officials actively promoted a list PR system, but were rebuffed by the PQ caucus and cabinet. Although this model was endorsed by the Commission de la representation électorale in 1984 following public hearings, it was decisively rejected in the fall of 1984 by the caucuses of both parties then represented in the Assembly.

In retrospect, support for electoral system reform by the Parti Québécois in their early years had much to do with the fear that their under-representation in the Assembly would demobilize their supporters, thus preventing the PQ from breaking the two-party mould. When it became obvious in the mid-1970s that the mould had been effectively broken and that the PQ was now in a position to win later, and to win big, the rank and file, though not Premier Lévesque, lost interest in the issue. Indeed, analysis has shown since then that the concentration of the Liberal vote biased the working of the plurality system in favour of the Parti Québécois, a feature that became obvious in 1998 when the party was returned to office despite trailing in the popular vote (Massicotte 2002, 2004a). Ironically, the party thanks to whom PR had become an issue was no longer interested. In no other province at that time was PR discussed so thoroughly.

4.3. Third Wave

We are now in the middle of what could be called a third wave of electoral system debates. What did reignite the debate? It is difficult to overlook that this occurred while incumbent politicians and existing institutions were facing a serious crisis of legitimacy. Starting in the 1980s, indicators of trust have plunged for elites, institutions, and political parties (Massicotte 1994). This has been followed since the 1990s by decreasing turnouts at all levels. Such developments led scholars and activists to argue that PR would restore public confidence and increase turnout.

Some election outcomes seemed anomalous to many. At the 1997 federal election, the Liberals emerged with a razor-thin parliamentary majority based on 38.5% of the vote, with each of the five contending parties leading in at least one province, which gave more salience to the regional cleavages problem. After it became plain, following the 1997 election, that the Reform Party was unlikely to expand beyond its Western bailiwick, while in Ontario Reformers and Progressive Conservatives would continue to be hanged separately, some suggested that AV would allow these two parties to improve their respective fortunes by exchanging second preferences, though empirical research cast doubts over this (Bilodeau 1999). Until the 1990s, New Democrats had kept hoping that they would one day emulate the British Labour Party and join the major leagues, as they had done in a few provinces, and did not support PR. The decline of National Democratic Party support in federal elections throughout the 1990s led many among them to an agonizing reappraisal from which they emerged, at least on the federal scene, as strong partisans of PR.

While federal outcomes remained within the normative expectations of the plurality system, some provincial outcomes could be criticized as what Shugart defines (see Chapter 1 in this volume) as systemic failures. Lopsided parliamentary majorities for the ruling party in some provinces stimulated the debate. In 1993 and 2000, the winning party in Prince Edward Island (PEI) failed by only 1,160 and 157 votes respectively to win *all* seats in the Assembly, and in 2001 British Columbia Liberals won all but two of the 79 seats at stake. In 1987, New Brunswick Liberals had won all 58 seats. Governments were elected with a smaller number of votes than their main challenger, another type of systemic failure that many find perverse. This occurred in Saskatchewan (1986 and 1999), in Newfoundland (1989), in British Columbia (1996), and in Quebec (1998), and most recently in New Brunswick (2006). Such 'spurious majorities' or 'wrong winner elections' sowed doubts even within established parties as to the virtues of first past the post. In a context of weakened deference for existing institutions, many questioned such outcomes and looked for alternatives.

Last, but not least, new parties have been emerging or are trying to. Some, like the Reform Party or the Bloc Québécois, have been able to break the mould right from the start in their respective regions thanks to the concentration of their vote, and did not press for PR, though some Reformers toyed with AV. For others, like the Greens, Action Démocratique du Québec (ADQ), or Québec Solidaire, the plurality system appears as a formidable obstacle, and a small party-friendly type of PR as the obvious solution. In 2001, BC Greens obtained 12% of the vote but failed to win a single seat. Mario Dumont's ADQ got a single seat both in 1994 and in 1998, with 6% and 12% of the vote respectively, and managed to get a disappointing four seats in 2003 with 18% of the vote. Only in 2007 was he able to break the mould by winning one-third of both votes and seats.

So far, reformers have been unsuccessful in all settings. However, it is obvious that this wave sharply differs from previous ones on many accounts.

4.3.1. A More Widespread Debate

In contrast with the 1970s, the debate is no longer confined to the federal arena and to Quebec. Unlike the 1920s, it has spread to every region in the country, though not to every jurisdiction. Electoral system reform has become an issue not only in Ottawa and in British Columbia, Ontario, and Quebec but also in New Brunswick and Prince Edward Island.

4.3.2. Different Discourses

The grounds for indicting the plurality system and replacing it with some form of PR also tend to differ from the previous wave. The claim that PR would reduce regional cleavages (Weaver 1997; Massicotte 2001) is more rarely heard, and is no longer at the forefront of electoral reform discourses on the federal scene. The plurality system is indicted for producing phoney majorities (all single-party parliamentary majorities relying on less than 50% of the vote are deemed 'phoney'), for hindering the entry of women and minorities in parliament, for driving turnout down, and for perpetuating an authoritarian structure of governance where the Prime Minister is all-powerful. Reformers tend to support PR without qualification and are not defensive about it. That PR might weaken the executive and substitute coalition governments for single-party majority governments is not only conceded, but hailed as a major improvement. It is alleged that PR would also bring more women in legislatures, increase turnout, make party lines more flexible, and produce a more consensual mode of governance. Whether they are firmly grounded in empirical reality or not, such arguments have been made widely. They aim at making PR attractive to new social movements, including women activists. A few notes of scepticism have been struck by some academics (Katz 1999; Courtney 2001, 2004; Lovink 2001).

In Quebec, discussions over PR have in addition been influenced by nationalist considerations.[3] Ironically, both support for and rejection of PR has often been couched in nationalist language, and both the most vocal supporters and bitterest critics of PR tend to be found among supporters of sovereignty. Whether PR will facilitate sovereignty or hamper its realization has emerged as a prime consideration in much of the discourse on PR.

When the issue was explored for the first time in the early 1970s, most nationalists felt that it was indispensable to have an electoral system that fully reflected the growing support for the Parti Québécois, otherwise they said at a time when the terrorist Front de Libération du Québec (FLQ was active), 'social peace' would be at risk. It was argued that plurality was an 'English' rule and as such ought to be rejected by a francophone society; that adopting PR in the Canadian context would evidence once more that Quebec is different; or that PR would allow all shades of nationalism, even the most radical, to be represented (Monière 1987). Others have argued that first past the post was bad for francophones because it allowed the anglophone minority to play kingmaker in not a few constituencies, and that Liberal Members elected in such conditions were 'controlled' by the English (Serré 2002). PQ Minister Jean-Pierre Charbonneau's support for PR was openly premised on the need to broaden support for sovereignty by allowing supporters of sovereignty from the hard left to be represented in the legislature.

The arguments do not seem to have swayed most supporters of sovereignty. Parti Québécois Members from rural areas (like many of their colleagues from other parties) are genuinely attached to the existing pattern of representation allowing for closer contacts between Members and voters. The existing boundary plan, the most unequal in North America (Blake 2005), is also praised for over-representing rural and remote areas. Some have argued that PR is a luxury that a minority nation like Quebeckers cannot afford because it would make coalitions or minority government the rule, thus weakening Quebec, or at least its government, surrounded as it seemingly is by countless enemies. Relying on unknown soothsayers, they have claimed that PR would entrench Liberals in office for decades. Whenever the electoral system returns a nationalist government with a smaller number of votes than its Liberal challengers, nationalists of all stripes are quick to point out that English-speaking voters supported the Liberals very heavily, but that

119

most francophones have got the government they wanted, though few would dare to repeat Daniel Johnson's candid post-election comment in 1966, that 'true, the Liberals have a plurality of the vote, but their plurality comes from the votes of the English and the Jews'.[4] More soberly, one can say that in its actual working, the plurality system has been helpful to the cause of sovereignty because it allowed the PQ to win a majority of seats while never securing a majority of the vote. Further, the electoral system has been heavily biased against the Liberal party for decades, first due to the over-representation of rural areas (until 1970) and thereafter by wasting thousands of Liberal votes in non-francophone constituencies, with the Liberals being deprived of power despite having a plurality of the province-wide vote, three times in 60 years (1944, 1966, and 1998). Few indeed would agree to be stripped of such an advantage.

The debate in Quebec is original insofar as in addition to the standard scenario of big incumbent parties pitting against small emerging political forces, it has the potential of setting the two larger parties against each other.

4.3.3. Process

A major difference with earlier waves of reform is the emphasis put on the reform process itself. The changes made in the 1920s, and the counter-changes of the 1950s, followed the familiar channels (Massicotte 2005). The government of the day came to the conclusion that a change was needed and pushed it through the legislature, with or without the support of the opposition. No attempt was apparently made to broaden the debate beyond the legislature, or to involve citizens in the decision-making process, though legislative committees sometimes conducted public hearings. Whether their motivations were high-minded or crassly partisan, reformers felt no need to go beyond the legislature, to hold a referendum, or even to subordinate the change to the consent of the parliamentary opposition. During the 1970s and 1980s, the public's feeling on electoral system reform was gauged at public hearings held by royal commissions (Pépin-Robarts, Macdonald), electoral bodies (Quebec), or parliamentary committees (Molgat-Cosgrove), yet the right of legislators to decide the issue in the end was not seriously challenged. It may be added that the few who did were sharply rebuffed by the political class, as Chief Electoral Officer Côté experienced in 1984 (Massicotte and Bernard 1985, 214–15).

Contemporary reformers are not of a single mind on this issue, and some governments still claim the right to follow the traditional way. Yet, the view has spread among reformers that incumbent legislators should be sidelined on the issue, on the assumption that they are sold to existing arrangements and that they are in a position of conflict of interests. The widely accepted view that parliamentarians should not be involved in electoral boundary changes has been extended to the electoral system itself. The strategy of short-circuiting incumbent legislators through various bodies elaborating reform proposals to be later voted on directly by the voters at referendums may look naïve, as such processes must be established in the first place by the very people they aim at circumventing. Yet, it has been tried in some settings.

In 2002, Quebec created a committee, chaired by Claude Béland and dominated by political outsiders, mostly on the Left. Regional hearings were held, culminating in February 2003 with 'États généraux' composed of participants selected by the Béland committee on the basis of their previous interventions at regional hearings. In its subsequent report, the organizing committee recommended that a referendum be held on its proposed new electoral system. Also in 2003, Prince Edward Island set up a one-man royal commission that elaborated a proposal. The proposal was later reviewed and fine-tuned following public hearings, and submitted directly to the people at a referendum in November 2005. In New Brunswick, the Lord government created a royal commission styled the Commission on Legislative Democracy. In its report, tabled in January 2005, the Commission also demanded that its proposal be submitted directly to the people at a referendum. By far, the most elaborate attempt in this vein has been British Columbia's Citizens' Assembly (CA) (see Chapter 5 by Carty, Blais, and Fournier). In Ontario, the McGuinty Liberal government set up a Citizens' Assembly that reported in 2007 in favour of an MMP system. A referendum will be held on this proposal simultaneously with the next election, scheduled for the autumn of 2007. The outcome of the referendum will be binding on the legislature only if the proposed system is supported by 60% of the votes cast, and by a majority in 64 ridings out of 107 (slightly less than 60% of the total).[5] The Ontario case is the only one where a reform process was initiated without evidence of systemic failure, as the plurality system neither produced a wrong winner nor resulted into lopsided majorities.

Even in Quebec, where the Charest government opted for a more classical approach by consulting informally political parties and experts on a specific proposal before tabling its own preferred model, the need was felt to go beyond the usual channels. In June 2005, a Special Committee of the Assembly was empowered to consult the public. In addition to members of the National Assembly from all parties, it included eight citizens acting in an advisory position. These people were selected by draw from among the people (actually some 2,500) who had expressed interest in participating to the work of the Commission by filling out coupons printed in the media.

The Law Commission of Canada, after commissioning academic research and having held public meetings, came up with a detailed report advocating MMP in 2004 (Law Commission of Canada 2004). The NDP took advantage of its pivotal position in the minority Parliament elected the same year to extract from the ruling Liberals, with the support of all other parties, an amendment to the Address empowering the Standing Committee on Procedure and House Affairs 'to recommend a process that engages citizens and parliamentarians in an examination of our electoral system with a review of all options'. The committee heard a few expert witnesses and travelled to various countries in order to get acquainted with the STV and MMP systems.

In June 2005 the Committee rejected the Citizens' Assembly approach, on the ground that it excluded legislators from the decision-making process on electoral system reform. In the words of Ed Broadbent, the CA's approach amounted to 'designing a hospital without consulting the doctors'. Instead, a complex process was proposed, involving a special committee of the House and a 'Citizens' Task Force' working in parallel, both later confronting their respective conclusions, with Parliament having the last word. The Task Force would report on the values and principles that Canadians would like to integrate in their democratic and electoral system. The special committee would be empowered to hold hearings throughout Canada. Both bodies were expected to meet later and discuss their respective findings. The Task Force would thereafter report its findings to the special committee, which would submit its recommendations to the House by the end of February 2006.[6]

The political maelstrom that toppled the Liberal government decided otherwise, but the new Conservative government is committed to deal with the issue. The Speech from the Throne of 4 April 2006, stated: 'Building on the work begun in the last Parliament, this Government will seek to involve parliamentarians and citizens in examining the challenges facing Canada's electoral system and democratic institutions.'

Discussions on the process have not focused only on public input. Some have tried to constrain as much as possible the decision-making ability of governments in this area. The Parti Québécois has claimed to enjoy a veto not only over any reform in this area, but over the very holding of a referendum thereon. Quebec's Citizens' Committee claimed in its report (2006) that while a referendum on its own model might not be indispensable, any other system should be supported by a two-thirds majority in the Assembly, on a free vote, with two-thirds concurring on *both* sides of the House. On such terms, it appears that the secession of Quebec would be easier to accomplish than reforming the electoral system.

In the area of electoral system reform, at least, the passion for participative democracy, consultation, deliberation, and referendums has reached recently unheard of levels. Such devices allow reformers to develop and to spread their arguments, to lobby parliamentarians, and possibly to prevail over them. The willingness of incumbent politicians to create such forums may be variously interpreted. Some may view these forums as allies whose reports can be cited in order to support their own reformist positions. Politicians opposed to reform may believe that consultations have the advantage of postponing decision, revealing unsuspected complexities or oppositions, while creating the exciting image of a government that reaches out to ordinary Canadians.

When politicians want to act, they do. When they instead appoint a royal commission or set up more appealing consultation processes, they may be playing for time. And time is very important. Whenever time elapses, sitting Members get absorbed into the system and the recollection of anomalous outcomes quietly fades away. Many assume that only referendums can break the deadlock and force politicians to introduce PR. They should remember that when it comes to reforming the Constitution, referendums were first advocated also as deadlock-breaking mechanisms, and have proved exactly the opposite. Supporters of the status quo may have come to an original understanding of Alf Smith's dictum that the solution to the evils of democracy is more democracy. The dream of some politicians is to see reform buried not by them, but by the will of the electorate. As the case for PR tends to be made by political parties sitting at the margins, referendums have the advantage of allowing supporters of large parties to keep the outsiders out.

Other approaches have been advocated. Since the coming into force of the Canadian Charter of Rights and Freedoms in 1982, electoral legislation has become a prime target for petitioners. Prison inmates, mentally deficient people, and even judges have been enfranchised by the courts. There have been important judicial decisions on the publication of opinion polls, third-party spending, electoral boundaries, and threshold for party registration. A British Columbia court decision of 1989 invalidated a provincial electoral boundary plan by invoking a right to 'equality of voting power'. Although this was later qualified by the Supreme Court of Canada, which rather proclaimed a 'right to effective representation', the *Dixon* case led some to believe that the plurality system might one day be declared unconstitutional because it violates equality of voting power (Knight 1999; Beatty 2005). Two court actions are currently on the rolls, one in Ontario and the other in Quebec.

Another possible scenario would be, in a minority Parliament, for a small party to make the adoption of PR a precondition for its own support for the incumbent government. Actually, this was tried only in Ottawa by the NDP following the 2004 election. But the NDP was not in a kingmaker position and, as mentioned above, all it led to was a committee studying ways to involve Canadians in the discussion of the issue. In no other setting has this approach been tried. From the point of view of an incumbent minority government, PR would entrench an uncomfortable situation for ever, while other contenders may feel that they are on their way to office. Revealingly, when the 2007 election resulted, for the first time since 1878, into a minority government, none of the three parties, then almost evenly matched in the legislature, insisted on electoral reform.

4.3.4. *A Debate No Longer Confined to the Political, Media, and Academic Classes*

A significant development of recent years is the creation of small organizations dedicated to electoral system reform, on the model of the British Proportional Representation Society. Both Fair Vote Canada (FVC) and Quebec's Mouvement pour une Démocratie nouvelle (MDN) were created in 2001. These organizations maintain websites, send newsletters, analyse various proposals, lobby parliamentarians, and intervene in public forums (Seidle 2002).

Earlier debates on electoral system reform used to take place within legislatures and in media columns, with a few political scientists being invited to testify in front of parliamentary committees. Now the public is invited to vent their feelings, and judging from some comments, experts should hope for little more than being part of the crowd or advising citizens' assemblies. Already in 1983, when the PR system favoured by Premier Lévesque was rejected by the caucuses of both political parties, Quebec's Commission de la Représentation électorale was empowered to hold public hearings in all regions on the issue. A total of 462 interventions were received, including 319 from individuals, 132 by associations, and 11 from incumbent legislators.[7] The hearings conducted in regions by the Béland Committee in 2002 gathered an average of 75 individuals each, so that in the end about 2,000 people were involved. In order to allow as many people as possible to intervene, participants were granted up to 4 minutes to make their point. Briefs were received from 146 individuals and 91 associations, including the 'Centre d'aide et de lutte contre les agressions à caractère sexuel', the 'Fonds d'Accès Musique Inc.', the 'École nationale d'aéronautique', and 'Mères avec projet de vie', along with the expected contributions from labour unions and nationalist organizations.[8] The États généraux themselves grouped some 1,000 participants. Quebec's standing committee on the Institutions received some 150 briefs during the autumn of 2002, but did not find time to hear any of their authors before the legislature was dissolved. Quebec's special committee on election law in 2005–6 received 362 briefs, and 1,080 individuals either emailed comments or answered a questionnaire on their views.

The Law Commission of Canada held public meetings in eight cities and organized or co-sponsored a series of forums jointly with women and youth organizations. New Brunswick's Commission on Legislative Democracy (2005: 6), in its report, acknowledged that general participation at its public hearings was low, but claimed greater success for the specific forums it conducted with young people, women, and francophones. The Commission on Prince Edward Island's Electoral Future (Prince Edward Island, Commission on PEI's Electoral Future 2005: 25) held 12 public meetings that attracted a total of 763 people. The most impressive figures come from British Columbia, where ~3,000 people attended the 50 public hearings held throughout the province, while 1,603 written submissions were made by 1,430 individuals.

4.3.5. To Focus on the Electoral System or Not?

Institutional reform can be addressed either globally, with the goal of producing a wide-ranging reform package, or be focused on a single item, in this case the electoral system. A prime example of the former approach is the Charlottetown Accord of 1992, which purported to deal not only with the issues included in the Meech Lake Accord but also with Senate reform and aboriginal self-government. The inauspicious fate of that reform has apparently convinced most Canadian politicians that such issues were best left dormant, while more focused efforts (e.g. the elimination of the constitutional privileges granted to denominational schools) if less exciting and dramatic, at least were successful.

Two reform processes were all-encompassing in nature. Quebec's États généraux were based on a document by Minister Jean-Pierre Charbonneau that addressed the following: a written constitution for Quebec, the US presidential system, regional decentralization, proportional representation, aboriginal government, direct democracy, fixed dates for elections, term limits, voting at 16, and increasing women representation.[9] As the term of the government that launched this consultation was nearing to its end, it was widely viewed as a preliminary brainstorming exercise on what the constitution of an independent Quebec would look like, and for that reason attracted minimal interest outside supporters of sovereignty. New Brunswick also adopted a broad approach, covering three areas: electoral reform (the electoral system, electoral boundaries, fixed election dates, and measures to boost voter turnout); legislative reform (enhancing the role of private Members and the Legislative Assembly, opening up the appointments process for agencies), and democratic reform (increasing public participation, referendums). This led the leader of the NDP to irreverently compare the report of the Commission to 'a kitchen sink full of things'.[10]

The other jurisdictions chose to focus on the electoral system. This was the case of the Law Commission of Canada, of British Columbia, Ontario, Prince Edward Island and Quebec under Charest. In the latter, the agenda for the public consultation that took place was enlarged so as to include proposed technical amendments to the Election Act and the reform process.

4.3.6. MMP Emerging as the Favourite Option of Most, but Not All

During the 1920s, the range of alternative electoral systems advocated was fairly narrow and was limited to alternative voting and the STV, often to apply separately in different parts of the country. While each one still has dedicated partisans (Flanagan 1999, 2001), the range of alternatives has broadened, reflecting in part the fact that it is no longer deemed indispensable as in older days for a credible model to have been tested first in the more familiar confines of Anglo America.

List PR systems like those used in most continental European states were first proposed in Quebec in the 1970s under the labels of 'Proportionnelle modérée' or 'Proportionnelle régionale'. Professor Vincent Lemieux appears to deserve credit for having first proposed this idea in 1971, and his proposal was later identified as a serious option by the Parti Québécois government in 1979 and in 1982–4. Quebec would have been divided into about 26 districts each electing between four and seven members, with open party lists (panachage). While this would have been a relatively moderate form of PR, it would have done away with single-member districts and for that reason was rejected by many. Reformers did not help their cause with legislators by trying to dismiss constituency work as unimportant. This formula came out of fashion afterwards, though it was resurrected by the Béland committee in 2003, and remains the favourite of the hard left in Quebec, provided that Swedish-style province-wide compensation seats mitigate the majoritarian tendencies fostered by a relatively small district magnitude. Yet, even on this side, MMP with province-wide compensation and two votes has been put forward recently.

Given incumbent legislators' attachment to single-member districts, it was widely believed that any proposal entailing wider multi-member districts, either list PR or list STV, was doomed to fail. Yet British Columbia belied the conventional wisdom, as well as the expectations of many, when the Citizens' Assembly opted for the Single Transferable Vote. The CA did not go through all the nuts and bolts of its proposal. While the model kept the Legislature close to its present size of 79, it provided for existing constituencies to be amalgamated with two to seven members to be returned from each new district. On the ballot paper, candidates would be grouped by party but randomly ordered within each party grouping.

By far, however, MMP has been the preferred reform option among reformers, reflecting the growing popularity of mixed systems since the beginning of the 1990s (Massicotte and Blais 1999; Shugart and Wattenberg 2001a). Even in British Columbia, it was advocated by 53% of submissions received by the CA, and by 52.5% of longer submissions. Support for STV was respectively 10.6% and 17.5%. STV in BC was not the outcome of a deep-seated popular pressure, but rather the fruit of the CA's deliberations. Like the legislators they try to substitute for, CA members (as well as the Béland committee and Quebec's Citizens committee) felt they were more than mere sounding boards for dedicated pressure groups that rushed to the consultations they held.

A mixed system was first proposed by Professor Robert Boily in 1966, and by the Parti Québécois in 1969. For federal elections, the idea was first aired in 1979 by the Pépin-Robarts Commission, based on the work of Professor William Irvine (1979). Dozens of variants of this model were proposed during the following years. This was also the approach selected recently by the Law Commission of Canada, the Quebec government under Charest, the New Brunswick Commission on Legislative Democracy, and the Carruthers Commission in Prince Edward Island. It must be pointed out that in all the mixed electoral systems proposed recently, list seats were to be distributed in a compensatory way (MMP), so that the ultimate outcome was roughly proportional to the strength of each party.

The details of the five MMP models proposed in recent years are outlined in Table 4.1.[11] All would keep the legislature pretty much to its existing size, with marginal increases in Canada, Quebec, and New Brunswick, and the status quo in PEI. Ontario's model would increase the size of the Assembly to 129 (from 103), but this would merely be a return to the size existing before the Fewer Politicians Act was passed in the late 1990s. As a consequence, single-member districts would be fewer in number and larger in size. The ratio of single-member district seats to list seats is much the same in each jurisdiction (about 2 to 1) though in Quebec it is more in the 3 to 2 range. Ontario has opted for a 70:30 ratio. None has dared to propose a 50:50 ratio, presumably for fear that the resulting constituencies would be found too large for voters' and Members' taste.

In single-member districts, Members would continue to be elected by plurality. No proposal envisages using the alternative vote, as the Jenkins Commission recommended for Britain.[12]

All MMP models but Ontario's (which opted for LR-Hare) use D'Hondt and all avoid overhang, even if this will work against smaller parties. In order to gauge to what extent each proposed model would reduce distortions; I computed the average Gallagher (1991) Index for the outcomes of simulations based on the two most recent elections in each jurisdiction. The MMP model that would produce the smallest amount of distortions (2.07, a figure comparable to Sweden) appears to be Prince Edward Island's. This makes sense, as list seats would be distributed province-wide among parties that obtained 5% of the party vote. Ontario's model, with

Table 4.1. Comparison of the MMP systems proposed in various jurisdictions

Feature	Law Commission	New Brunswick	Quebec	Prince Edward Island	Ontario
Size of legislature	304	56	127	27	129
Number of SMD seats	197	36	77	17	90
Number of list seats	107	20	50	10	39
Ratio of SMD to list seats (%)	65 to 35	64 to 36	61 to 39	64 to 36	70 to 30
Number of districts for list seats	16	4	24 to 27	1 (province-wide)	1 (province-wide)
Effective district magnitude	19	14	4.7 to 5.3	27	129
Number of votes cast by voter	2	2	1	2	2
Formula for allocating seats	Unspecified	D'Hondt	D'Hondt	D'Hondt	LR-Hare
Overhang seats	None	None	None	None	None
Party lists	Voters may endorse party list, or select candidates on a list	Closed	Closed	Closed	Closed
Threshold	Candidates in one-third of SMDs in province	5% province-wide	None	5% province-wide	3% province-wide
Dual candidacies	Allowed	Forbidden	Allowed	Forbidden	Allowed
Filling vacant seats					
SMD seats	By-election	By-election	By-election	By-election	By-election
List seats	Next on list	Next on list	Next on list	Next on list	Next on list
Average level of distortions for two most recent elections (Gallagher index)	3.57	3.01	6.86	2.07	2.75

Abbreviation: SMD: single-member district.

a 3% threshold, has an index of 2.75. The highest level of distortions (6.86, about what is found in the PR systems existing in Spain and Greece) would occur in Quebec, despite the absence of an explicit threshold in the proposal and a ratio less favourable to constituency seats. This is slightly less than the comparable index for the Jenkins proposal (7.08). By using D'Hondt within 24–27 districts, most having three constituencies and two list seats, the Quebec model would impose an implicit threshold of about 14% of the vote within each district and would provide the leading parties with a modest bonus. The Law Commission of Canada (LLC) (3.57) and New Brunswick (3.01) models stand in-between, but are much closer to PEI's and Ontario's. New Brunswick and Prince Edward Island proposed a 5% threshold province-wide, while the LCC would exclude from the apportionment of list seats parties that did not present candidates in at least one-third of single-member districts within each province or territory. In both cases, the district magnitude is high enough to guarantee fair representation to smaller parties provided they cross the threshold.[13]

All models but Quebec's provide for the casting by voters, in addition to a vote for a candidate in a single-member district, of a second vote for a party, a feature that allows voters to split their votes between two parties if they wish. In Quebec, list seats would be allocated based on the votes cast for the candidates of each party in single-member districts, because research established that rejected votes tend to be higher wherever two votes are cast, and for fear of a manoeuvre that occurred in Italy in 2001, that eliminated the compensatory element of the system and transformed it into a parallel system.

Most models opted for regional party lists. One may feel that the size of the Canadian territory precludes province-wide allocation of list seats, yet this was proposed for both the smallest (Prince Edward Island and the second largest (Ontario) province. This feature of the PEI model led some voters to fear that the best positions on each party list would go to candidates from the Charlottetown area, and that the representation of rural areas would accordingly be diminished. Party lists would be closed in New Brunswick, Quebec, Ontario, and Prince Edward Island, with candidates being elected on the basis of their ranking on the list of their party (unless they had been elected in a single-member constituency). The LCC was torn between the greater freedom granted to voters by open lists, and the assumption that women representation would be higher with closed lists. In the end, it recommended that voters be allowed to choose between both options.

Dual candidacies, that is the possibility for candidates to stand both in a single-member district and on a party list, provided they deleted from the list in case of success in a district, were controversial. They were found acceptable by the LCC, by the Ontario, and (initially) by the Quebec government, while in New Brunswick and Prince Edward Island they were prohibited rejected because public hearings suggested they were unpopular with the public.[14]

Objections from the ruling party caucus have led the Quebec government to cant against dual candidacies.

When it came to filling vacant seats, all models opted for the solutions adopted in New Zealand, Scotland, and Wales: a by-election for vacancies occurring in single-member districts, with list seats being filled by the next unelected candidates of the same party on the list.

These are not the only variants of MMP put forward. In BC, the model put to the CA bore similarities with the Jenkins model, with two votes, alternative voting used in single-member constituencies, list seats apportioned province-wide and being afterwards re-allocated among the provinces' regions, on the basis of open lists. Despite these refinements (or maybe due to them), the model was roundly rejected by the Citizens' Assembly. In Quebec, the model put forward by PR activists from a coalition of small left-wing parties and social movements provided instead for a 60:40 ratio, province-wide compensation, two votes, and closed party lists. Quebec's Citizens' Committee (subject to two dissents within its ranks) tried to reconcile the conflicting views they had heard by proposing a 60:40 ratio, two votes, closed party lists, a 5% threshold, province-wide apportionment of list seats followed by the re-allocation to the administrative regions of seats won by each party. It is interesting that the vast majority of proposals made to the Special Committee were variants of MMP.

4.3.7. So Far, Everybody Failing?

Machiavelli's famous quote that nothing was more difficult than changing a country's constitution has often been found fitting for Canada. On surface, changing the electoral system looks much easier because this can be made by an ordinary statute both in Ottawa and in the provinces, and because the government party normally can do this alone. The main challenge for reformers is to overcome the instinctive preference of legislators for the status quo. Once they have, the deed is done.

Some hoped that the year 2005 would be the year of a great break-through. This was not the case, and the prospects for success now look bleak, though referendum victories in Ontario (2007) and British Columbia (2009) might reverse the tide. None of the models described above has been adopted so far. Only Quebec's has been couched in legislative language, but it has not yet reached Bill status.

In Prince Edward Island, the issue was settled for a while by a referendum held on 28 November 2005. Despite last-minute alterations designed to appease opponents, MMP was roundly rejected by 64% to 36%. The formula was opposed by virtually every legislator from both sides of the House, and found support only from the NDP. The Commission on PEI's Electoral Future had ignored the preference of legislators for a BC-type threshold and had recommended not to derogate from the standard 50% plus one rule. However, Premier Binns made it clear during the campaign that he would feel bound by a positive vote on MMP only if support reached 60% of the vote, and if turnout was high enough. The referendum was not held simultaneously with a general election, but in isolation, shortly before winter, which helped to drive turnout downwards. Ostensibly for budgetary reasons, the government decided that the number of polling stations would be reduced by 90%, which implied that many more voters would have to queue at each polling station, and that the latter would be more distant from each voter's home. Further, no list of electors was used, which meant that before being allowed to vote, electors had to answer four questions. Turnout was actually in the 30% range, though there is no evidence that a higher turnout would have yielded a different outcome.

The Law Commission of Canada's proposal was dealt with more expeditiously. A parliamentary committee heard the testimony of the members of the commission in January 2005 and Members made it plain that, with the exception of the NDP, they did not agree. In view of the tone of the debates held on electoral reform in the House of Commons in February 2001 and September 2003, this came as no surprise. A recent study found that most parliamentary candidates at the 2006 election, except among the NDP and the Greens, are opposed to PR (Black and Hicks 2006).

In New Brunswick, the only action taken by the legislature was to order an electoral redistribution based on the procedural recommendations of the Commission on Legislative Democracy (CLD), but for an Assembly of 55 *single-member* districts. The Lord government, whose hold on the Assembly was quite precarious, waited until June 2006 before tabling its answer to the CLD Report. A referendum was promised 17 months after it was released. Premier Lord has not yet promised to hold a referendum on MMP. He is on record as having said that a referendum, if held, would take place simultaneously with the 2008 municipal elections, and that a threshold higher than 50% would not be imposed.[15] Ironically, Lord's government lost the ensuing election while securing more votes than the winning party, and the new Liberal Premier later buried the idea.

The prospects seemed better in British Columbia, as the legislature had agreed in advance that the system proposed by the Citizens' Assembly would be submitted to a referendum held simultaneously for the May 2005 election. However, the 60% threshold was missed, with 58% supporting the proposal. Another referendum will be held simultaneously with the next general election, and meanwhile a map of proposed electoral districts for STV has been prepared. Whether a more specific proposal will look more attractive, or less, remains to be seen.

In Quebec, Premier Charest promised in 2003 to reform the system within two years. During the summer, it was announced that the government intended to introduce an MMP system. In September, however, it was announced that the new system would not be in force for the next election. The schedule was for the government proposal to be disclosed in June 2004, but following meetings of the government party caucus; this was postponed to next autumn. In December 2004, the government unveiled a draft bill setting out in detail its preferred model, as well as the working document that contributed to its preparation (Massicotte 2004b), but pointedly insisted that this was a mere basis for public debate. During the public consultation that followed, the government refrained from defending its own proposal and rather emphasized the need to consult widely. The vast majority of those who appeared supported MMP with province-wide compensation. A minority supported the status quo, arguing that electoral reform would hamper the representation of rural areas. Two reports were issued in 2006. Both agreed on the need to have an MMP system, while rejecting all the features of the model proposed by the government in its draft bill. The group of citizens proposed a highly complex model combining province-wide distribution of list seats with regional allocations. Members of the Committee were unable to agree on any specifics. It was announced that no action, if any, would be taken before next autumn. The possibility of holding a referendum simultaneously with the next general election was aired, but this option was rejected by the cabinet. In December 2006, the issue was referred to the Chief Electoral Officer for further study, to report by December 2007.

Yukon ordered a report on electoral reform that was tabled in April 2005. It came to the conclusion that no reform was needed.[16] In Saskatchewan, no party beyond the Greens seems to consider electoral reform as a priority.[17] Manitoba, Alberta, Nova Scotia, and Newfoundland have shown no interest whatsoever.

4.4. Obstacles to Electoral Reform

While it has been discussed more intensely than before, electoral system reform has not become a priority issue in the Canadian public debate and remains by far overshadowed by other issues (Bricker and Redfern 2001). It is difficult to agree with the comment made recently by a dedicated reformer, that electoral reform in Quebec is second only to sovereignty when it comes to catching the public mind.[18] One is closer to reality when saying that in Quebec and elsewhere, electoral system reform is discussed intensely, but within relatively small circles, that a deep commitment to PR does hardly extend beyond supporters of small parties, and that electoral reform has failed so far to become a burning issue. This may explain why nationwide media have paid little attention to the issue so far.

Opinion polls conducted on the issue suggest that the public is some-what receptive to reform, but not keen on it. Outside the public forums held for that purpose, electoral system reform is rarely discussed. Following the BC referendum campaign, the Director of Fair Voting BC wrote that polls showed 60–70% of the population knew little or nothing about the referendum question. 'The campaign', he said, 'was hampered by the difficulty to engage people in a subject too abstract by far for most.'[19] A most troubling finding was made in a poll conducted following the BC referendum. The view that STV should be accepted was shared by only 39%, while 47% agreed that because the YES side failed to reach 60% of support, STV should not be accepted. One may wonder why so many people are willing to concede that their own vote should be ignored.

Despite the cautious attitude taken by most mainstream politicians during those debates, it is becoming obvious that attitudes among legislators on PR mostly range from lack of enthusiasm to bitter hostility. The emphasis put on public consultations may stem from a laudable concern for having the purest decision-making process imaginable. It can also be read as an astute way for legislators to play for time and to postpone reforms they do not feel comfortable with. As most sitting Members, except in Ottawa, have refrained from expressing their concerns too openly, one can only guess how they really feel, but the following may be important considerations.

Any PR formula, be it STV or MMP, would facilitate the entry of new political parties in the Assembly and make the attainment of a legislative majority by a single party much more difficult. Yet, Canadian politicians prefer by far having single-party majorities, and are willing to accept that this rule works for their opponents as well. It guarantees full power, untrammelled by blackmail from coalition partners or the necessity of sharing the spoils of office. It is revealing that whenever a minority Parliament is elected, Canadian politicians mostly opt for a single-party minority government rather than for a majority coalition. The former may have a shorter life expectancy, but the 'ins' keep full control over the machinery of government. The normal order of things is preserved as much as possible, until electors be provided with an opportunity to repair the 'mistake' they have made. Forming a coalition means accepting the absence of a single-party majority as a normal situation, to last the full term of the legislature, while opting for a minority government may amount to interpreting it as an unfortunate lapse to be remedied at the earliest opportunity.

It is becoming more and more clear that the instances of systemic failure recorded in recent elections, while helping to put PR on the political agenda, have failed to shake support for the plurality system within the larger parties. This author is under the impression that even the most anomalous outcomes produced by first past the post raise less genuine anger among the politicians who suffer them than among the PR activists who quote them repeatedly. In Prince Edward Island, Conservatives and Liberals were each in turn almost shut out from the Assembly in recent years, yet neither did support the model that was put at a referendum in 2005. When PR was examined in 1984 and in 2002, there was a strong likelihood that the Parti Québécois would be wiped out from the Assembly at the ensuing election, yet the party did not seize the opportunity to alter the rules of the game and in 1984, incumbent Members were convinced they would survive the wave that, polls predicted, would soon engulf their party (Milner 1994). In Ottawa, Progressive Conservatives were smashed in 1993, yet few on that side made any noise about changing the electoral system. Ultimately, they solved their problem by merging with the Canadian Alliance.

The 1998 'wrong winner election' in Quebec is even more revealing because in the context of Quebec electoral politics, this specific harm can only happen to the Liberal party. Yet, a political columnist disclosed a few months later, without being contradicted, that even Liberal legislators had privately swallowed the outcome and were not willing to insist on electoral reform. During the Address debate that took place a few months after the election, no Liberal Member, except the party leader and the party's critic on election law issues, made any mention of this anomaly, and none expressed outright indignation. They did not press the PQ government on this issue during the legislative term, and the PQ's decision in 2000 to postpone the introduction of PR until after sovereignty went virtually unnoticed. When three academics were invited to talk about electoral reform at a Liberal General Council meeting barely six months after the election, it was revealed that in the future the PQ was bound to get the same number of seats as the Liberals even if the latter led by as many as 7.5 points in the popular vote. The audience reacted with such equanimity that one academic pointed out that it was up to party militants, not professors, to be infuriated by such outcomes.[20] In 2001, when the Standing Committee on Institutions was empowered to examine the issue, the first thing the parties agreed among themselves was that no change should be made before the next election. In the information booklet that was distributed to participants at the hearings of the province's Special Committee on Election Law, the linguistic gerrymander was not even mentioned, and Liberals pointedly stayed away from the hearings, leaving the floor to other parties and to the social movements.

So smaller parties apparently remain the most committed to PR. But here again, one must look closer. The Parti Québécois was highly vocal on electoral system change in its early years, but becoming a major player led to a reappraisal, and in recent years the party's repeated calls for consultations and a referendum on the issue hardly dissimulated its intention to kill any proposal the Liberals might come up with. Mario Dumont's ADQ seems well on its way to the same path. The federal NDP, having now lost hope of becoming a major player, supports PR, but intriguingly this sudden zeal for reform has not spread to its British Columbia, Saskatchewan, and Manitoba wings, which have reached major party status or are in power. The late Eugene Forsey once quipped that PR is something you support when you cannot implement it, and that when you can, you no longer support.

As discussion focuses on alternative models, parliamentarians have little difficulty finding in any model features they do not like. STV might create tensions within each party because each candidate will be running not only against other parties, but against other candidates from the same party as well. The presence of Members belonging to different parties might generate tensions within districts. MMP means fewer single-member constituencies. Incumbent legislators are facing the unpleasant prospect of playing musical chair to be renominated as constituency candidates. Single-member districts will be larger than they now are, and not everybody agrees that list Members will share constituency work with their constituency colleagues. Indeed, many fear that if they do, there will be tensions between both groups of legislators especially if they belong to different parties. Even if such tensions are absent in Germany, the country with the longest experience of MMP, many feel that the tensions that have arisen in Scotland and Wales are inauspicious. Closed party lists are viewed by many as undemocratic, putting Members under the yoke of party leaders. The consequences of split-voting are unknown, and might adversely affect some parties.

In short, Shugart's outcome-contingent factors for reforming the electoral system are weak, as larger parties do not believe they will be better-off under alternative rules. As to his act-contingent factors, there is no evidence that any ruling party has gained much additional support, either by including electoral reform in its platform, or by launching public consultations thereon. However, one must note how cautious legislators have been in venting their feelings, thereby avoiding a possible backlash among the voters. The latter remain mostly uninterested. There is nothing in Canada at present like the sheer rage that New Zealanders felt at their politicians when they supported MMP in 1993.

There is no doubt that the third wave of electoral system reform has so far generated innovating deliberative and consultative processes, attracted greater (though not overwhelming) public interest, produced detailed models, and stimulated academic research. The jury is still out on what it will achieve in the end.

Notes

1. These experiences were short-lived as STV was soon repealed everywhere except in Calgary, Vancouver, and St. James, where STV survived until the 1970s.
2. *Journals of the Legislative Assembly of Saskatchewan*, 9 March 1933, pp. 72–3.
3. Lysiane Gagnon, 'Sovereignty colours electoral reform', *The Globe and Mail*, 3 April 2006, p. A13.
4. Pierre Godin, *Daniel Johnson*, tome 2, Montréal, Éditions de l'Homme, 1980, p. 118. Massicotte and Bernard 1985, 104.
5. *Electoral System Referendum Act 2007*, Statutes of Ontario, 2007.
6. In separate reports, both the Conservatives and the Bloc Québécois highlighted how slim the consensus among parties was. The former supported a Citizens' Assembly on the BC model, while the latter expressed concerns about the creation of a Citizens' Task Force.
7. Québec, Commission de la Représentation électorale, *Pour un mode de scrutin équitable. La proportionnelle territoriale*, Québec, 1984, p. 15.
8. Québec, *Prenez votre place. Rapport du Comité directeur sur la réforme des institutions démocratiques*, March 2003, pp. 79–84.
9. Jean-Pierre Charbonneau, *Le pouvoir aux citoyens et aux citoyennes. Document de réflexion populaire*, Québec, June 2002.
10. Mary Moszynski, 'Report touts fixed provincial election dates', *The Moncton Times and Transcript*, 20 January 2005, p. A4.
11. When there were successive versions of the same model, as in Prince Edward Island and Quebec, the most recent version of the model has been selected.
12. This was also proposed by the supporters of MMP in British Columbia.
13. No authoritative simulation has been conducted for BC-STV, as no specific boundary plan was proposed, and as it is difficult to gauge how second and subsequent preferences will be distributed. Based on a simulation conducted by Dave Ferguson of the Green Party (http://members.shaw.ca/greenparty/gpbc/STV/), we found the Gallagher Index to be 9.38 for the 2001 election, which would mean that the distortions might be higher than Quebec's. Remember, however, that the huge lead for the Liberal party at that election has the effect of inflating the leading party's bonus, especially with districts electing between two and seven Members. In its report (British Columbia Citizens' Assembly on Electoral Reform 2004a: 7), the Citizens' Assembly offered a graph that assumed that each party except the 'others' would have won seats in proportion to their respective votes.
14. In New Brunswick, the issue of dual candidacies was framed the following way by the Commission: 'Should candidates be able to run both in a constituency and on a list? This is the norm in Germany and is allowed in other MMP systems—it is roundly criticized in some jurisdictions. As discussed earlier, it

creates the "Zombie" politicians problem. On the other hand, it allows parties to virtually ensure the election of their leading candidates by placing them high on their list (eg. party leaders who may lose a riding).'

15. Kathy Kaufield, 'Only 50 percent plus one would likely be needed to accept proportional representation, premier says', *The Telegraph-Journal*, 1 December 2005, p. A4.

16. The report can be found at http://www.gov.yk.ca/files/electoral_reform_final _rpt.pdf. See Julia Skikavich, 'Politicians, citizens push for electoral reform discussions', *White Horse Daily Star*, 21 April 2005.

17. James Wood, 'Electoral reform stalls in Saskatchewan', *The Leader Post* (Regina), 19 May 2005.

18. Paul Cliche, 'Nouvelle tentative du PQ pour que la réforme du scrutin s'enlise'(www.pressegauche.org/imprimersans.php3?id_article = 97), 17 April 2006, p. 3.

19. Nick Loenen, 'British Columbia's Electoral Reform Referendum: Lessons Learned', email message, June 2005, p. 5.

20. Contrast with the reaction of the party who lost the Malta election (held under STV) in 1981 with over 50% of the vote. Their Members boycotted the meetings of the newly elected legislature for months until the government had agreed to pass a constitutional amendment remedying at such outcomes should they occur again in the future (as they did).

5

When Citizens Choose to Reform SMP: The British Columbia Citizens' Assembly on Electoral Reform

R. Kenneth Carty, André Blais, and Patrick Fournier

Canada has long embraced majoritarian electoral politics and remains one of the few major established democracies to cling to the first past the post politics of a single-member plurality (SMP) electoral system. Despite proposals for change from a few enthusiasts and some political scientists, the call for electoral reform has had very little traction and, as Louis Massicotte notes in Chapter 4 of this volume, the issue has rarely long appeared on the country's public agenda. It is perhaps all the more surprising then, that in the space of two years, half of the country's provinces should suddenly have engaged in serious reform exercises. Matthew Søberg Shugart (in Chapter 1) seeks to explain this by answering the questions When and Why are reforms away from majoritarianism considered? But even if these questions are answered, we are still left with Who, How, and What questions. Who proposes reform? How do they put electoral reform on the political agenda? And What do they recommend as an alternative to the existing system? Answers to those questions are likely to be critical to any successful electoral reform.

To date there have been specific proposals drafted to reform the single-member plurality systems in Quebec, New Brunswick, Prince Edward Island, Ontario, and British Columbia (BC) (Carty 2006). All but British Columbia recommend forms of a mixed-member proportional (MMP) system. That is not surprising for, as Blais and Shugart indicate (see Conclusion in this volume), MMP is perhaps the least radical direction which reform might take, and the examples of New Zealand (described by

Vowles in Chapter 6) and the new Scottish and Welsh assemblies are often held up as working examples of this alternative. Thus British Columbia seems the unusual case—its reform exercise led to a recommendation for the adoption of the single transferable vote (STV), a proposal that was supported by 58% of the electorate in a province-wide referendum at the time of the 2005 general election. In this chapter, we explore the Who, How, and What aspects of British Columbia's electoral reform process. It is not over, and so we conclude with a word about next steps.

5.1. Electoral Reform in British Columbia

Shugart's analysis of the situations in which reform of the single-member plurality system is proposed suggests that movement to reform the electoral system in British Columbia was almost inevitable. The province's politics was marked by the two most dramatic instances of inherent systemic failure—a 'wrong winner' (which Shugart less contentiously calls a 'spurious majority') and a 'lopsided' majority—in quick succession. With a political party, previously disadvantaged by the system, swept into office on a platform of change, both of Shugart's inherent and contingent factors were in place, and electoral reform quickly moved onto the active agenda. In British Columbia's case, this was advanced by a Liberal party government which had promised to take up the issue after losing the 1996 election to the New Democrats despite outpolling them by 42 to 39%. The Liberals' subsequent overwhelming victory in 2001, when the party won all but 2 of the legislature's 79 seats with only 57.6% of the votes, may have only confirmed the view of many that the electoral system was unable to meet the minimum requirements for effective Westminster-style parliamentary governance.

During the subsequent legislative debate on the proposal to establish a *Citizens' Assembly on Electoral Reform*, neither the Premier nor the leader of the opposition made reference to those two elections, although both were aware that widespread frustration at those results lay behind the interest in electoral reform in their parties and among the wider public.[1] Much of the discussion focused on a perceived general democratic malaise and declining levels of public trust in political institutions, particularly the first past the post electoral system.[2] Premier Campbell spoke about the need to 're-establish the critical link between our democratic institutions and those they are supposed to serve' and reminded the House that his party's election manifesto had explicitly promised to give people 'the right to demonstrate how they want to elect their MLAs'.[3] For her part, opposition leader MacPhail specifically pointed to an Institute for Research on Public Policy study by Howe and Northrup (2000) that documented British Columbians' increasing dissatisfaction with the electoral system. Both major parties then voted to support the unique idea of creating an assembly of citizens especially mandated to consider the issue of electoral reform.

While serious consideration of electoral system change was taken up after the 2001 election, it is worth noting that it was but one element of the new government's wider democratic and institutional reform agenda. The Liberals saw it as part of a package of changes which included reforming governmental accounting practices to make them more transparent, establishing fixed election dates (a first for Canadian legislatures), and the opening of cabinet meetings to public scrutiny by broadcasting some of them on the parliamentary television channel. The new Liberal government saw itself as leading a broader democratic reform movement in response to public opinion calling for change.

Whatever the status of single-member plurality electoral regimes in other political systems, it was hardly revered in British Columbia where electoral reform had occasionally been advocated as a tool for depriving the socialists of an opportunity to form a majority government. To do just that, the province conducted two successive general elections in the early 1950s using a majority rule preferential ballot system in districts returning between one and three representatives. Multi-member electoral districts persisted even after the province reverted to the plurality rule in 1956. Some three-member districts were used until the mid-1960s, and two-member districts were used until 1987 when half of the legislature's members were elected in them. In fact, the election of 1991 was the first in the province's history in which all members of the legislature were elected by a plurality rule in single-member districts: it was also the year in which over 80% of the electorate supported a referendum to institute a provision to provide for popular recall of members of the legislature.

Thus, it seems clear that the inherent and contingent factors necessary to stimulate electoral reform were in place in British Columbia and that the historical context provided an openness to using other electoral systems. What was less obvious was how a reform agenda might be advanced.

The really revolutionary aspect of the British Columbia process was the politicians' decision to exclude themselves and hand the problem over to ordinary citizens. Premier Campbell noted that the plan called for 'an act of true citizenship' on the part of those who would make up a citizens' assembly. That had never been done before in any democracy and so the outcome was quite unpredictable.

5.2. A Citizens' Assembly

The idea to use a citizens' assembly to deal with the issue of electoral reform seems to have evolved in popular discussions around a perceived democratic deficit and no one individual can legitimately claim parentage.[4] Certainly the growing interest in and experimentation with citizen juries, deliberative polls, and new forms of civic engagement were well known to reform advocates. At the same time, the frustrating failures of the early 1990s to resolve outstanding Canadian constitutional issues by traditional means led a number of political activists to consider whether new processes to advance a reform agenda needed to be developed. The Canada West Foundation led in the development of this work, studying and advocating the use of constituent assemblies as a vehicle for change. Electoral reform enthusiasts in British Columbia—led by a former MLA and Social Credit party government caucus chair, Nick Loenen—began a campaign to convince politicians that an assembly of ordinary citizens might be the best mechanism to deal with fundamental political reforms. To maintain popular control, he advocated that one be coupled with a referendum, as used in New Zealand during its successful electoral reform process.

The prospect of electoral reform actually occurring took a major step forward when Liberal leader Gordon Campbell, speaking to a party policy convention in April 1999, indicated that he favoured creating a citizens' assembly to look at the issue.[5] His party was then in opposition, and no doubt unhappy about having lost the previous (1996) election while having obtained more votes than the then re-elected New Democratic Party. The Liberals made Campbell's reform proposal part of their election manifesto and, after winning a 'lopsided' victory in 2001, the new Premier moved to create an assembly process. Campbell's argument for turning the issue over to the public was simple. He argued that 'the rules of democracy should be designed by the people they serve, not by the power brokers who may wish that the democracy worked in their interests'

(2003: 4). By power brokers he meant politicians who were engaged in the electoral game and so were in a conflict of interest over the rules governing their activities.

Once safely in office, the Liberals had to decide what to do about the issue. The new caucus members had learned in their pre-election party candidate school that, if elected, their leader fully intended to see the promises made in the election manifesto document implemented.[6] It was clear that Campbell was personally committed to the assembly idea for it was his leadership that put and kept it on the agenda—without his direct efforts there would have been no assembly. Thus, when the issue came to the new Liberal government's legislative caucus for discussion, members recognized that the principle of holding an assembly was settled: the question they wrestled with was how they might proceed.

In short, there was a Citizens' Assembly in British Columbia because the Premier was determined that there should be one and was freely prepared to relinquish some of his own power to a group of citizens. That decision is in many ways surprising for it does not fit the standard depiction of politicians as power-seekers. It is a reminder that politicians have a variety of motivations and that ideological preferences or personal commitments can override narrowly defined power-seeking.

Premier Campbell started a process that could lead to an overhaul of the first past the post electoral system that clearly benefited the two main parties including his own Liberal party. As Blau suggests in his analysis of veto players (Chapter 2), we might expect a strong objection from caucus members in such a situation. However, there was no caucus resistance for the simple reason that the party's leader, and now the new Premier, had firmly and publicly established his position before and during the election campaign. In that case, any attempt to block the Premier's initiative from a caucus member would have been interpreted as a direct challenge to the leader, a position no MLA was willing to take.

Promising to hold a citizens' assembly was one thing, creating one was another for, as Campbell (2003: 4) said on introducing the enabling bill to the legislature, 'no government in the history of British Columbia, in the history of our country' had done it before. He could have added no government anywhere had ever done it before. The basic idea was to involve the province's public as fully as possible in discussions about what sort of electoral system it wanted. To do so there were to be three dimensions to the reform process. First, there would be the meetings of the Assembly itself. Having debated the issue, the Assembly would then engage the population in a set of community hearings to provide for the greatest possible public input. The third dimension would be a referendum on any recommendation the Assembly made. Each stage was to be as transparent as possible and independent of any government direction or control.

With no previous experience or a blueprint outlining how a citizens' assembly might be constructed at hand, the government commissioned Gordon Gibson, a one-time MLA turned public affairs commentator and a Senior Fellow of the Fraser Institute, a Vancouver-based think tank, to develop a model.[7] Gibson produced a detailed plan and budget that was accepted in large part by the government: the major modification it made to his proposal was to increase the Assembly size in order to enhance the prospects that it would be fully representative of the provincial electorate.[8] The key features of the final Assembly plan were as follows:

(1) *Random selection of members.* All British Columbians on the voters list (with the explicit exception of active politicians and their partisan agents) were to be eligible for random selection for membership. Participation would not be compulsory so that an element of self-selection was inevitably involved.

This feature was important to establish the legitimacy of the Assembly, both among the members and with the wider public. Though members were selected from individual electoral districts to ensure geographic coverage of the entire province, they were to come to the Assembly as representative individual British Columbians, not as the local delegates of any community or group.

(2) *Gender balance.* There was a deliberate decision taken to provide for equal numbers of men and women.

This feature marked the Assembly out as unique for no legislature elected (or appointed) in Canada had ever come close to being gender balanced. For members, this feature strengthened their claim to being legitimately representative. Many argued that it strengthened the propensity for collaborative and consensual deliberation rather than adversarial debate of the sort seen in the legislature.

(3) *Narrow and clear mandate.* The Assembly was charged with considering the electoral system defined simply as 'the manner in which voters' ballots are translated into seats in the Legislative Assembly'. Other issues, however germane to electoral competition, were excluded.

This focused the Assembly on a specific and particular task and allowed it to develop and work to a manageable agenda. If the Assembly chose to make a recommendation for change, it had to recommend one specific alternative which would be 'described clearly and in detail'. This helped to concentrate the Assembly's attention. By requiring that the recommendation had to be specific and detailed, the mandate ensured that Assembly members would have to develop a fairly sophisticated and detailed knowledge of electoral systems.

(4) *Any recommendation to go to public referendum.* This feature of the Assembly plan gave Assembly members a strong sense of responsibility and motivation. They knew that they were being watched by their fellow citizens and that their report would not simply be deposited on some neglected government library shelf. This led to all their work being public so that voters would be able to see the basis and process that led to any recommendation.

(5) *Full independence from government.* Not only were working politicians (and their agents) excluded from participation, but the Chair was given complete authority and financial resources to appoint staff, recruit members, and lead the Assembly. As it happened, there was never any suspicion of government interference or direction throughout the entire exercise.

With the plan in place, the legislature unanimously agreed to the government's nomination of Dr. J.P. Blaney as Assembly chair. A former President of Simon Fraser University in Vancouver, Jack Blaney had been instrumental in the establishment of its Wosk Centre for Dialogue and had a passionate commitment to adult education and public dialogue. Described by Premier Campbell as both 'a conceptual thinker and a consensus builder', he proved to have the right balance of skills to recruit a dedicated and independent staff[9] and to lead 160 disparate citizens through the year-long work.

5.3. The BC Citizens' Assembly on Electoral Reform

Recruiting 160 citizens to participate in a year-long public policy process on a subject of tangential interest to most people presented a challenge. The Assembly's staff had British Columbia's Chief Electoral Officer select names from the voters list in each of the province's 79 electoral districts. The names were drawn at random with provisions for equal numbers of men and women and stratified to match the age distribution of the district. Those so selected were sent letters informing them of their opportunity to participate in the Assembly and inviting them to indicate their interest. Individuals who responded positively were then able to attend a local community meeting, where they heard a detailed presentation about the scope and obligations of the project and again asked if they still wished to be considered. Those who signalled willingness had their names placed in a hat, and one man's name and one woman's name were then drawn for each electoral district. When it was discovered that no members of the province's First Nations communities had been chosen, a subsequent draw of such individuals who had attended a selection meeting was held to add one man and one woman from that population.

The process ultimately saw 23,034 initial information letters sent out to inform the selected individuals about the Assembly and indicating the eligibility requirements.[10] Only 1,715 individuals (7.4%) responded to this first invitation, so there was obviously a high degree of self-selection. Of those, 1,441 were invited to 1 of the 27 local selection meetings held around the province: 1,105 (76.7%) accepted the invitation and 964 (66.9%) actually attended. Thus, of the over 23,000 individuals randomly drawn by the BC Electoral Officer's computer, 4.2% ultimately came to a selection meeting at which the final 160 (0.7%) were chosen to be members of the Assembly.[11] The self-selection involved— first to respond to the initial information letter, second to accept an invitation to a local meeting, and then third to allow one's name to go into the hat—appears to have produced a strong commitment to the project. Only one member dropped out before the year-long exercise was completed.

This protracted selection process produced an Assembly that was evenly gender balanced and somewhat more age representative than the voters' list itself.[12] Like the provincial population, the Assembly had a very diverse multicultural and linguistic cast with members from all kinds of working, middle class and professional occupations and backgrounds. Given that the Assembly was to start with a learning phase designed to introduce members to the variety and mechanics of alternate electoral systems, the educational backgrounds of the members were potentially important. And it was extraordinarily varied: members with only a few years of elementary schooling (sometimes years ago in a far-off country) found themselves sitting beside colleagues who had advanced university

Table 5.1. Views of Citizens' Assembly members[a]

	Pre-Assembly	Mid-Assembly	Post-Assembly	BC public (Post-Assembly)
Self-assessment of general politicization[b]				
Interest in politics	7.0	7.5	7.7	5.7[c]
Informed about politics	6.0	6.7	6.9	—
Informed about electoral systems	4.4	8.1	8.8	—
General satisfaction with existing system[d]				
Satisfied with BC democracy	47	31	34	65
Satisfied with BC electoral system	35	19	14	63
No preferred electoral system for BC[d]	90	47	—	—
Knowledge of alternate electoral systems[d]				
Unable to identify a PR country	73	14	17	—
Unable to identify a preferential vote country	95	20	8	—
Unable to identify a two-vote country	85	31	24	—
Specific views on electoral system principles[d]				
Seats should be proportional to votes	69	86	90	59
Strong MLAs needed to defend local interests	95	72	85	—

Abbreviations: BC: British Columbia; PR: proportional representation; MLA: Member of the (provincial) Legislative Assembly.

[a] Don't knows or no responses have been excluded in the calculations reported.

[b] Mean based on a 0–10 scale.

[c] Question asked specifically about interest in BC politics: those for Assembly members simply mentioned politics.

[d] Percentages.

training, one with a doctorate in theoretical physics from Oxford University.

Despite the varied and broadly representative character of the membership, the self-selection dimension to the recruitment process had the potential to generate an Assembly of individuals with well-established and strong views about the electoral system and a propensity for reform that was not typical of the wider electorate. The data in Table 5.1 allow us to explore the extent to which this was the case. They are taken from a series of surveys of Assembly members conducted at various stages of the process.[13] Comparative data describing the views of the wider electorate come from a rolling cross-section conducted between the release of the Assembly's final report and the subsequent May 2005 referendum.[14] As they gathered to begin their work (column 1), Assembly members described themselves as 'moderately' political: on a 0–10 scale, they rated their average interest in politics at 7.0, which was somewhat higher than the average reported by the public (5.7).[15] Members judged themselves even less informed (than interested) about politics (6.0) and considerably less informed (4.4) on the subject of electoral systems.

Most of the individuals recruited to participate in the Assembly were not mistaken when they gave themselves a low rating on their existing knowledge of electoral systems. Few had any real understanding about the variety or the working of electoral systems used in other democracies. When asked, 73% said they could not name a country that used a proportional electoral system, 95% could not name a country where voters got to rank order candidates, and 85% could not name a country where electors got two votes—one for the party and one for a candidate.

Although the Assembly members claimed to be only moderately interested in politics, they were uncharacteristically active citizens. Virtually all reported having voted in the previous provincial and federal elections as compared to just 71 and 63% of the BC electorate. The great majority of them (85%) indicated that they were involved in some form of volunteer work with more than one (the average was 2.1) community or professional organization. This suggests that these were individuals with high levels of social capital and an underlying sense of civic duty that provided the basis for their decision to take part in the Assembly.

These high levels of civic engagement did not translate into high levels of satisfaction with the state of British Columbia's democracy or the working of the province's electoral system. As Table 5.1 indicates, only a minority of Assembly members described themselves as satisfied with either. This was in sharp contrast to substantial majorities in the public who declared themselves satisfied with both. Here is a hint that the self-selection aspect of the recruitment procedure may have led to disproportionate numbers of more dissatisfied individuals being recruited into the Assembly process. However, these Assembly members appeared to be agnostic—or perhaps they were simply declaring themselves open minded—on the question of what electoral system would be best for BC: as they arrived to begin their work, 90% reported that they had no preferred system for the province.

Any decision about an electoral system ultimately will rest upon a set of values that can be articulated in terms of principles that structure an institutional design. Table 5.1 reports the views of members and the public on two such principles that would prove to be critical to the citizens' assembly reform exercise in British Columbia. First, there is the question of proportionality. As Shugart (Chapter 1) rightly notes, proportional representation (PR) systems operate on 'opposing principles of representation' to constituency-based winner-take-all systems. It is striking therefore that, knowing little about other electoral systems or how they worked, 69% of Assembly members (and close to two-thirds of the wider electorate) expressed support for the principle that a party's seat share should be proportional to its vote share. At the same time, undoubtedly reflecting the geographic impulses that have long been central to Canadian political practice, 95% indicated that they believed voters needed a strong MLA to defend local interests. Here were the seeds of a tension that would lie at the heart of the Assembly's struggle to decide what sort of electoral system it ought to recommend for the province.

As the Assembly started, its members were demographically reasonably representative of the province. Although they were active citizens, most appeared to be generally dissatisfied with the system, but were relatively clear and broadly agreed about the principles that should underlie a more acceptable one. What they lacked was information or knowledge about the world of actual electoral systems, and so they were unable to identify a preferable alternative to their existing single-member plurality institution. The first two phases of the Assembly's work were designed to change this.

5.4. Learning about Electoral Systems

Before they could debate and decide about what electoral system would be best for British Columbia, Assembly members had to learn about both the working of the first past the post system (while most knew how voting was conducted, many knew little else about the details of the electoral, legislative, and constitutional system within which it was nested) and the range of alternate electoral systems available. To help them do this, the staff organized six residential weekends in Vancouver spread from mid-January to the end of March 2004—a kind of political science boot camp.[16] Supported by David Farrell's (2001a) excellent and accessible comparative textbook on *Electoral Systems*, they provided a series of plenary presentations supplemented by regular discussion groups and occasional talks by visiting experts on specific topics. For most members, this was a daunting agenda and only half could say at the end of the first weekend that they felt confident that they were going to be able to cope with the material: by the end of the six-weekend learning phase, only about 15% were still not confident. About 10% later reported that they had 'seriously considered withdrawing from the Assembly' at one time or another during this period but none did so—an indication of the collective commitment members appear to have made to the project and to one another.[17]

The learning phase has been described in detail elsewhere (see Ratner 2004). One feature that bears notice is the members' claim that, of nine different learning activities they engaged in over the period, ranging from plenary presentations through discussion in small groups, personal study, and web forums, the general lectures from the research staff were the most useful (British Columbia Citizens' Assembly on Electoral Reform 2004b: 69). This may reflect the low information base from which most started, for it was those lectures which provided members with a foundation on which to build. But it also raises the possibility that their final decision was then overly influenced by the views and preferences of the staff. In the post-Assembly questionnaire, members were asked if they thought 'the presentation of options by the Assembly staff was biased' and whether 'the Assembly's research staff had a preference about which electoral system would be best for BC'. Eighty-eight per cent of those responding said they thought the presentations were unbiased; their views about the staff's own preferences were more mixed. Thirty-seven per cent said they did not think the staff had a preference, 32% claimed they did not know, 18% thought that the staff liked STV, and 10% said that they preferred MMP. Thus, while it is impossible to rule out the possibility that the staff may have had some influence, an overwhelming majority of members perceived the staff to be neutral.

The members did an extraordinary amount of work and research on their own. One member 'translated' Farrell's book into 'simple' English, another devised a program to run hundreds of computer simulations of alternate electoral system scenarios, others did web research, and many organized public discussions and events in their communities: all shared what they were doing with their fellow Assembly members. Not surprisingly then, Table 5.1 (column 2) reports dramatic improvements in knowledge of electoral systems as well as considerably higher levels of interest in and information about politics after they had gone through this program. At the same time, the proportion of members expressing dissatisfaction with the existing system increased. There were no particularly striking alterations in their views about what basic principles ought to structure an electoral system, although support for the proportional principle clearly increased.

The learning sessions were followed by a set of 50 public hearings held across the province. All members attended those in their home district and most went to at least one in another corner of the province—often in a community they had never visited before. Members hoped that these meetings would give them a clear indication of what the public wanted in an electoral system. Instead they quickly discovered that most members of the public knew far less about the details of electoral systems than they (i.e. they were like the members had been when they started), but they also heard expressed, time and again, a marked appetite for change. It seems likely that these hearings attracted disproportionate numbers of those who wanted to see a change to the electoral system. Ultimately then, their major contribution beyond publicizing the Assembly was to convince Assembly members that a recommendation for change would be welcome, but that the members themselves would have to do the hard work of designing and deciding upon the details of an alternative themselves.

As they came to the end of this first half of their work, the members were reflecting on a wide range of criteria by which they might make an assessment about electoral systems. Asked to rank nine different criteria on a seven-point scale (with 7 = extremely important and 1 = not important), members gave all of them relatively high scores (the highest mean score, 6.2, was assigned to voter choice and the lowest was local representation with a mean rating of 5.1). Although Shugart might emphasize that opposing principles underlie different electoral systems, it appeared that Assembly members were not anxious to choose between them. They did not see any single principle as pre-eminent and looked to electoral systems that might find ways to accommodate and 'balance' apparently competing principles.

Beyond a consideration of general representational and governance principles, the learning phase had also led to Assembly members developing clear views about the respective merits of different types of electoral systems. When asked to rate nine different ones 'in terms of how good you personally think each system would be for BC' on a seven-point scale

(7 = very good, 1 = very bad), Assembly members gave the highest mean rating to MMP (5.4), followed by open-list PR (5.3) and STV (5.1). All other systems were rated much lower, including SMP with a mean score of only 2.9. Obviously, their comparative assessments found the existing first past the post system wanting as they expressed a marked preference for systems with proportional and preferential features. By the end of the learning phase, about half claimed that they now had a preferred electoral system (up from 10% at the beginning) and while 69% thought it very likely that the Assembly would reach a consensus, many (44%) thought it would be difficult to do so.

5.5. Choosing an Electoral System

The mandate of the Assembly required that if it was to recommend a change in the electoral system, it had to present a detailed alternative. Simply recommending 'proportional representation' or 'preferential voting' would not be acceptable. The logic of this requirement was that for a recommendation to go to referendum the electorate would need to know precisely what it was voting on and, if it passed, the legislature would have to know what had been agreed to. To move towards a recommendation, the Assembly decided to first identify key principles it wanted institutionalized as part of the fundamental structure of an electoral system. Breaking into small discussion groups, members debated what elements would be necessary features of any electoral system acceptable to the province. All the groups came to the same conclusion identifying three characteristics:

(1) *Voter choice.* This element reflected the members' constant ranking of increased or maximum choice for individual voters as their most highly regarded value. It was to be articulated in a system that provided for preferential and/or multiple ballots.

(2) *Proportionality.* Members believed that the first past the post system was inherently unfair because it provided no direct or logical connection between vote and seat shares. They concluded some degree of proportionality was desirable although there were differences among members about just how proportional a system needed to be to be fair.

(3) *Local representation.* There was less agreement about the importance of local representation. Many, especially those from rural and

sparsely populated areas, believed it an essential element of any acceptable system; some urban members thought it a completely spurious issue. Debate on this principle was ongoing and individual members' estimates of its importance varied over time (Blais, Carty, and Fournier 2008). Ultimately, the Assembly agreed that local representation would have to be a structural feature of any system on which they might reach a consensus.

As they approached the task of designing an alternative electoral system, members faced the challenge of determining which system would provide an acceptable trade-off among their three, sometimes competing, elements. The collective recognition that all three would have to be accommodated and balanced ruled out both majority systems, given their lack of proportionality, and PR list systems, given their weakness in providing for local representation. This left Mixed Member Proportional (MMP) and Single Transferable Vote (STV) systems as the two most plausible alternative types.

Figure 5.1, which charts Assembly members' comparative rankings of these two types over time, indicates that in the early period of the Assembly's work there was a distinct preference for MMP over STV. However, it was also the case that, well into the process, a third or more of the members did not rate one of those systems better than the other. Nevertheless,

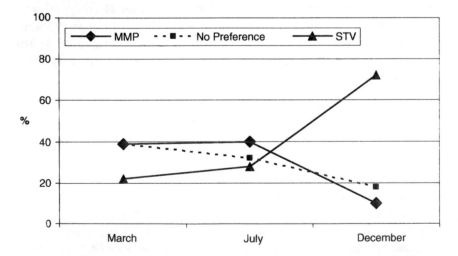

Figure 5.1. Assembly members' preferences for mixed-member proportional (MMP) or single transferable vote (STV)

as members moved into the final deliberative stage of the process, a major shift occurred—the number of indifferent members (those with no preference as between the two systems) dropped. As the debate sharpened, STV emerged as a clear winner over MMP. When it came to a final vote to decide between the two, the members ended up choosing STV by a 4:1 ratio.

In making this choice, Assembly members appear to have been governed by their views on the three principles they wanted to see in an electoral system. An analysis of members' views reveals that those who gave priority to the value of *voter choice* preferred STV with its preferential ballot.[18] That predilection had emerged by the midpoint of the Assembly process and persisted until the end. By the time members came to make their decision, those who gave priority to the *proportional* principle had come to see that the particular MMP model they had created was not going to be substantially fairer (i.e. more proportional) than their STV plan. This reflected both the specific features of the MMP system they thought would be acceptable—a 3% province-wide threshold and regionalized lists—and the conclusions of the computer analysis one member conducted comparing the experience of other MMP and STV systems. It appears that views on proportionality played relatively little part in structuring the Assembly's choice between its MMP and STV alternatives. More critical was the assessment of the place of *local representation* in electoral politics. Members who were particularly concerned with it moved to support STV, partially on the grounds that STV induces politicians to do a lot of constituency work (on this, see Katz 1980; Carty 1981; Marsh 2000), and partially because STV does not reduce the absolute number of local members in the way MMP does.

Thus, each of the three values played into members' evaluations and contributed to the Assembly's choice of STV. Proportionality, though perhaps most important in leading to the basic decision to recommend an alternative to SMP, was least important in the choice between alternatives as neither was perceived as much fairer than the other. For its part, STV was preferred by those most concerned for voter choice, and it ultimately became the choice of those for whom local representation was particularly salient. This latter group may have been slow to decide that STV offered them the better of the two alternatives, but when they did their preferences were critical to shaping the wider Assembly's final recommendation.

5.6. The Surprising STV Choice

In comparing MMP and STV, Blais and Shugart (see Conclusion) suggest that STV is a more radical reform and rightly observe that most of the jurisdictions opting for reform are opting for MMP. That judgement echoes the views of political science experts who, in response to a survey by Bowler, Farrell, and Pettitt (2005), rated MMP as the 'best system'. So the decision to recommend STV can be seen as surprising. It raises the question of why ordinary people who constituted the membership of the BC Citizens' Assembly opted for it rather than MMP, the typical choice of reformers and the option recommended by reform commissions in other parts of the country. Could it be that STV has greater appeal among 'ordinary' citizens than among the 'experts'?[19] And if so, why?

While there are differences in the judgements of experts and ordinary citizens, it must be conceded that they are modest. Of the experts who responded to the invitation to rate many different electoral systems, 52% ranked MMP as their first choice, but STV was the second most frequently (by 38%) preferred system (Bowler, Farrell, and Pettitt 2005). In a subsequent survey we conducted with Bowler and Farrell, in which professional experts were again asked to rate different electoral systems, the highest mean rating was given to MMP (5.5), followed by STV and open-list PR (5.1). At the end of their work, the new 'citizen-expert' members of the Assembly gave mean ratings of 6.2 to STV and 5.2 to MMP.

Experts and BC's Assembly members both clearly liked STV and MMP, preferring them to all other systems, but they did not rank them in the same order. Two factors may be at play. First, Bowler, Farrell, and Pettitt did not ask their experts to consider the value of voter choice yet we know it was consistently the most highly rated value of the BC citizens and important for many in their choice of STV. A second important difference between the experts and the Assembly membership is that the latter paid more attention to the issue of local representation. The choice of STV in British Columbia reflected the fact that its citizen decision-makers were more concerned with local representation, and how it would work in practice for them, than experts typically are. Important as it was, however, the difference should not be overstated. Assembly members, like the experts, had positive evaluations of both systems. The choice between STV and MMP was a difficult and contested one and the Assembly's decision reflected a collective assessment of how best to balance the competing claims of the two principles for British Columbia.

5.7. Electoral Reform in British Columbia?

When the Assembly was created, the government had wanted to do more than simply respond to the anomalous results (instances of what Shugart calls inherent systemic failures) of the two previous elections. It intended to provide an opportunity for the public as a whole to pass judgement on what kind of politics it wanted for the indefinite future and saw this as requiring more than a simple majority. After internal debate, the government proposed a standard of 60% acceptance for any change. Liberal caucus members do not appear to have seen this as a mechanism for ensuring defeat: many apparently expected a recommendation for change and one that would pass that threshold.[20] At the same time, however, it was agreed that there ought to be a second criteria for acceptance, namely, that any recommendation win majority approval in 60% of the electoral districts. The clear intent of this was to ensure the urban majority in the Victoria and Vancouver districts would not be able to impose its will on the rest of the province. For many, this was thought to pose the more difficult hurdle. The legislature responded by amending the province's referendum act to establish this new double standard for success.

Many Assembly members felt that the standard was unreasonably high. However, they appeared to accept it as part of the political trade-off involved in establishing a Citizens' Assembly allowed to make a recommendation that would bypass the government and legislature and go directly to referendum. Their decision led the members to draft a Yes/No question 'Should British Columbia change to the BC-STV electoral system as recommended by the Citizens' Assembly on Electoral Reform?' that went to referendum at the time of the provincial general election (17 May 2005), five months after their report was finalized. The result was clear: 57.7% of those voting said Yes, and the question received majority support in 77 of the province's 79 electoral districts. Thus the referendum, despite having unexpectedly easily met the second test, narrowly failed the first, and so was declared lost. In the aftermath, the newly returned government recognized the broad support for change and Premier Campbell announced there would be another referendum. Arguing that not all citizens had learned much about the proposal and its implications, he pledged that public funds would be made available to support (For and Against) publicity during the next referendum campaign and that voters would have the benefit of a map indicating how STV electoral districts would be structured. The province's independent electoral boundaries commission was directed to design an STV electoral map for that purpose.

Gibson's original report establishing the basic plan for the Assembly process had argued that 'there is no need for "Yes" and "No" [referendum campaign] committees' on the grounds that 'political parties, academics and pundits will no doubt provide for all the debate required'. That proved to be a serious misreading of the province's political dynamics, especially given the decision to hold the referendum on the same day as a general election. When it created the Assembly, the government made it clear that it would not take a position on any recommendation. This echoed the Premier's clearly defined position that the electoral system was a matter for citizens, not party politicians who had a direct and personal stake in it. As a consequence, the Liberal party and cabinet took no position on the issue. Some individual caucus members spoke out both for and against the recommendation during the campaign in their local districts, while others simply argued that they were strong supporters of the Assembly process itself.

With the government silent on the substance of the issue, the main opposition party, the New Democrats, opted to do the same. The party was preoccupied with rebuilding after its electoral debacle of 2001 and had only one incumbent MLA standing for election. Thus, it had no established caucus position, and while the new leader had advocated change to a more proportional system at one of the Assembly's public hearings, she had been silent on details. With individual party members likely divided on the issue, the New Democrats took advantage of the Liberals' silence to do the same. As a result, the issue received little attention in the media war between the two main parties and so quickly disappeared from public attention. For its part, the Green party (which had captured 12% of the vote in 2001 and was seen by some as a relevant political force) spoiled its opportunity to send a clear message when its leader, disappointed in the Assembly's preference for STV over MMP, announced she would lead a campaign against the recommendation, only to be forced to back down by large numbers of party members keen on any kind of proportional system.

The media attempted to generate some interest in the issue: the press provided coverage of the Assembly and its preferred STV system with most major newspapers ultimately recommending a Yes vote. With few resources, small groups of advocates and opponents staged a low-key campaign and the Assembly members themselves emerged as perhaps the most aggressive campaigners for their recommendation. They quickly formed an alumni group and 88% of them reported taking an active part in the campaign: 15 indicated they had given 20 or more public talks in the five-month period between the release of the report and referendum day, while many reported doing radio and TV interviews, writing letters, staging debates as well as other events to capture attention.[21]

The real black hole in this entire reform process was the large number of British Columbians who simply did not know about it. Despite the best efforts of those in favour of change, the absence of a high-profile publicity campaign meant 44% of the electorate claimed to know nothing about BC-STV by the time of the referendum vote. This was crucial for, as Cutler and Johnston (2008) demonstrate, 'the more they [the electorate] knew, the more they voted Yes'. And in particular, the more they knew about the Assembly and its process, the more likely they were to support the recommendation.

5.8. Conclusion

The British Columbia story is remarkable in many respects. First and foremost, the process that was put in place was extraordinary. Letting a group of ordinary citizens propose a new electoral system after an intense period of learning and deliberation was an extraordinary experiment. No such comprehensive exercise had ever been conducted anywhere. But so dramatic, and successful, was the example that two other jurisdictions— the Netherlands and the Canadian province of Ontario—soon followed suit and established their own Citizens' Assemblies on Electoral Reform.

Of course the most surprising aspect of the British Columbia approach to reform is that it was instigated by a government which had full power to enact any reform it deemed desirable. Why would politicians, who are generally assumed to be power-hungry, come to the conclusion that it is in their best interest to allow others to choose the rules that could affect their chances of being re-elected? Our conclusion must be that there are instances where politicians do not think exclusively in terms of their own interests. All the evidence points to the verdict that Premier Campbell established a Citizens' Assembly simply because he thought this is how things should be done. Of course, the Premier could hope that he could reap some electoral benefits from establishing an independent process (Shugart's act-contingencies), but we doubt that this was the crucial consideration. The BC case reminds us that there are these exceptional instances where the pursuit of the public interest is a paramount consideration.

British Columbia is also exceptional in the reform proposed by the Assembly, for in virtually all other recent instances MMP has been the option preferred by reformers trying to replace SMP. As we have indicated, this reflected the stronger concerns that Assembly members had with the issue and practice of local representation. But the proposal may also have reflected lesser risk-aversion among the members. Blais and Shugart (Conclusion) suggest that MMP may appear to be a less 'radical' option because it retains some elements of first past the post. Could it be that ordinary citizens engaged in a bold reform experiment pay less attention to considerations of that sort than seasoned politicians?

For all its uniqueness, it is also true that the British Columbia story confirms much of what we know about electoral reform. When the members looked for alternatives to first past the post, they looked to systems that incorporate the opposing principle of proportionality. They struggled to find a system that would be fairer, though not necessarily absolutely proportional, while allowing voters the option of expressing their preferences for individual candidates. The same dual concern has emerged in all other attempts to reform SMP and appears well justified, as empirical evidence indicates that preferential voting mechanisms are associated with higher levels of voter satisfaction (Farrell and McAllister 2006*b*).

The BC case also supports our understanding, clearly articulated by Matthew Søberg Shugart in Chapter 1, about both the conditions that initiate reform processes. Clearly the outcome of the 1996 election, which allowed the New Democratic Party to win a majority of the seats even though they had fewer votes than the Liberals, was significant in convincing Liberal leader Campbell that there was something basically wrong with the existing system.

Finally, for the time being at least, first past the post still prevails in British Columbia. Not surprisingly, most reform attempts fail. In many cases, as Blau points out (Chapter 2), the status quo is maintained because it is not in the interest of majority of elected politicians to change the rules under which they have performed rather well. But this was not the case in British Columbia, where politicians have decided to give voters a second chance. This next round, scheduled for the 2009 provincial general election, ought to tell us something about the electoral appeal of electoral reform.

Notes

1. See the debate reported in the British Columbia *Hansard* for 30 April 2003.
2. Dalton (2004) claims that one of the consequences of declining political support is increased demand for institutional reform.
3. MLA—a Member of the (provincial) Legislative Assembly. There is no common appellation for this office across the Canadian provinces and a variety of other titles are in use. The government's manifesto, to which the Premier referred, was known as the *New Era* document.
4. This paragraph draws on conversations with a number of those involved in these early informal activities and discussions.
5. Earlier discussions had referred to constituent assemblies—Campbell appears to have been the first to use the term 'citizens' assembly'.
6. The discussion here, and later in the text, on the role and response of the caucus at different stages of the reform process draws on confidential interviews with involved members.
7. When plans were subsequently being made for the Dutch government's *Burgerforum* and the Ontario Citizens' Assembly on Electoral Reform, both jurisdictions drew heavily on the BC model and experience.
8. Gordon Gibson, Report on the Constitution of the Citizens' Assembly on Electoral Reform, 23 December 2002. The report can be found on the Assembly website at: http://www.citizensassembly.bc.ca/public/inaction/history. Gibson had recommended 79 members (one per electoral district) and suggested some top-up members might have to be appointed to ensure representativeness. The government was opposed to appointing any members in principle so doubled the proposed size to enhance the prospects of achieving a fully representative Assembly with a random draw process. In the end, two additional members were drawn to guarantee First Nations participation. Together with the chair, this meant there were 161 members in total.
9. The permanent, full-time staff ultimately included the Chair, a Director and Associate Director of Research, a Director and Associate Director of Communications, a Chief Operations Officer and Office Manager, and five support staff who aided in all areas of the work. All members of the staff were very careful to betray no sense of their personal views about the current, or any alternate, electoral system.
10. The Assembly was designed to be as inclusive as possible: members had to be BC residents on the voters list and able to use the English language—this latter requirement probably had the effect of excluding an indeterminate number of members of some immigrant communities. As noted above, the only formal exclusions were for holders of a number of clearly specified political positions.
11. Full details of the selection process can be found in the Assembly's *Technical Report* (British Columbia Citizens' Assembly on Electoral Reform 2004*b*: 31–64).

12. Data on age distributions are in the *Technical Report* (British Columbia Citizens' Assembly on Electoral Reform 2004*b*: 40).
13. The surveys were conducted by the authors at the time of the Assembly. All together there were 13 surveys of Assembly members—three major mail questionnaires done before the Assembly first met, at the midpoint of its work, and then after it made its final report; nine short questionnaires completed at Assembly meetings; and one telephone survey conducted after the referendum.
14. The survey was conducted by the Institute for Social Research at York University under the direction of Fred Cutler, Richard Johnston (both of the Department of Political Science, University of British Columbia), and the authors. There was a weekly rolling cross-section from 17 January to 30 April and a daily rolling cross-section from 1 May to 16 May 2005. A total of 1,286 interviews took place from January to April and 1,057 in May.
15. The questions were slightly different. Those put to the public referred specifically to 'BC politics', while those to the Assembly members referred to 'politics in general'. This may account for some of the variation.
16. A full account of this, and the subsequent two phases of the Assembly's work, can be found in its *Technical Report* (British Columbia Citizens' Assembly on Electoral Reform 2004*b*: 65–94).
17. Attendance at Assembly meetings was always 95% or better and the Assembly reported only one drop-out which occurred as it started its deliberative meetings months later in September.
18. This paragraph draws heavily on the analysis in Blais, Carty, and Fournier (2008).
19. Although note that the citizen members of the Dutch Burgerforum recommended very few changes to its country's electoral system and those in the Ontario Citizens' Assembly subsequently recommended its own version of an MMP system.
20. We are relying on confidential interviews. It would seem that many caucus members expected an MMP recommendation (a system the Greens had been promoting and perhaps the only other one they knew) and believed it would attract much support.
21. It should be noted that four members reported taking part in the campaign on the No side.

6

Systemic Failure, Coordination, and Contingencies: Understanding Electoral System Change in New Zealand

Jack Vowles

In 1993, New Zealand held its last election using a single-member plurality (SMP) electoral system. Its next election in 1996 took place under a mixed-member proportional (MMP) system. The change was triggered by two referendums. The first was held in 1992, with electoral system as the only subject of the ballot. It presented a choice of change or no change, with a menu of choice options, the choice between these to take effect if change won the day. Change won, with MMP as the most preferred change option, and at the next referendum in 1993, concurrent with a general election, MMP emerged as the victor in a contest with the SMP system.[1] As an almost completely unexpected case of radical electoral system change in a country with a long established history of SMP elections, this course of events has inevitably attracted international interest. Two research programmes have analysed the process and its aftermath: Victoria University's Political Change Project[2] and the New Zealand Election Study.[3] Other analysis of the change has a New Zealand focus (Nagel 1994; Jackson and McRobie 1998; Denemark 2003) or is located in the context of the adoption of mixed-member systems in various countries (Gallagher 1998; Sakamoto 1999; Shugart 2001a, Rahat 2004).

Most of the literature addresses the consequences. Some work develops explanations of change (Mulgan 1995; Vowles 1995; Boston et al. 1996b; Lamare and Vowles 1996; Denemark 2001), or analyses the reasons for electoral change theoretically and comparatively across several cases

(Dunleavy and Margetts 1995; Boix 1999; Sakamoto 1999; Shugart 2001*a*, 2001*b*; Chapter 1 in this volume; Siaroff 2003; Benoit 2004). This chapter revisits the explanations for change within the framework of recent theory.

6.1. Theorizing Electoral System Change

Most analysis of electoral system change assumes with rational choice theory that key players are political parties that are unitary actors (Dunleavy and Margetts 1995; Boix 1999; Benoit 2004). In the context of shifts from SMP systems to proportional representation (PR), Colomer hypothesizes that changes will move 'mostly' towards 'more inclusive formulas' representing a larger number of parties. Changes will be more likely to occur the shorter the life of the current electoral system, and will be triggered by growth in the number of parties (Colomer 2004: 5).

Matthew Shugart supplements rational choice theory by identifying normative explanations that account for the placing of the electoral system on the agenda with rational-actor assumptions addressing what happens next. Change moves on to the agenda when systems fail according to their own norms: one or other of the two main sets of principles of representation, plurality and proportionality (Lijphart 1999; Powell 2000). Reform to PR will not happen because its virtues are appreciated on their own merits, but because SMP elections fail to deliver on their expectations. Under an SMP system, a large majority of seats may be generated out of a vote minority but is expected so long as it rests on a vote plurality. Systemic failures are 'the incapacity of the electoral system to deliver the normatively expected connection between the vote and the formation of executive authority' (Shugart Chapter 1 in this volume). In an SMP system, 'the election of the second largest party (by votes) to a position of full executive power could be considered a systemic failure, as it calls into question the ability of voters either to re-elect or to replace an incumbent government if the outcome after the election is that the party with the most votes is in opposition'. Another example of failure 'would be the decimation of the opposition in the form of an overly lopsided majority for the largest party' because 'the majoritarian model of democracy carves out an important role for the opposition as the only institutional monitor... on the government' (Shugart Chapter 1).

Rational choice assumptions apply when a reform process is in motion. Following Reed and Thies (2001), Shugart distinguishes between outcome- and act-contingent reform motives. In outcome-contingent circumstances, actors feel they will be better off under new rules. In act-contingent circumstances, actors see short-term benefit in proposing a reform even if it is not in their long-term interest.

Another recent contribution to the debate develops the beginnings of an even more nuanced approach, also drawing on rational choice theory while acknowledging its limitations. Rahat (2004: 461–2) observes that rational choice models may be designed to accommodate a more realistic world of unstable preferences and behaviours, non-unitary collective actors, and imperfect and biased information. However, it is difficult to build in all these assumptions to a formal model. He proposes a multistage historical comparative approach, like Shugart, drawing on the concept of agenda-setting. Each stage in a reform process takes place in a different context, in which actors and their goals may differ considerably. Rational choice insights continue to be of value, but set in a historical-comparative framework, not in an all-encompassing model (Rahat 2004: 465–76).

The analysis that follows implicitly accepts the need for such multistage analysis, but its main arguments address the general inadequacy of the elite-centred rational choice approach. Most theoretical literature on electoral system change is weak on three points crucial to the New Zealand case. Parties were divided, normative values continued to motivate actors after the agenda was set, and mass opinion was a key element. Indeed, this chapter argues that mass opinion is more important than all current theories concede, particularly, and rather obviously, if the decision moves to referendum. Even in other circumstances, mass opinion is likely to provide the framework for act-contingency at the elite level. Otherwise, why would elites imagine their actions should gain favour in public opinion? Recent work on the effects of winning and losing elections on elite and mass attitudes to institutions is particularly helpful in theoretically linking partisan interests to the attitudes and perceptions of the mass public (Anderson et al. 2005: 171–80; Bowler, Donovan, and Karp 2006). Voters for losing parties must consent to the rules of competition and are less likely to do so the more they vote for a party that consistently loses.

Shugart's concept of systemic failure is also useful because it seeks to explain how reform moves on to the political agenda. But it can be met by a sceptical critique: did the system fail, or did actors within the

165

system simply fail to understand its inbuilt incentives and thus fail to coordinate? The concept of coordination is a major theme of analysis of strategic voting (Cox 1997). A failure in the ability of an SMP electoral system to deliver according to the norms expected could simply be the failure of elites and voters to coordinate effectively. Opposition party B splits into parties B1 and B2. Together in an election, these parties gain more votes than the government of party A, but the likely consequence of plurality elections will be a government of party A returned by a majority of seats. Therefore, the answer to the problem is not electoral system change, but a return to more effective elite coordination with the merger of the two opposition parties or failing that, electoral accommodations between them. Short-term party-led coordination strategy can be distinguished from voter-driven or grass-roots coordination by means of strategic voting (Blais and Carty 1991: 83; Cox 1997: 70). At the grass roots, more voters need to realize the consequence of failing to concentrate their votes in the most competitive opposition party. Taking this argument to the extreme, there is no such thing as systemic failure: the problem is the failure of actors to behave according to the rules.

This voluntaristic use of the concept of coordination failure is rarely fully developed, and for good reasons. Taking rational actor assumptions to the limit, it assumes unrealistically high levels of information and ignores social and political constraints. If successful coordination requires the construction of a two-party system, social cleavages and path dependence may prevent this, or at least slow it down. SMP systems were not designed to produce the government and opposition parties that underpin the norms associated with them. Before the invention of parties, SMP methods developed to elect single representatives from spatially defined communities. As Cox and others have shown, Duvergerian theory explains how candidate competition in a single district works much of the time. There are incentives to vote for the candidates expected to take first and second place, and for only two candidates to stand. Yet, non-Duvergerian equilibria can emerge at the district level (Johnston and Cutler 2006). Incentives to coordinate may not be effective. How this happens still needs more research. Voting could be expressive, representing a protest or at least a rejection of the two most viable candidates, rather than any expectation of having an effect. Or people could be ignorant of the candidates' chances and thus choose a candidate with no chance of winning in the absence of any sense of wasting a vote.

Moreover, there is no convincing theory that explains why SMP system incentives towards two-candidate district competition should transfer to two-party politics nationally, nor any evidence that this consistently happens (Cox 1997: 186, 273). Some strategic non-entry may be encouraged by institutional incentives such as a strong Presidency or path dependence. But where the Duvergerian model of a two-party SMP system exists in the real world, it is the result of contingent not systemic factors. Outcomes of SMP national elections are determined as much by where the votes are cast as by how many votes are cast for the contending parties (Kim and Ohn 1992). If those separated by a single major social cleavage are spatially distributed, a dominant two-party system may emerge (Taagepera and Grofman 1985). Otherwise, multi-party politics may prevail.

If a spatial cleavage weakens, and two-party politics give way to multi-party politics, this can open up risks of systemic failure resistant to coordination. Cox theoretically and empirically analyses coordination under SMP conditions, but reports consistently successful attempts to coordinate only where there are additional institutional incentives (Cox 1997: 181–202).

6.2. Electoral System Change in New Zealand

The subtitle of the most comprehensive analysis of electoral system change in New Zealand reflects three themes emphasized in the literature: accident, design, or evolution (Jackson and McRobie 1998), summing up the debate but not resolving it.

6.2.1. *Evolution and Systemic Failure*

The argument from evolution is consistent with Colomer's hypothesis that electoral system change will move towards a more inclusive PR system, triggered by an increase in the number of elective parties. The SMP system was used consistently and continuously in New Zealand from 1914 onward. A two-party alignment consolidated from the late 1930s. From mid-century, the two-party vote began to decline and the non-major party vote and thus the effective number of parties increased. Proportionality of seats to votes and turnout both fell. The data in Table 6.1 indicates a process of partisan dealignment and an increased risk of systemic failure (Vowles 1995, 1997; Denemark 2001).

Table 6.1. Disproportionality, effective number of parties, volatility, and partisan seats–votes differences in New Zealand under the SMP system, 1914–93

	Disproportionality	Effective elective parties	Age-eligible turnout	Two-party vote	Volatility	Seat–vote differences			
						Liberal	Reform	National	Labour
1914	3.8	2.4		82.8	15.5	-1.9	4.4		-1.8
1919	18.8	2.9		86.5	39.6	-2.7	22.8		-13.8
1922	5.1	2.8	82.3	75.3	6.1	1.2	6.9		-2.5
1925	18.3	2.7	85.8	90	16.9	-6.7	22.3		-12.3
1928	3.5	3.1	87.4	64.9	24.2	4	-1.1		-2.5
1931	8	2	82.3	65.7	18.4			8.4	-4.3
1935	18	2.4	86.8	73.8	42.4			-10.1	20.2
1938	9.8	1.9	92.3	64.6	26.6			-9.1	10.5
1943	6.9	2.2	85.8	89.7	16.7			-0.3	8.7
1946	1.1	2	91.4	79.9	13.7			-0.9	1.2
1949	5.2	2	90.1	96.1	7.8			5.6	-4.7
1951	8.4	2	87.7	90.4	3.8			8.5	-8.3
1954	11.5	2.5	85.6	88.4	22.6			12	-0.4
1957	6.4	2.3	86.6	92.5	8.2			4.6	3
1960	9.3	2.4	84.4	91	9.8			9.9	-0.9
1963	8.6	2.3	82.2	90.8	1.6			9.2	0
1966	12.5	2.6	78.6	85	12.6			11.4	2.4
1969	8.9	2.4	80.9	89.4	9.9			8.4	2.2
1972	12.1	2.4	79.7	89.9	12.3			-4.7	14.8
1975	12.9	2.5	80.2	87.2	18.8			15.6	-2.8
1978	15.6	2.8	82.1	80.2	20.1			15.6	3.1
1981	16.6	2.8	83.1	77.8	9.7			12.3	7.7
1984	15.4	2.9	85.5	78.9	32.5			2	17
1987	8.8	2.3	80	92	27.3			-2.8	10.8
1990	17.4	2.5	76	82.9	34.5			22.3	-6.2
1993	18.2	3.3	76.7	69.8	27.8			15.4	10.8
mean	10.8	2.5	83.9	82.9	18.4	-0.2	10.2	6.3	2
SD	5.2	0.4	4.3	9.2	10.9	4.1	10.9	8.6	8.6

Notes: Disproportionality is estimated by Gallagher's index (Lijphart 1994: 61), volatility by Pedersen's index (Bartolini and Mair 1990: 20), and the effective number of elective parties as defined by Laasko and Taagapera (1979); see Lijphart (1994: 68).

Abbreviation: SMP: single-member plurality.

At the 1978 and 1981 elections, the centre-right National party secured fewer votes but more seats than the Opposition Labour Party and continued to govern. Two consecutive 'wrong winner' elections sparked off an electoral reform debate. Electoral reform was no longer just a concern of small parties that would benefit from PR. But the situation could be reasoned away. Both elections were held under the boundaries drawn at the 1977 electoral redistribution. Some blamed those boundaries. But to other observers, the experience confirmed a perception that over the long term the parties of the right had done better out of the SMP system than Labour.[4] Indeed, in relation to votes cast since 1946, of years in government Labour enjoyed less, and National more than would have been the case under 'proportional tenure' (Castles 1985: 41; Vowles 2004: 174). Translating votes into seats, the main beneficiaries of the SMP system in New Zealand appear to have been the Reform and National parties. Table 6.1 shows that Labour's average seat–vote advantage due to the 'mechanical effect' (Duverger 1954: 224–6) has been 2%: but Reform's was 10% and National's just over 6%. For example, at the 1993 election Labour and National almost tied in votes at ~35%, with National only marginally ahead. Yet, National's greater seat bonus gave it a five-seat margin over Labour.

Yet, the evidence for bias is not immediately clear, as at other times Labour also gained greater seat bonuses under the SMP system. Sophisticated methods have been developed to estimate bias and more generally the shape and form of votes and seats relationships in SMP systems. Setting electoral boundaries has been used to either minimize or maximize bias, depending on whether control of the process is political or administrative and bound to remove or at least reduce bias. First, one estimates the extent to which the number of seats for the winning party is exaggerated by the system. Early research identified empirically a relationship to the power of three, 'the cube rule' (Kendall and Stuart 1950). But exaggeration tends to vary, and an exponential curve is usually its most appropriate functional form (Taagepera and Shugart 1989: 161). Over and above exaggeration there is partisan bias. If each party has the same share of votes, does each get the same amount of seat share exaggeration? Or across the range, or at critical points, does one party get more than the other, and thus benefit from bias?

Figure 6.1 strongly suggests bias, plotting seat shares against vote shares for Labour and the parties of the right and drawing the two exponential curves that best fit the form of the models through the data-points. The right parties' vote curve strikes the 50% seat line at about 44%,

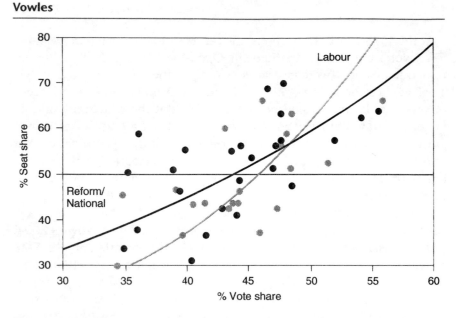

Figure 6.1. Differences in the exaggeration of votes into seat shares between Labour and Reform/National, 1914–93

and Labour's at about 46%. At 40 and 35% of the votes, the curves are much further apart. Comparing the data-points in the scatter, under the SMP system Labour formed a majority government just once with a vote of under 45% (1984), while Reform and National won seat majorities with less than 45% on six occasions (1919, 1922, 1954, 1966, 1978, and 1981).

Biases under an SMP system are often found because of the spatial distribution of voting support. As is well known, if one party's votes are more concentrated in some areas, it will win those seats with big margins but fail to win enough closely contested seats to gain as big a seat share as it would with votes evenly distributed across all seats. The drawing of electoral boundaries can either reduce bias or enhance it where dominant parties control redistricting.

New Zealand's electoral boundaries have been determined by non-partisan means since 1887. A 'country quota' assigned country electorates a target of 28% fewer registered voters than those in urban areas until 1946. At the same time determination of boundaries was changed from total to adult population, further reducing the weight of votes in rural areas, where there were higher proportions of children. In 1950, a new National government restored the total population basis, but not the country quota. Tolerance within the target was established at plus or minus 5% in 1956. Up until then, although reducing as electorate populations grew bigger, tolerance for variations could be quite high, up to a further 20% in some rural electorates on top of the country quota.[5] Given all this, one might expect some electoral boundary-induced bias in the early period after 1914, but very little from 1946. In fact, the effects of the country quota were marginal, at one or two seats at most, at least in the crucial period of three-party politics between 1919 and 1931 (Chapman 1969: 66–8).

Methods to identify exaggeration and bias in electoral systems have evolved over several decades. Initially applied to two-party systems, they have been developed for multi-party systems (King 1990). Analysis has tended to move away from multi-election models in favour of analysing bias through successive elections, using data at the district level (Gelman and King 1994; Jackman 1994). Multi-election methods are criticized because of their insensitivity to short-term changes generated by partisan control of boundary changes, a problem relatively absent in New Zealand.

Here our interest is in the long term. Given this, Table 6.2 reports the results from simple time series models in which vote share percentages for Labour and the parties of the right are regressed, first on the natural logs of two seats of percentages of seat shares. This assumes an exponential relationship but also adds vote share for the other major party to the model plotted in Figure 6.1. In a second model, the two major party vote shares are regressed on unlogged seats. The results are very similar, indicating that while an exponential curve may be the best fit, a linear relationship works almost as well. A linear model has the advantage of providing parameter estimates that are easier to interpret.

However, both models 1 and 2 include constant terms that indicate the percentage of seats expected when vote shares are 0. However, they are not 0. In model 2, one of these constant terms is not statistically significant, making estimation of predicted probabilities unreliable. Models 3 and 4 remove the constant term, forcing it to be a realistic 0.[6] As noted earlier, an explanation put forward for the 1978 and 1981 election results lies in the 1977 distribution of seats they had in common. The fourth unlogged and suppressed constant model drops both of these elections and those prior to 1946, and still predicts the 'wrong winner' outcomes at a hypothetical election when both major parties received 40% of the votes.

171

Table 6.2. Exaggeration and bias in New Zealand elections, 1914–93

	1: Logged		2: Unlogged		3: Unlogged		4: 1946–75, 1984–	
	b	SE	b	SE	b	SE	b	SE
Right seats[a]								
(Constant)	2.94	0.29**	7.03	12.96				
Right vote	0.03	0.01**	1.38	0.28**	1.51	0.13**	2.11	0.23**
Labour vote	−0.01	0.00*	−0.41	0.16*	−0.38	0.14*	−0.97	0.24**
Adjusted R^2	0.50		0.52		0.98		0.99	
SE Estimate	0.18		8.07		7.95		5.04	
Durbin-Watson	1.44		1.76					
Predict 40:40		44.2		45.8		45.2		45.4
Labour seats								
(Constant)	2.45	0.32**	21.08	9.30*	1.55	0.11**	2.15	0.21**
Labour vote	0.05	0.00**	1.46	0.11**	−0.46	0.11**	−1.07	0.20**
Right vote	−0.02	0.01*	−0.86	0.20**				
Adjusted R^2	0.87		0.88		0.98		0.99	
SE Estimate	0.20		5.79		6.27		4.43	
Durbin-Watson	1.99		2.02					
Predict 40:40		40.4		45.2		43.5		43.4

[a] Reform 1914–28, Coalition 1931, National 1935–.
* Significant at 0.05 (two-tailed test).
** Significant at 0.01 (two-tailed test).

On top of all this, the predicted probabilities for all the elections in all models match the actual rankings of winner or loser: that is, when Labour wins more seats than Reform/National, the predictions match this, as they do in reverse. Under the SMP system, there has been a larger impact of minor parties on Labour's chances of gaining seats. When the two major parties dominate the votes, Labour has a slight advantage over National in gaining a majority seat bonus. With non-major party voting up, and a vote share below mid-to-low 40%, Labour is far less likely to gain a seat majority than National. The pattern is time-consistent because of stability in the urban–rural cleavage that is the foundation of New Zealand's electoral geography (Chapman 1962; Vowles 1989, 1997). Smaller parties to Labour's centre or left chipped away at votes it needed in marginal electorates. The geography of non-Labour/non-right party voting has made it harder for Labour to form governments than for National to do so.

6.2.2. Coordination: Could Systemic Failure Have Been Avoided?

Figure 6.1 indicates a wide scatter of data-points around the curves. Unlike those implied in the models in Table 6.2, the curves do not take into account voting for the other major party. But some of the scatter also reflects coordination strategies. For example, both a one-variable Figure 6.1 and most of the two-variable Table 6.2 models predict a bigger seat gap between Labour and National in 1993. There is some evidence that people who would otherwise have voted for the alternative left coalition, the Alliance, decided to vote strategically and thus reduced the gap.

Someone rejecting the concept of 'systemic failure' could apply a coordination argument to the two 'wrong winner' elections. Indeed, had relatively small numbers of votes been transferred from the third party, Social Credit, to the Labour Opposition in a small number of electorates, Labour could have won a seat majorities in both elections. The numbers are 1,117 votes in 1978 (0.41 of a percentage of the Social Credit vote). In the right places it could have shifted six seats. Only 306 votes in 1981 (0.08% of the Social Credit vote) could have shifted three seats. However, this prospect seems plausible only in retrospect, and out of context. The Labour and Social Credit parties had little in common on which to generate coordination, either between their organizations or among voters.

Party-led coordination has two main forms: short-term, or long-term by merger. Short-term coordination takes place in a three-party system, where one party stands down in a district to make possible a straight fight between the other two, perhaps as the result of another reciprocal deal elsewhere. Under the SMP system in New Zealand significant numbers of seats were uncontested by one or other of the three main parties up to the late 1930s. This made sense in terms of the three-party system, but competing political elites do not always embrace short-term coordination strategies. It seems more than likely that actors were primed to do so because the 1908 and 1911 New Zealand elections were conducted under a Second Ballot system. This would have accustomed political elites to withdrawal of candidates for a straight fight between the two more likely contenders, a nice example of path dependence. Table 6.3 shows that with a Parliament of 80 members over the period, the number of seats uncontested by these parties was quite substantial.

However, there is only fragmentary information about the extent to which these candidate withdrawals were reciprocal and coordinated. Even Labour, the party most organized during the period, did not begin to take effective central direction of its candidate entry decisions until the late 1920s. The other parties were even less centralized (Chapman 1969: 40). However, there were negotiations between Labour and the Liberal party in 1922 to adopt proportional representation if those parties together were

Table 6.3. Numbers of seats not contested by significant political parties 1914–38

	Labour	Reform/National	Liberal
1914	61	1	9
1919	26	15	16
1922	38	5	24
1925	20	9	30
1928	21	6	20
1931	25	2	—
1935	4	6	—
1938	2	3	—
Total	197	47	99

to control Parliament after the election. While the negotiations came to nothing, Labour may have run fewer candidates in rural electorates than it would otherwise have done, to the Liberals' advantage. In 1925, the Liberal and Reform parties discussed a possible merger. This again came to nothing, but the Liberals did not run candidates in some rural Labour-held seats, allowing Reform to recapture them (Chapman 1969: 17–18, 25).

The other coordination strategy is long-term, where parties merge. But the practical difficulties of negotiating such coordination are well illustrated by the 10-year gap between the first perceptions that vote-splitting was to the detriment of Reform and the Liberals, both occupying more or less the same space on the right, and action to solve the problem (see Bassett 1982). Having formed a pre-election coalition in 1931, Reform and the Liberal party, renamed United, at last applied a consistent policy of standing candidates down to benefit each other. Indeed, they are counted as one party in Tables 6.2 and 6.3 from 1931. But reflecting a continued deficit in central coordination, significant numbers of recalcitrant supporters of each party continued to stand against the other party's coalition-endorsed candidates. It was not until 1938 that the centre-right fully merged into the National Party. Another example occurred at the last SMP election in 1993, when five centre and centre-left parties formed the Alliance. Under MMP, however, that grouping soon fell apart.

From 1938 until 1993 the major political parties ran candidates in every seat. When Social Credit Party entered the party system in 1954, some voters did begin to vote strategically, coordinating at the grass roots. The first effective case was in the Northland electorate of Bay of Islands, later Hobson after a redistribution of boundaries in 1946. From 1928

Table 6.4. Strategic voting in Hobson 1954–66

	Social Credit vote percentages	
	Hobson	New Zealand
1954	28.8	11.1
1957	22.9	7.2
1960	36.4	8.6
1963	44.3	7.9
1966	48.0	14.5

to 1935 the electorate had elected a Country Party MP. The Country Party did not contest the seat in 1938, and it fell narrowly to Labour. National picked up the seat in 1943. Social Credit beat Labour into second place in Hobson in 1954, and as Table 6.4 shows despite no upward trend in national support for Social Credit, its candidate increased its votes in 1960 and 1963 as people hitherto voting Labour switched to Social Credit.

In 1966, Social Credit took the seat only marginally assisted by a national swing. Later, by-elections were the best opportunity for grass-roots coordination that benefited Social Credit, making it possible for people to choose the more viable opposition party but without threat to the government remaining in office. Thus in 1977 and 1980 Social Credit won its next two seats at by-elections, again by collapsing the Labour vote, and then held each seat at the next two general elections. This, and a few other cases, nicely illustrates the Cox take on Duverger: coordination can happen at the local level. Nationally, Labour and Social Credit cooperation was never on the agenda, and enormous information and collective action problems prevented voters from filling the gap, even assuming significant numbers might have wanted to, in itself debatable.

Candidate withdrawals would have had some effects on seat–vote ratios in the 1920s. Without these some people would have voted differently. Estimates of disproportionality will be slightly biased as a result. Nevertheless this history as detailed in Table 6.1 indicates that party candidate withdrawals or voter coordination did not greatly enhance proportionality or the interests of the parties that might have benefited, except in one case of party merger. Otherwise it mattered only on the margins making it possible for smaller parties to have token seats. Coordination could not correct the bias as it affected the major parties in the formation of governments after 1935.

There is another further claim sometimes made against systemic failure. Given that the seat predictions for the two 'wrong winner' elections were close, and that in 1984 Labour managed to gain a seat majority on 43% of the votes, perhaps actors were to blame in a different way.[7] In 1978 and 1981 Labour should simply have put more effort into winning the crucial marginal seats it lost. The easiest response to this is to suggest that Labour put as much effort into that task as it perceived necessary and could at the time. Had it known the results beforehand, no doubt it could have targeted its resources better! The case for systemic failure of the SMP system due to a consistent partisan bias associated with multi-party politics appears a firm one. It confirms key hypotheses derived from Shugart and Colomer.

6.2.3. *Intent and the Constitution*

However without further explanation, New Zealand experience is inconsistent with another Colomer hypothesis: the older the system, the least likely the change. Dating from 1914, New Zealand's SMP system was surely old enough to be relatively immune. In itself, the bias in the party system under multi-party politics might have been enough to put electoral system change on the agenda, but not necessarily enough to carry through a 'reform process'.

Another element was needed. In 1979, Labour MP and constitutional lawyer Geoffrey Palmer published *Unbridled Power? An Interpretation of New Zealand's Constitution and Government* (Palmer 1979). In it he advocated electoral system change to a supplementary member system that would have been at best semi-proportional. His most important argument was a fundamental critique of New Zealand's political institutions. Palmer criticized a concentration of excessive power in Cabinet and the Prime Minister. He was not alone in his views. Political scientist Keith Jackson had earlier pointed out that New Zealand combined three features found together in no other democracy at the time: the absence of fundamental constitutional law, a single-Chamber legislature, and an SMP electoral system, adding up to 'a total lack of restraints' (Jackson 1978: 17). To those, one could add a unitary state with only weak local and regional governments. And, in addition, with a relatively small Parliament, 'fortress' Cabinets (Chapman 1989, 1992) could control a majority of the government party's MPs, and could govern without significant impediments other than the need for their party to face re-election.

Political theorist Richard Mulgan had argued a pluralist case against Palmer's liberal critique of the constitution (Mulgan 1980). After becoming a member of the Royal Commission on the Electoral System, like many others, Mulgan's position changed, and he became an advocate of MMP. Mulgan later borrowed the concept of 'elective dictatorship' that had originated in Britain to launch another powerful critique of New Zealand government under the SMP system (Mulgan 1992). In the meantime, Arend Lijphart's international comparisons of democratic institutions had identified New Zealand as an extreme case of highly majoritarian government: as he put it, 'a virtually perfect example of the Westminster model of democracy', outranking even Britain on that dimension. Richard Rose also weighed in, describing New Zealand as 'the only example of the true British system left' (Lijphart 1984: 16, 19; 1987).

This debate was not just academic. It began when Robert Muldoon was Prime Minister in the National government of 1975–84. Muldoon often preferred his own judgement to that of expert advisors. He attacked his political critics aggressively. By taking the portfolio of Minister of Finance, he was able to dominate his government like few Prime Ministers before or after him. When the Labour Party defeated Muldoon's government in 1984, it went on to adopt his 'take no prisoners' approach by rapidly adopting a programme of market liberalization it had not signalled in advance. Despite opposition within the Labour Party, the 'fortress Cabinet' went on to transform New Zealand from one of the most highly regulated to one of the least regulated economies in the western world.

In the broader sense of systemic failure, perhaps the Westminster system was operating under expected norms. But the norms of conduct within New Zealand's centralized political institutions had another leg. Governments were expected to be responsive and accountable to public opinion, making election promises and keeping them. An implicit social contract had been broken (Mulgan 1990; Chapman 1992; Gibbons 2000). It was in this context that normative arguments for PR took hold, to the effect that changing the electoral system was the key to bridling government power and thus rebalancing New Zealand's constitution.

6.2.4. Contingency and 'Accidents'

One of the key contingent conditions outlined by Shugart applies well to New Zealand: alternation to a previously disadvantaged party, when Labour took office in 1984 (Shugart Chapter 1). But the party did not take an outcome-contingent approach. During the 1980s few among Labour's leaders believed that a change to PR would benefit the party. Then Deputy Prime Minister Geoffrey Palmer was the key figure in establishing a Royal Commission on the Electoral System. Palmer might have approached the idea of reform with some 'outcome-contingent' assumptions, but his public arguments were normative. The majority of Labour's leaders, who contributed to that decision either deferred to Palmer, thought that it would not matter, or saw the Royal Commission benefiting Labour through act-contingency.

The Royal Commission's recommendation of MMP was unexpected, and gave rise to a social movement to promote electoral reform, the Electoral Reform Coalition (ERC). The Royal Commission gave legitimacy to one electoral reform option and opponents of the SMP system eventually united around it. Labour rejected the Royal Commission recommendation of change to MMP subject to referendum. During the 1987 election campaign, Prime Minister David Lange announced in error that Labour had a policy of a referendum on electoral system change. Labour did not deny this 'act-contingent' commitment until after the election, giving a further indignant boost to the campaign for reform.

Much is made of this event, some explanations portraying it as a catalyst, without which electoral system change would not have happened. Yet the mistake was made in a context of ongoing pressure for a referendum on the electoral system, increasing public dissatisfaction with the political process, and intensifying concern about the government's willingness to override public opinion. Lange would not have raised the issue if it had not been current, and its salience is confirmed by the fact that it was seized upon and made an issue. Hypothesizing a counterfactual scenario in which Lange had not made the error, it is possible that electoral system change could still have occurred.

Again in accord with an act-contingent logic, seeking to embarrass Labour, the National party promised a referendum. And Labour was by then willing to match the promise. Palmer had become Prime Minister and also supported MMP on the basis of the Royal Commission's Report. Lange's misstatement may not have been necessary for these developments. Labour had reason to be embarrassed about its failure to deliver an electoral system referendum regardless of the Lange error. That error, after all, received so much attention and was not immediately repudiated because of that prior history. And with Palmer as Prime Minister favouring MMP, and seeing defeat looming at the 1990 election,

Table 6.5. Support for MMP/PR and FPTP/Alternative by party voters

Referendum vote 1993	National	Labour	NZ First	Alliance
MMP	24	68	69	82
FPP	74	28	26	15
N	635	631	151	329
% vote	35.1	34.7	8.4	18.2

Abbreviations: MMP: mixed-member proportional; PR: proportional representation.

Source: Lamare and Vowles (1996).

Labour could well have made a referendum commitment if National had not, and National could then have followed suit, simply reversing the order in which the two parties triggered the process. Meanwhile most of the Labour and National leaders agreeing to the referendum believed that their promises posed little risk of change. They could not believe that New Zealand voters would opt for PR. At this level, it may seem reasonable to describe electoral system change in New Zealand as unintended (Benoit 2004: 372) or a mistake (Hunt 1998). But this only follows from a narrow assumption that the only significant actors were political party elites, and ignores the context in which those party elites were so much out of touch with public opinion in large part because of their insulation from effective electoral competition outside the two-party club. While the deterministic language of necessity and sufficiency helps distinguish between systemic and contingent causes of change, a probabilistic model is more likely to be a better fit in terms of explaining the final outcome.

The experience of electoral system in New Zealand change poses a further challenge, this time for those seeking to pursue a rational choice approach. First, only one significant party, the Alliance, took an explicit position. The Labour or National parties remained officially neutral, although their most prominent politicians opposed change. By 1993 it was deemed counterproductive for established politicians to oppose MMP. The case for SMP was taken up by a business-funded group set up only a few months before the referendum. Most politicians stood by making only *sotto voce* contributions to the debate. Many members of the mass public held strong opinions critical of the political process and of politicians that originated in a mixture of cultural values and institutional expectations (Table 6.5).

Lamare and Vowles (1996: 329–30) provide the only attempt to explain in probabilistic terms the 1993 referendum results, by establishing the limits of the party interest approach and reconciling it with the effects of values, culture, and institutions. As expected, Alliance voters almost unanimously voted for MMP and their degree of partisan identification enhanced that support further. The most important puzzle is why supporters of the two major parties voted for electoral system change. In the absence of explicit cues from the key parties, Lamare and Vowles hypothesized that people would vote in the referendum to promote the political success of the party they voted for. Given mixed messages, voters would have to construct that perception to some degree for themselves.

Senior Labour politicians were giving cues to vote against MMP, but those in closer touch with Labour's voters did not agree with them. Just over 70% of Labour's key activists and candidates who responded to a survey of party elites indicated support for MMP, and almost the same proportion of Labour voters. The existence or extent of their partisanship made no significant difference to Labour voters' referendum choice. The rationale for a Labour vote for change could have relied to some extent on the recollection of the two reversed plurality elections. Expectations of future political success probably played the major role. At the 1993 election the anti-National vote was badly split and despite some voter-driven strategic voting in 1993 with only marginal effects, there was no coordination strategy between Labour and Alliance. MMP would have the effect of encouraging coordination on the left, even if the leaderships of the two parties initially resisted it. Contrary to a hypothesis that left-leaning Labour voters would be more favourable to coalition with a party to Labour's left, this desire for coordination through centre-left coalition government was the same among right-leaning Labour voters as it was on the left. The intent was to maximize the odds of government for the centre-left rather than maximize seats for one or other centre-left party. One could go so far as to suggest that after the change to MMP Labour's senior elites ultimately followed their voters, rather than the reverse.

Few members of the National Party supported change. But the referendum margin over the SMP system required the quarter of National Party voters that did vote for MMP. Those who did so were more likely to have a weak identification or no identification with the party. Among non-partisans, less committed National party voters, and among Labour voters in general, there were other dimensions of opinion. Key predictors of support for MMP were normative preferences for coalition government and belief in government policy-accountability to the electorate. This expressed the reaction to nearly 20 years of 'unbridled' Cabinet power. In 1992, after a raft of other market-orientated reforms, including welfare cuts and a dramatic weakening of the legal status of trade unions, the National Party had sunk to the lowest polling support ever experienced by a New Zealand government. The time was ripe for electoral system change as a result of perceptions of abuse of power. Public rejection of the very idea of single-party government was a key factor. The extreme nature of the New Zealand constitution—to which the SMP system had made an important contribution—was another systemic cause of change.

The importance of a preference for coalition government also throws some doubt on Shugart's assumption that systems are seen to fail only in terms of their own norms. Norms associated with PR did enter the debate in New Zealand under the influence of the Royal Commission's Report. Opinion-leaders began to support PR because they believed it would enhance democratic representation, and the SMP system began to be evaluated according to PR norms. Norms continued to shape the process beyond an agenda-setting role, and those norms were changing.

Three governments in a row—National, Labour, and National again—had used their constitutional powers to override public opinion with radical policies. The shift of votes away from major parties was the result, and further promoted change. At the 1993 election the combined vote for National and Labour dropped below 70%, their lowest combined vote since 1928, increasing the pool of voters for parties with an interest in PR. In this sense party interest still had a role to play.

6.3. Conclusions

Partisan bias was systemic under the SMP system in New Zealand, and not merely contingent on two anomalous elections. Without additional incentives coordination failures under the SMP system in New Zealand were inevitable without full-scale party mergers. Empirically satisfying the requirements of norms for systemic success under SMP systems requires a single cleavage, other institutional incentives, and/or a spatial distribution of votes that facilitates unbiased two-party competition. Multi-party politics in an SMP system greatly increases the risks of systemic failure, and may make it inevitable if multi-party politics persists for a significant time.

Special features of the New Zealand case suggest that a definition of systemic failure should extend beyond the electoral system and take into account other institutional features such as the country's unique constitutional structure that concentrated power in a 'fortress' Cabinet with 'unbridled power'. By greatly reducing the odds of single-party majority government, electoral system change weakened the ability of New Zealand governments to rule without having to seek more broadly based support for their policies. In the category of contingent causes of change, a mixture of outcome and act-contingent factors can be identified.

In common with other recent examples of the process, the New Zealand case challenges theorists of electoral system change to move beyond the assumption of self-interested politicians and unitary political parties to consider the reasons why ordinary people should vote for or against change in referendums or citizens' assemblies. Here the task is to specify the conditions under which voters will simply take cues from parties or other elites, and where they will have their own reasons for their referendum vote choices that may reflect broader normative concerns about the political process—that may also influence elites either sooner or later. Perceptions of the need to enhance the normative performance of New Zealand democracy brought 'systemic failure' into the picture as a justification for change beyond an agenda-setting role.

Notes

1. See McRobie (1993) for a range of opinions and interpretations focused around the 1992 referendum.
2. Boston et al. (1996a); Boston (1998); Ward (1998); Barker and McLeay (2000); Barker et al. (2001); Boston and Church (2002); Boston, Church, and Bale (2003).
3. Vowles et al. (1995, 1998, 2002, 2004); Banducci, Donovan, and Karp (1998, 1999); Banducci and Karp (1999); Karp and Banducci (1999); Vowles (2000, 2002, 2005); Karp and Bowler (2001); Karp et al. (2002); Johnston and Vowles (2006); Vowles, Banducci, and Karp (2006). McLeay and Vowles (2006) bring data and analysis from both projects together.
4. Professor Robert Chapman, New Zealand's pioneering election analyst, took both positions at different times. In 1969 he noted 'a mild favouritism for

National against Labour (1999: 271) but in 1979 emphasized the effects of the 1977 boundaries on the 1978 result (1979: 86).

5. In 1914 the tolerance was plus or minus 550 votes. From 1920 it was raised to 1,250 in rural electorates (Atkinson 2003: 138). In 1946 a 500-vote tolerance was established for all electorates that amounted to about 5% given enrolments at the time.

6. There is no antilog of 0 so regression through the origin is not reported for model 1. However, as 0 is the antilog of 1, close enough to 0 for these purposes, models were also run on this basis and their results were consistent with those of the other models.

7. The 1984 and 1935 elections were the only cases where a party to the right of National got significant votes, and this almost certainly explains their outlier status.

Conclusion

André Blais and Matthew Søberg Shugart

The preceding analyses have demonstrated that the path of electoral reform in first past the post (FPTP) electoral systems is a complicated one, that it varies immensely across countries and over time, and that a great number of factors are at play. A detailed understanding of the various cases ought to make us wary about bold assertions about necessary and/or sufficient conditions for electoral reform. Still it is possible to discern general patterns, and these patterns suggest that reform is more likely to occur under some conditions.

It is appropriate to distinguish at the outset the process of reform initiation and that of reform implementation. It could be that some factors make it more likely that reform is on the political agenda but that other factors are responsible for the final decision to change the system or not. In this regard, it is important to keep in mind that Shugart's analysis in Chapter 1, while broader in coverage, focuses primarily on the initial stages by which a formal review of the electoral system gets on the agenda, while country-specific chapters consider the full sequence.

This raises the question of the link between the various stages of the reform process. We would make two apparently contradictory claims on this point. First, starting the process of reform is not the same thing as actually doing it, and so we should allow for the possibility that the factors at work at the two stages are different. But, second, the two steps are not independent of each other. It is not clear, for instance, why a government that has no intention of changing the system would want to initiate the reform process. This raises questions about the motives of those governments that seem willing to contemplate reform. How committed are they to reform? Is this only a way to dodge the issue and 'buy' time? Or are they ambivalent and struggling to define their positions?

At the theoretical level, one may distinguish three types of interpretation for why governments keep or change the electoral system: *interests*, because they are advantaged or disadvantaged by the existing system; *ideas*, because they believe that first past the post is 'good' or 'bad'; and *institutions*, because it is easy or difficult to change the rules. These three types of interpretation are not mutually exclusive. This is particularly the case with respect to institutions, which presumably come to play a role only if there is a willingness to consider reform.

The interpretation of electoral reform that is based on interests is typically associated with rational choice. In such a model, best represented by Benoit (2004), politicians are rational actors who attempt to maximize their utility, which in this case is equated with being elected (Downs 1957). According to such an approach, each actor determines whether she would do better or worse under another electoral system and decides to support reform if she comes to the conclusion that she would gain from changing the rule, and reform takes place only if a majority of legislators decide that it is in their best interest to adopt a new electoral system. This is, essentially, what Shugart in Chapter 1 refers to as 'outcome-contingent' motivations for parties to promote electoral reform.

The second approach is based on ideas. The claim is that the impetus for electoral reform is driven by the belief that first past the post is a 'bad' system that needs to be replaced. The system is 'bad' either because it is unfair, it is biased against smaller parties (see the Introduction to this volume) or because it is perceived to have failed to sustain the normative model expected of it, that is a strong majority government formed by the party that has a plurality of the vote and a strong opposition (see Shugart Chapter 1). For instance, the widespread shift towards proportional representation (PR) at the beginning of the twentieth century was in good part the result of an almost consensual perception at the time that PR was the most 'democratic' system (Blais, Dobrzynska, and Indridason 2005). Likewise, Bowler, Donovan, and Karp (2006) find that among politicians who responded to their survey, post-materialists as well as those on the left are more favourable to electoral reform, suggesting that preference over electoral systems may be correlated with broader ideological positions.

Those who argue that ideas matter do not dismiss the role of interests. Bowler, Donovan, and Karp (2006: 443), for instance, recognize that 'self-interest is a major determinant'. They insist, however, that 'it is not the entire explanation', and that 'values and ideology play an important but not quite as predictable a role'. The debate, therefore, is between those who think that the choice of an electoral system hinges 'almost' entirely on interests and those who believe that ideas or values count 'almost' as much. In this volume, Chapter 1 by Shugart represents a synthesis of these approaches, inasmuch as it suggests that parties may perceive reform to be in their electoral *interest* when voters are open to the *idea* that the current system is illegitimate or that an alternative normative model of democracy is 'better'. When a party expects to gain electorally by attaching itself to a popular case of reform, we have what Shugart refers to as an 'act-contingent' motivation—a possibility that we return to below.

The third interpretation focuses on the role of institutions. As mentioned above, institutions cannot be the whole story. The institutionalist account starts when some actors push for electoral reform while others resist, and it does not attempt to explain the sources of demand for change (or for the status quo), which is presumably driven by interests and (perhaps) ideas. The basic intuition is that the probability of success (electoral reform) depends on the rules of the game (Massicotte, Blais, and Yoshinaka 2004).

The institutional perspective leads us to consider the relative power of the government versus that of the legislature, the role of the upper house (when there is one), and the courts, as well as the presence or absence of direct democracy instruments through which electoral reform can be imposed or blocked. The general hypothesis inspired by this approach is that the chances of electoral reform are inversely related to the number of veto points (see Blau Chapter 2): the more players have the capacity to block reform, the more likely the status quo is to prevail.

From a veto-points perspective, existing FPTP systems should be among the 'easiest' electoral systems to change, because most of the jurisdictions in question typically have one party in the majority over the one powerful legislative institution. If that party makes a commitment to reform the electoral system, the vetoes on it are minimal. Of course, as we develop further below, there may be intraparty obstacles to developing a commitment to reform, in that leaders and backbenchers may have opposing interests. However, once internal debate has worked itself out in favour of pursuing reform, the set of FPTP parliamentary democracies places few obstacles in the ruling party's path to reform implementation. The Canadian Senate theoretically could block a reform passed by the House of Commons. The British House of Lords could do the same to that country's House of Commons (though the lower house could invoke the Parliament Acts to override the Lords, as it did on the electoral system for British Members of the European Parliament). On the other hand, the Canadian provincial legislatures, like that of New Zealand, are unicameral; thus institutional opportunities to veto a majority party's proposal are practically non-existent in these cases.

Given that the institutional obstacles to reform are so few in the parliamentary FPTP systems where replacement of the electoral system has been considered, there is something truly striking about the actual reform processes so far: *none has gone forward without a referendum*. Even though the majority party in a Westminster system could enact electoral reform without subjecting itself to a veto, in New Zealand, British Columbia (BC), Ontario, and Prince Edward Island (PEI), referendums took place pitting a reform proposal against the status quo. Likewise, referendums were contemplated in the UK and New Brunswick, though the reform processes there were aborted prior to a public vote. This contrasts with reforms in countries whose pre-reform systems were other than FPTP. For example, in Italy, the ultimate decisions to change the electoral system for the 1994 election, and a subsequent decision to change it yet again in 2006, were taken exclusively in parliament.[1] There were also no referendums to adopt new electoral systems in Japan (Reed and Thies 2001), Colombia (Shugart, Moreno, and Fajardo 2007), Venezuela, or Bolivia. Outside of the world of the FPTP democracies, Ireland may be the only case in which a major proposed electoral reform was submitted to referendum: twice, attempts by Fianna Fáil to replace single transferable vote (STV) with FPTP were defeated by the voters in referendums required by Ireland's constitution.[2]

Why would the one electoral system that most empowers a single party (in most parliamentary systems that use it) universally have a referendum as part of its (actual or planned) reform process, while more 'consensual' political systems would seldom have referendums on a final proposal to replace something as fundamental as the electoral system? One interpretation takes us right back to the ideas approach: FPTP and its attendant majoritarian pattern of parliamentary democracy have a serious underlying legitimacy problem. A change to the way future governments are elected may simply be too big a step for a party to take without consulting more widely, as in a referendum. If this interpretation is correct, it is, of course ironic: calling a referendum puts a veto in the path of reform that would not otherwise be there, and thus may make the retention of the less 'legitimate' FPTP system more likely. We return below to the question of legitimacy of FPTP, but first we take stake of how the framework developed by Shugart in Chapter 1 performs in light of the case studies of this volume.

1. Assessing the Framework of Inherent and Contingent Factors

Shugart in Chapter 1 sets out to identify the factors that lead to the process of reform initiation. He argues that the process hinges on a combination of 'inherent' and 'contingent' factors. According to Shugart, there are inherent tendencies for FPTP to produce 'systemic failure', that is not to deliver what it is supposed to deliver. When this inherent tendency comes into the open through anomalies, such as spurious or lopsided majorities, Shugart argues, an electoral reform process may proceed, provided contingent factors are also present. The two contingencies he identifies are the coming to power shortly after the anomaly of the party that was disadvantaged by it (an outcome contingency) and the presence of public sentiment for reform that either or both major parties might wish to cultivate in electoral competition (an act contingency).

1.1. *Inherent Conditions: Anomalies as a Spur to Reform?*

As noted by both Shugart (Chapter 1) and Vowles (Chapter 6), FPTP originated in a pre-democratic context in which the only concern was to provide local representation (see Vowles Chapter 6). Nowadays, FPTP is expected to lead to the formation of a one-party majority government, the governing party being the party with greatest support (i.e. with a plurality of total votes), with a 'strong' opposition to make sure that the party in power is accountable to the people. From that perspective, 'anomalous' outcomes may occur, which may lead, on the one hand, to parties reassessing whether the current system is advantageous to them (an *interests* interpretation), and, on the other hand, to legitimacy problems for the current system (an *ideas* interpretation). Chapter 1 identifies two types of anomaly: plurality reversals, where the party with most votes does not get to form the government, and lopsided majorities, where one party wins an overwhelming majority of seats in Parliament and the opposition is decimated.

There is strong evidence that plurality reversals and/or lopsided majorities were crucial in New Zealand, British Columbia, Prince Edward Island, Quebec, and New Brunswick. In this volume, Carty, Blais, and Fournier (Chapter 5) note that the origins of the process of electoral reform in British Columbia are consistent with the framework presented by Shugart (Chapter 1): consecutive elections produced a plurality reversal and then a lopsided majority (with the latter marking the coming to power of the party that had been disadvantaged in the previous election). Vowles likewise notes (Chapter 6) that the ultimate replacement of FPTP in New Zealand was driven in large part by failures of the former electoral system; however, he suggests that, somewhat contrary to Shugart's interpretation (Chapter 1), the performance of the system was not being judged only with respect to its own normative values (i.e. majoritarianism). Rather, he notes, New Zealand's democratic values were undergoing a substantial change such that the model of 'unbridled power', as a widely read book described the system, was already being questioned.

If it is accurate to say that anomalous outcomes at least increase the probability of electoral reform—even if they cannot be said to be either necessary or sufficient—it is an indication that ideas matter. If we followed a rational-choice approach, we would expect parties to decide to keep or change the electoral system on the basis of their own self-interest. Shugart contends that interests are not all that matter. It makes a difference whether the system is judged to be 'acceptable' or not. It is well known that FPTP favours big parties over small parties. It would seem that many are willing to live with such a bias provided that the system is not unduly 'unfair', that it allows the most popular party to form the government, and the 'second' most popular party to provide 'strong' opposition.

How much impact these anomalies, and more specifically normative reactions to these anomalies, actually have is more difficult to ascertain. We would venture three propositions. First, the impact of anomalies and of values and norms is stronger at the initial stage of the process (as Shugart in Chapter 1 suggests). Anomalies usually lead to some parties and/or groups questioning the legitimacy of FPTP and putting the issue of electoral reform on the political agenda. Second, ideas matter but, in the end, they seldom trump interests.

Third, ideas come to play a major role especially when interests are ambiguous.

When discussing the role of interests and ideas, it is important to specify *whose* interests and ideas. We will assume here that the main actors are the parties, the party leaders, the government, the prime minister, and individual legislators. We will also refer to politicians in general.

The first assumption is that politicians want to change the electoral system only if and when they believe that their chances of being re-elected would be higher under a different set of rules (Benoit 2004). The second assertion is that the politicians who hold power benefited from the electoral system in the previous election and expect to benefit in the next one. It follows from these two propositions that most elected politicians oppose electoral reform because they reason that their chances of being re-elected are higher under FPTP than under alternative rules. The outcome, of course, is no reform.

However, as we discuss below, some of these assertions may not be as obvious as they first appear to be. Nonetheless, these propositions are basically right. Interests are crucial. Most of the time it is in the interest of most elected politicians to oppose electoral reform and for that basic reason the most likely outcome in any particular instance is...the status quo. Politicians are unlikely to adopt a new electoral system that will clearly decrease their chances of being re-elected. Yet, there are cases when interests are ambiguous and in these cases there is a window of opportunity. The occurrence of anomalies opens one such window, in that in both cases, the party with the second most seats after the anomaly (or individual leaders or legislators within it) may now see FPTP not only as normatively troubling but also as working against their own party. This is where the 'outcome contingency' comes into play, and as Chapter 1 showed, five of the seven reform processes were initiated when the party that had been previously disadvantaged by a spurious or lopsided majority came to power in the first or second election thereafter.

1.2. Outcome Contingency: Reform Because Politicians Expect a New System to Benefit Them?

To approximate a fuller and more nuanced explanation of electoral reform, we really need to disaggregate the notion of party or 'politicians' more generally, for individual party leaders and backbench members of parliament (MPs) may have interests or preferences that diverge from those of their co-partisan colleagues, or from aggregate party interests. Let us deal first with party interests, thinking of 'party' as if it were a unitary actor. In Duvergerian equilibrium[3] where there are only two parties and the party with most seats gets to form the government, it is clearly in the interest of both parties to keep FPTP. This is a very efficient way to keep potential new competitors out of the race. The same situation prevails if there are two major parties and a few minor parties. The minor parties should push for reform and the major parties, which control the legislature, should oppose it. What if there are three 'major' parties, of about equal size? The parties should espouse reform only if they expect their support to decrease in the future. This could be the case of one of the three parties (though perhaps the most likely scenario is that all three parties will be 'optimistic', because partisans engage in wishful thinking (Blais and Bodet 2006)), but the bottom line is that at least two of the major parties (again with a majority of the seats in the legislature) are prone to conclude that they have a vested interest in keeping FPTP.

An interesting case occurs when FPTP seems to favour one of the two major parties over the other. The system was biased against Labour in New Zealand (Vowles Chapter 6) and it is biased against the Conservatives in Britain (Blau Chapter 2) and the Liberals in the province of Quebec (Massicotte Chapter 4). Then is it not in the disadvantaged party's interest to change the electoral system? We should consider the cases in which the theory articulated in Chapter 1 implied there would be electoral reform, yet there was not. The Quebec Liberal party (PLQ) is instructive in this regard. The PLQ is perhaps the clearest instance of a major party being disadvantaged over its main rival by the electoral system. Twice in just over 30 years, the provincial Quebec Liberals had more votes than their main competitor and yet they had fewer seats and they did not form the government. Is it not in their interest to change the system?

In the 13 elections that took place since 1956, the Liberals had a plurality of the vote nine times and in seven cases they benefited from FPTP and could form a single party majority government. Under a PR or mixed system, they might have been in government more often (perhaps nine times instead of seven) but most of the time they would have had to share power with other parties under a minority or coalition government. So what is to be preferred: To be in government slightly more often while having to share some of that power with another party or to be in government slightly less often while being in full control? Most politicians, presumably, prefer the latter. Anomalies, like 'wrong winners', are the exception and, over the long haul, 'disadvantaged' major parties still benefit from the system most of the time. As suggested by Shugart (Chapter 1), a party that sees itself as the 'natural governing party', or at least as a periodic governing party over the longer run, is much less likely to perceive electoral reform as being in its interests, even if it is disadvantaged in ways that cost it substantially in those elections that result in its being in opposition. In addition to the Quebec Liberals, this explanation of long-haul benefits to being periodically in government alone probably account for the lack of interest in electoral reform by the New Democratic Party (NDP) of Saskatchewan (as discussed in Chapter 1). The NDP or its predecessor, the Cooperative Common-wealth Federation, has had the most seats at 12 of 16 provincial elections since 1944. Such a party is rather unlikely to perceive an interest in proportional representation, even it is suffers from an occasional anomaly.

The conclusion must be that the long-term interest of major parties in FPTP is to keep the system, even in the case of major parties that are structurally disadvantaged relative to their main competitor. As Massicotte (Chapter 4) says, 'even the most anomalous outcomes produced by first past the post raise less genuine anger among the politicians who suffer them than among the PR activists who quote them repeatedly.' Most party leaders most of the time probably expect anomalies—even ones that disadvantage their party—to be aberrant in an electoral system that, at almost any given election, gives them a fairly high probability of being able to exercise full power. One—perhaps the only—circumstance where it would be in the interest of a major party to espouse a shift towards some dose of proportionality is if and when, and only if and when, it expects to become a 'minor' party in the not so distant future (Boix 1999). Yet, no such situation appears to explain any of the cases of reform initiation discussed in this volume: all of the parties that put reform on the agenda appear to have had strong prospects for remaining one of the two leading parties indefinitely.

If the emphasis is on the long-term interest of parties, any large party that opens up the possibility of electoral reform would seem to be acting against its own interests. Might the perspective be different if one thinks in terms of party leaders' short-term interest? The leader of the Quebec Liberal party or the Saskatchewan NDP could well reason that it is in his/her best interest to change the electoral system if he/she expects a close race (with respect to votes) in the next election. The Quebec Liberals, for example, need to get many more votes than the Parti Québécois in order to win more seats (and form the government). If the leader is focused on the very next election (her whole career hinges on the outcome of the next election) and if there appears to be a close race, then her interest is to change the system.

Sometime, therefore, the short-term interests of a party leader may clash with the long-term interests of the party. That could be the case for leaders of major parties that are structurally disadvantaged relative to their main competitor, if and when they expect a close race in the next election. Under the existing FPTP, a close race (in terms of vote support) entails an electoral defeat (fewer seats than the other major party). Under some kind of proportional representation, the leader may hope to win a plurality of seats and head a minority or coalition government. Note, however, that three necessary conditions must be met simultaneously: the party leader must believe that her party is likely to have more votes but fewer seats in the next election under the existing system, she must be the prime minister (he/she has the capacity to bring about reform), and she must be able to persuade MPs (from her party) to accept reform. This is bound to happen very infrequently. And when it happens, additional hurdles are likely to emerge, as we indicate below.

Another situation that is often thought to be propitious to electoral reform is the presence of a minority government. This is what the Liberal Democrats have been hoping for in the UK. Clearly it is in the Liberal Democrats' interest to move to some kind of PR. If they have the balance of power they could try to impose electoral reform on Labour as a condition of support (see Blau Chapter 2). The problem, of course, is that it is in Labour's interest to keep FPTP. So the Liberal Democrats could get a deal only if they could credibly threaten to go with either Labour or the Conservatives, if they made electoral reform their top priority, and if the Labour or Conservative leader was short-term oriented (the major parties' long-term interest is to keep the system; the leaders' short-term interest is to become the Prime Minister). There are many 'if' and so the probability of changing the electoral system increases, at best, only slightly under a minority government. In any event, Shugart (Chapter 1) found no cases in his data of a reform process having been initiated when there was no party with a majority in parliament.

The upshot of this discussion is that it is always in the major parties' long-term interest to oppose electoral reform but that, in exceptional circumstances, it may be in the short-term interest of the party leader to change the system. This raises the question of the relative power of the Prime Minister (or party leader) versus that of individual MPs.

What, then, about individual MPs' interests? The first observation to be made is that most of the time individual MPs' interests coincide with those of the party and of the leader. The most immediate interest of each MP is to be personally re-elected in her constituency. But things are much more interesting if one is on the government side. Among other things, one's chances of being a member of the cabinet are of course nil if one is in opposition. There are many more opportunities if one's party forms the government.

Nonetheless, as Blau notes (Chapter 2), there may be times when the perspectives of leaders and rank-and-file members diverge, on account of policy motivations. Blau cites two instances, one actual and one hypothetical. When electoral reform became part of the Labour manifesto before the 1997 UK election, it was partly because Labour leaders expected any future majority for their party to be slim and thus their own centrist ('New Labour') policy agenda to be threatened by left-wing MPs in their own caucus. Given such a scenario, which proved to be pessimistic with respect to their future electoral success, cooperation with centrist Liberal Democrats appeared to be attractive. Of course, the Liberal Democratic Party would be more in the mood to cooperate if a reformed electoral system gave it more seats and more bargaining power. Thus, Labour leaders appear to have raised the issue of electoral reform out of anticipated intraparty policy conflicts. The hypothetical scenario mentioned by Blau reverses the potential impetus with Labour for electoral reform: some members of the party believe that the 'centrist incentives' of FPTP mean that majorities for their party come 'at a cost to some of our radical aspirations', as Blau suggests, leading them to think that a PR system could give them more leverage within prospective coalition governments than they now have within a majority party. Both of these possibilities suggest an inherent condition for reform that Shugart (Chapter 1) did not consider: intraparty tensions between leaders seeking to promote a centrist national agenda and MPs whose own constituencies might demand different sorts of policy priorities.

A potential source of conflict may arise if and when it is in the leader's short-term interest to change the electoral system while it would be in the interest of some MPs to keep FPTP. This would occur when the party in power expects to lose a close election to its main rival under FPTP even if it gets more votes. In this case, MPs occupying safe seats could object to electoral reform because any change in the electoral system is likely to decrease their probability of re-election. But should they? It all depends on how much the probability of a party 'victory' increases under a new system, on how much the probability of their own re-election is reduced, and on how much they value being an opposition and a government MP (plus their relative aversion to risk).

The bottom line, however, is that most of the time few MPs will have a strong interest in steadfastly opposing their party's position on electoral reform. That implies not only that MPs are unlikely to push reform if their party leaders do not want it, but also that if their party wishes to go towards reform, the conventional wisdom that electoral reform is impossible because it would involve turkeys voting for Christmas must be questioned (see Blau Chapter 2). Basically, MPs' interests coincide with those of their party. There may be special occasions when the two sets of interest clash but when they do this would involve a minority of MPs. The main reason why electoral reform is unlikely, as Blau (Chapter 2) and Massicotte (Chapter 4) argue, is that the major parties' long-term interest is to keep the system.

This analysis of outcome contingencies, which might result in major-party politicians pushing for reform because they expect a new elec-toral system to be in their interests, assumes that political actors are well informed about their 'true' interests. This is a fair assumption most of the time. Politicians have a large stake in making the right decision. The electoral system has direct consequences on their careers and they have all the incentives to assemble the relevant information required to maximize the probability of coming to a 'correct' assess-ment of how various options would affect their probability of winning. And we indeed observe that the major parties in FPTP systems almost always oppose electoral reform, which is entirely consistent with their interests.

At the same time, one should not assume that politicians are always perfectly informed about the consequences (for them and their party) of moving to another electoral system. Pilet (2007) shows that the Belgian party elite devoted little time and attention to developing a coherent position on issues of electoral reform and that in some cases their posi-tion was not consistent with their 'objective' interest. This is particu-larly the case when interests are ambiguous (or when there is tension between long-term and short-term interests). It is quite possible that in some cases incumbent politicians whose values lead them to favour a change in the electoral system will downplay the negative consequences of such a change. In the same fashion, Katz (2005: 62) notes that in post-communist Europe there 'appears to have been a strong tendency to misread the relative strengths of the likely competitors' as well as 'a very simplistic understanding of the political consequences of electoral laws'.

Our verdict, nevertheless, is that in the great majority of cases in established democracies politicians perfectly understand where their interest lies and they stake a position accordingly. This means that minor parties systematically support electoral reform and major parties systematically oppose it. Yet, errors of judgement are bound to happen from time to time.

We have supposed that the cost/benefit calculus that politicians make when they decide to support or oppose electoral reform entails determining how much better or worse off they would fare under an alternative system, and that parties want to maximize their seat share and (even more) their chances of being in government, alone if possible. We have also assumed that the positions they take on this issue have no impact on their chances of being re-elected; the 'act contingency' motivation that we turn to now suggests that there may be circumstances when position-taking on electoral reform impacts re-election.

1.3. *Act Contingency: Will Parties Support Reform Because Voters Want It?*

There is the possibility that politicians might gain votes and seats by promising a change in the electoral system, or at least conserve expected losses by not appearing to be anti-reform. This is what Shugart (Chapter 1) calls 'act contingency'. When public opinion is favourable to reform, politicians have an incentive to be on the 'good' side of the issue; they hope to reap more voter support in the process. Blau (Chapter 2) and Vowles (Chapter 6) argue that these considerations have been at play in Britain and New Zealand.

Whether or not public opinion might lean in favour of electoral reform, it can hardly be overstated how unimportant the electoral system is to voters most of the time. The public is concerned about health, education, taxes, war, and peace, or highly symbolic issues such as the flag or the recognition of a nation, but it hardly gets excited by the choice of an electoral system. As Massicotte (Chapter 4) notes, few people care much about this issue, so the probability of a party gaining or losing substantial votes in an election because of its position on the electoral system may appear close to nil. Nonetheless, we do not have to imagine a political scientist's fantasy in which the public rates the electoral system among the very biggest problems facing the nation or province in order to see that parties may gain strategically at certain critical junctures from branding themselves as 'pro-reform' in a general sense, including electoral reform. We agree with Katz (2005: 69), who lists 'the importance of public outrage' as the first of his three generalizations that explain why major electoral reforms occur. As he further notes, electoral reform may even become a 'safer' issue from the politicians' point of view than attacking the really substantive underlying sources of public outrage. If voters are dissatisfied with politics as usual, a party may attempt to promote electoral reform as a way to show that it is 'doing something'. Or it may fear the appearance of being anti-reform (on the importance of this factor in Japan, see Reed and Thies 2001).

In any event, there is anecdotal evidence that politicians sometimes support electoral reform in the hope that this will increase their popu-larity. Perhaps more tellingly, most major parties do not unequivocally and steadfastly oppose electoral reform, as their interest would seem to dictate. They tend to dodge the issue, they waver, and, as we have seen in the various chapters of the volume, they indeed sometimes do initiate a reform process that they may not be able fully to control through creating a commission of inquiry (UK and New Brunswick) or tabling a proposal (Quebec). Yet at other times (including New Brunswick, Quebec, and the UK, again), there often appear to be no real costs to letting the issue drop even after a proposed 'official' reform proposal has been made public.

British Columbia and New Zealand are cases where, the chapters in this volume suggest, the act-contingent factors have been most engaged. Carty, Blais, and Fournier (Chapter 5) note that the debates in the BC Legislative Assembly mentioned 'democratic malaise' in the province, and that electoral reform was but one of many aspects of the Liberal government's wider democratic reform agenda. The government thus can be said to have been seeking to brand itself as the party that would tackle the 'malaise' felt by voters, even if public opinion was by no means engaged on the specific issue of the electoral system. Vowles (Chapter 6) notes that in New Zealand by the 1990s, there was such a pervasive sense that 'an implicit social contract' about how democracy was to function had been broken that both parties found themselves competing over who would do something about it. Whether or not Prime Minister Lange's claim that his party was committed to a referendum on the electoral system was a simple mistake, there is no doubting that their National opponents would later use the lack of follow-through in the next campaign against Labour. There was thus a pro-reform vote to be cultivated in New Zealand, as a perspective based on 'act contingency' would expect.

That major party leaders are sometimes willing to put electoral reform on the agenda and unwilling or unable to stop movement towards actual reform suggests that major party leaders themselves feel uneasy with FPTP. Because of its inherent tendency to produce political outcomes that are hard to justify on normative democratic grounds, appearing to be too favourable to an electoral system that benefits their own pursuit of political power may be risky, at least if there is some element of 'democratic malaise' or 'public outrage' at the time. As Shugart notes in Chapter 1, some of the inherent effects of FPTP—specifically, inflating the seat totals of the largest parties and regularly 'manufacturing' majorities—are precisely consistent with the majoritarian pattern of governance associated with FPTP. Nonetheless, while such outcomes are consistent with the prevailing democratic model, they are not necessarily consistent with contemporary democratic norms. And this legitimacy problem arises even in the absence of anomalies (spurious and lopsided majorities).

As a result of these aspects of FPTP, many politicians may share the verdict that the system is neither fair nor reliable. And so there is the temptation to find out whether something could be done about it, a temptation restrained by an understanding that the party is doing fine under the existing rules. The outcome is sometimes a prudent opening of the reform process, followed with lesser interest as time goes on and as it becomes clearer and clearer where party interest lies (the status quo, normally).

2. So, Is Electoral Reform an 'Accident'?

The foregoing analysis leads to the conclusion that electoral reform occurs only if and when one of the major parties come to support electoral reform even though it is against its best self-interest to do so. Electoral reform could be seen as an 'accident', although that is not to say that it cannot be explained systematically.

There could be two types of accident. The first is when the prime minister's short-term interest is to change the system so that his/her party can remain in power after the next election. The problem is that this happens very seldom and that when it happens timing may make reform impossible (Blau Chapter 2). Not only does the leader have to come to the conclusion that it is in her interest to change the electoral system but she must reach that conclusion early in the mandate to prepare and pass the necessary legislation, and she must be willing to make this issue a top priority.

The second type of accident is when a party leader 'mistakenly' supports electoral reform. Such mistakes must be exceptional, but they occur from time to time. They occur when a party leader has formed strong normative values about the pros and cons of proportional representation, values which prevent her from 'coldly' calculating her interests.

As alluded to in Chapter 6, the shift to mixed-member proportional (MMP) in New Zealand may have been at least partly the result of a mistake. Vowles argues, correctly, that much more was involved. Perceptions of the need to curtail the power of the Prime Minister and of the Cabinet were absolutely crucial, both at the beginning (when the issue was put on the agenda) and at the end (during the referenda). But mistakes there were. Prime Minister Lange made an error when he announced that Labour had a policy of referendum on electoral system change. The two major parties were wrong in their assessment that voters would not vote for electoral reform. These 'errors' are only part of the story, but if the two parties had decided to kill electoral reform, that might have been the end of it.

The situation is more complicated in the case of British Columbia, where Premier Campbell initiated a process (the Citizens' Assembly), by which he no longer would control the final decision about whether to change the electoral system (though there was a safeguard, a referendum with a required threshold of 60%). The premier seems to have come to that conclusion on the basis of strong convictions on the matter (Carty, Blais, and Fournier Chapter 5). We do not know whether Mr. Campbell had thought at all about the possible consequences of electoral reform for his party and himself. The impetus for reform may have been the conviction, spurred by the frustration of having lost the previous election while having obtained more votes than his opponent (the NDP), that the rules of the game should be set by the people, not by politicians. This is a very rare instance, we would argue, of values trumping interests, or more precisely of values leading to the neglect of interests (defining 'interests' in terms of Campbell's party's prospects of enjoying full power under FPTP).

According to this perspective, then, FPTP is bound to produce, from time to time, anomalies that undermine its perceived legitimacy, certainly among minor party supporters, to a certain extent among the mass public and even within the major parties' elite. These anomalies spur a movement in favour of electoral reform. This movement is often, though not always, resisted by the major parties that have a vested interest in maintaining the status quo. That resistance is not steadfast, however, because major party leaders themselves have serious doubts about the legitimacy of the system. As a consequence electoral reform remains on the agenda. At the end, however, interests usually trump values and the status quo is maintained.

Because major party leaders are normatively ambivalent on the issue, they are prone to make mistakes from time to time. They sometime do not take the time to think systematically about the consequences of reform for their party and themselves, and they endorse a reform that will reduce their chances of being re-elected and/or forming the government. Such mistakes are rare but supporters of electoral reform do whatever they can to make them happen.

3. What New Systems Are Proposed: The Advantage of STV and MMP

If a decision is made, whether in a commission or a citizens' assembly or some other forum, to replace FPTP with some form of proportional representation, obviously there remain many options. 'PR' is a diverse category. Yet there is a striking regularity in the processes so far. Among the many variants of proportional representation, only two appear to have been given serious consideration in the plurality jurisdictions. One is the mixed-member proportional (MMP) system. The other is the single transferable vote (STV). When the New Zealand Royal Commission was making its recommendations, it came very clearly down in favour of MMP. When first given the opportunity to vote on FPTP and various alternatives in 1992, voters strongly favoured MMP, with an option for STV a distant second. More recently, the British Columbia citizens' assembly favoured STV (while also considering MMP) and a similar body in Ontario recommended MMP (while also considering STV). Commissions in Prince Edward Island and New Brunswick also settled on MMP as their recommended replacement for FPTP. (The details of the proposals in each Canadian province are given in Massicotte's Chapter 4.)

Pure list forms of PR—whether open or closed—apparently have not received serious consideration in any of the FPTP jurisdictions.[4] The most likely reason is that a shift to electing all members from party lists is seen as too big a break from the FPTP tradition of local, constituency-based representation. That is, both MMP and STV promise substantially proportional results among political parties, but also retain a strong element of familiarity with the tradition of FPTP elections. In the case of MMP, the continuity is evident in the election of half or more of legislators from single-seat districts. In the case of STV, districts tend to remain small, albeit considerably larger than under the plurality system, and candidates continue to be elected on the basis of their own individual ability to attract votes from within a geographically defined constituency. Of the two systems, STV arguably represents the more 'radical' reform, because it injects intraparty competition as well as proportionality into the electoral process, and thus may tip the balance farther in favour of local representation than the FPTP status quo, whereas the party list component of MMP may tip the scale in the other direction, in favour of more centralized political parties. In their Chapter 5 in this volume on British Columbia, Carty, Blais, and Fournier suggest that concern over party control might have been precisely why members of that province's citizens' assembly favoured STV. In all the other jurisdictions with a reform proposal to date, the proposal has been some variant of MMP.

Interestingly, a survey of experts' evaluations of the various electoral systems supports the citizens' and commissioners' preferences regarding specific forms of PR. Bowler, Farrell, and Pettitt (2005) found that MMP and STV were the two most highly rated systems by the experts, well above the other options. Open-list PR was a clear third. FPTP comes only sixth out of nine in terms of mean rating. (Closed-list PR also fared poorly.) Thus the preferences of commissioners and those citizens who have been most engaged on the issue of alternative electoral systems are generally in line with those of the academic experts, with MMP and STV being preferred to the FPTP status quo or to other potential reform options.

4. The Future of Electoral Reform in FPTP Jurisdictions

As of mid-2007, whatever momentum there once appeared to be in Canadian provinces towards replacing first past the post may be sputtering, and there is no currently active reform process in the UK. Only New Zealand has actually made the change to a PR system among all the jurisdictions where the idea has been publicly debated. While a passage of the referendum in Ontario in October 2007, could yet put other processes in Canada back on track, the 2005–7 period has not been a successful one for reform. The BC referendum failed to meet the required hurdle for change (although a second referendum is planned), the PEI referendum was soundly defeated, and a scheduled referendum in New Brunswick was cancelled. Meanwhile, in Quebec, the ruling Liberals were reduced to minority status in an election in 2007, and while that might appear to increase the demand for electoral reform, it actually may not. As we have noted here, there are no cases on the record in recent decades of proportional representation having been adopted (or even subjected to formal consideration) on account of a minority government. Now is a good time to take stock of the prospects for additional FPTP jurisdictions to consider electoral reform.

In Chapter 1, Shugart lists Saskatchewan, Trinidad and Tobago, and the UK as potential cases, based on patterns of vote-to-seat translation that raise the risk of anomalies. Nonetheless, as noted previously in this chapter, Saskatchewan has already had some anomalous outcomes, yet the New Democrats probably see the system as remaining favourable to them over the longer haul, given how frequently they have governed. Trinidad and Tobago held three general elections from 2000 to 2001, in a quest for stability, and each was closer in votes that the previous one, although the latter resulted in a one-seat majority. This sequence suggests that the FPTP system is not delivering the expected 'strong' governments, but at the same time, with two parties combining for more than 94% of the vote in each election since 1995, and with more than five percentage points between them only once in the period, it is likely that each party will see itself as able to benefit from the system in the foreseeable future. In the UK, as Blau (Chapter 2) notes, it is currently the Conservatives who are penalized by FPTP, yet there is little interest in electoral reform in that party, which expects to benefit again from FPTP in the near future. Electoral reform could come on to the formal public agenda again as a result of a hung parliament, but as we have pointed out, that scenario is not as favourable to reform as it is sometimes perceived to be.

We should consider the prospects for electoral reform in India and the USA, as these are by far the two largest jurisdictions in the world to use FPTP. Is either of them a candidate for replacement of the system? As Shugart noted in Chapter 1, both countries have, albeit for different reasons, a political process in which the aggregate national votes for parties are of diminished salience, compared to Canada (and its provinces), New Zealand, the UK, and the Caribbean island nations. India's party system is dramatically different from those of all the other jurisdictions covered in the volume. Whereas the others typically have two, or at most, three major parties, in India, the two largest national parties have combined in recent elections for barely half the national vote. Each of these parties, Congress and the Bharatiya Janata Party (BJP) (Indian People's Party), has numerous alliance partners at the state level, and state-based parties (whether in alliance with a national party or not) comprise most of the remainder of the aggregate national vote. This pattern of alliances and state parties suggests that nationwide vote totals are less important than are shifting regional political coalitions. Indeed, India has had some serious-looking anomalies recently if we focus only on national party vote totals. After both the 1998 and 1999 elections, the BJP led the government despite Congress having more nationwide votes (by a margin of almost five percentage points in 1999). Yet, when Congress and its allies came to power in 2004, there was no process of electoral reform initiated. The patterns of Indian politics—summarized as state-based competition within national alliances—may be uniquely suited to FPTP elections (Carroll and Shugart n.d.), given that any PR system would potentially open up electoral competition and legislative bargaining to parties with very different and more dispersed constituencies.

As for the USA, as Shugart notes in Chapter 1, it is hard for any 'anomalies' in terms of the relationship of seats to votes to become an issue when aggregate national party votes for Congress are not even reported in the media.[5] The US congressional electoral process remains fundamentally more in tune with the old adage, 'all politics is local', than any of the other FPTP jurisdictions discussed in the volume. As long as elites and voters alike respond mostly to local considerations in congressional contests, the legitimacy of FPTP is unlikely to be called into serious question. That is not to say that the American electoral system does not have serious normative issues. Partisan and bipartisan gerrymandering is a salient issue in many states, but the reforms that are discussed by politicians and even most non-governmental reform groups are not changes towards proportional representation or other alternatives to FPTP, but rather changes *within* FPTP. For instance, with most states allowing their legislatures to redraw district lines for the national House as well as for state chambers, the most commonly promoted reforms concern the creation of various models of 'independent' redistricting committees. As Bowler and Donovan (Chapter 3) note, there are many examples of electoral reform, broadly defined, at various jurisdictional levels in the USA, and there have been changes to the federal reapportionment process (also a change within FPTP), but the possibility of replacing FPTP with some form of PR is, with few exceptions, not one of them.

5. Reform *to* FPTP?

Our focus in this volume has been on the factors that increase or decrease the probability of electoral reform in countries (or provinces) with a first past the post electoral system. We may wonder, at the end of this journey, whether the same factors might increase or decrease the probability of a shift in the other direction, that is from some kind of proportional representation to first past the post.

Because we have no empirical instance of such a shift, the exercise is necessarily more conjectural. It is, however, quite appropriate to ask ourselves why major parties in a PR system do not attempt to adopt first past the post? Clearly some parties, the major parties or those with a strong geographic concentration of their vote, would do better under FPTP. From a rational-choice perspective, should they not push for electoral reform? Yes, of course. Why do they not?

These questions take us back, again, to the role of ideas and interests. We would argue that PR has proven more resilient to change than FPTP, over the long haul, because it is more ideologically consistent with the dominant conception of democracy, with its heavy emphasis on equality. Over the long haul, then, values matter as much as interests, especially when it comes to bringing about change. It is possible for major parties in FPTP to resist electoral reform on the basis of interest; it is more difficult normatively for major parties in PR to impose a new electoral system that is clearly to their advantage. On the other hand, it is also more difficult institutionally. Many PR democracies are consensual in respects other than the electoral system (Lijphart 1999), in that they have some combination of strong bicameralism or supermajority requirements. Some of their constitutions mandate proportional representation of some form. In fact, as noted above, it was just such a constitutional requirement for a referendum that twice has allowed the voters of Ireland to 'save' STV from attempts by Fianna Fáil governments to change it to FPTP. This is one concrete example of how veto points in countries that currently have proportional representation might make it daunting for any one party—or even a 'concert' of two large parties— to attempt a shift to FPTP or another disproportional system. For that matter, even if only the decision of two large parties would be enough to change the electoral system by a majority vote in parliament, it is likely that each party has existing coalition partners that might abandon the party as soon as electoral reform was broached. As Katz (2005: 73) put it, 'even if parties are motivated by self-interest, and unrestrained by any normative commitment to democratic principles, they might still find abstaining from even the appearance of electoral manipulation to their advantage.' This argument appears to work in PR systems, regardless of whether we take an *ideas* or an *interests* approach to the question.

6. Concluding Thoughts

All in all, then, an explanation based on *interest* appears to perform satisfactorily when it comes to explaining electoral system reform or the lack of it. Its basic prediction is that major parties that benefit from FPTP will want to keep it and that minor parties, which are disadvantaged, will support electoral reform, and that because major parties have more leverage than small parties, the most likely outcome is the status quo. Most of the time such an approach will yield an accurate prediction (FPTP remains), but it clearly cannot account for the few instances of reform that do occur nor for the fact that there are more instances of FPTP being replaced by PR (or mixed) than the reverse. FPTP prevails where it used to prevail a century or so ago, but in recent history there appears to be no case where FPTP was adopted to replace PR (or mixed).

Blais, Dobrzynska, and Indridason (2005) argue that PR was adopted in most European countries at the turn of the twentieth century in good part because it was then widely perceived to be 'the' democratic voting system. Such a perception has mostly disappeared. The dominant view now is that PR has both merits and limits. Yet, FPTP is rarely seen as the 'best' system, and in the (admittedly few) cases in which citizens have been engaged in processes of study and deliberation about FPTP and other electoral systems, they have uniformly preferred PR to FPTP. The three citizen assemblies on electoral reform that have taken place recently in British Columbia, Ontario, and the Netherlands each recommended substantially proportional systems (Blais and van der Kolk 2007). Ontario and BC citizens wanted to replace FPTP with STV or MMP and did not spend much time debating other possible systems. Dutch citizens wanted to conserve proportional representation, but to introduce more opportunity for candidate preference voting to matter for which candidates are elected, making lists more open. Additionally, as we noted above, the academic experts agree in placing FPTP far down the ranking of normatively desirable electoral systems.

All of this suggests that FPTP is still perceived to be unsatisfactory on normative grounds and that variants of PR, provided they have some form of candidate voting, are perceived as superior. Because of this normative shortcoming of FPTP, demand for electoral reform is always present in most jurisdictions that use it (though not, as noted, in India and the USA, for the most part). But it is in the interest of major parties to keep the system, and so reform rarely occurs. Nevertheless, FPTP has lost the battle of ideas and it is always under attack. It takes an exceptional set of circumstances for these attacks to be successful but such exceptions do occur, and so FPTP is sometime replaced. In the short term, interests almost always trump values but over the long haul values matter as much as interests.

Notes

1. There was a citizen-initiated referendum that got the process started by making a seemingly minor, but actually fundamental, change in the upper-house electoral law. However, there was never a vote at the end of the process, pitting a proposed new system against the status quo. See Katz (2001).
2. The other exception is Switzerland, which had two referenda on a proposal to replace the multi-member majority system with PR at the beginning of the twentieth century. The second was successful. See Carstairs (1980).
3. The concept of Duvergerian and non-Duvergerian equilibria comes from Cox (1997).

4. However, list PR is used in Britain for elections of Members of the European Parliament.

5. The electoral college reversal—a clear anomaly—in 2000 has received wide attention, but the constitutional status of the presidential election process and the high hurdles for constitutional amendments means that reform or replacement of the electoral college would be quite different, procedurally, from legislative electoral reform, even in the US House (where a federal statute, in principle, probably would be sufficient).

References

Anderson, C. J., Blais, A., Bowler, S., Donovan, T., and Listhaug, O. (2005). *Losers' Consent: Elections and Democratic Legitimacy*. Oxford: Oxford University Press.

Andrews, J. and Jackman, R. (2005). 'Strategic Fools: Electoral Rule Choice under Extreme Uncertainty', *Electoral Studies*, 24/1: 65–84.

Ashdown, P. (2000). *The Ashdown Diaries. Volume One: 1988–1997*. London: Penguin.

Atkinson, N. (2003). *Adventures in Democracy: A History of the Vote in New Zealand*. Dunedin: University of Otago Press.

Bale, T. (2006). 'PR Man? Cameron's Conservatives and the Symbolic Politics of Electoral Reform', *The Political Quarterly*, 77/1: 28–34.

Banducci, S. and Karp, J. (1999). 'Perceptions of Fairness and Support for Proportional Representation', *Political Behavior*, 21: 217–38.

——Donovan T., and Karp, J. (1998). 'Citizen's Attitudes about Democracy after Electoral Reforms', *Legislative Studies Quarterly*, 23: 153–4.

——————(1999). 'Proportional Representation and Attitudes About Politics: Results from New Zealand', *Electoral Studies*, 18: 533–55.

Barber, K. L. (1995). *Proportional Representation and Election Reform in Ohio*. Columbus: Ohio State University Press.

Barker, F. and McLeay, E. (2000). 'How Much Change? An Analysis of the Initial Impact of Proportional Representation on the New Zealand Parliamentary Party System', *Party Politics*, 6: 131–54.

——Boston, J., Levine, S., McLeay, E., and Roberts, N. S. (2001). 'An Initial Assessment of the Consequences of MMP', in M. Shugart and M. Wattenberg (eds.), *Mixed-Member Electoral Systems: The Best of Both Worlds?* Oxford: Oxford University Press, pp. 297–322.

Bartolini, S. and Mair, P. (1990). *Identity, Competition and Electoral Availability*. Cambridge: Cambridge University Press.

Bassett, M. (1982). *Three Party Politics in New Zealand 1911–1931*. Auckland: Historical Publications.

Baston, L. (2005). The *UK General Election of 5 May 2005: Report and Analysis*. London: Electoral Reform Society.

——(2006). *The Great Local Vote Swindle: The Local Government Elections on 4 May 2006*. London: Electoral Reform Society.

Beatty, D. (2005). 'Making Democracy Constitutional', in P. Howe, R. Johnston, and A. Blais (eds.), *Strengthening Canadian Democracy*. Montreal: Institute for Research on Public Policy, pp. 129–36.

Benoit, K. (2004). 'Models of Electoral System Change', *Electoral Studies*, 23: 363–89.

——and Schiemann, J. (2001). 'Institutional Choice in New Democracies: Bargaining over Hungary's 1989 Electoral Law', *Journal of Theoretical Politics*, 13/2: 153–82.

Bilodeau, A. (1999). 'L'impact mécanique du vote alternatif au Canada: Une simulation des élections de 1997', *Canadian Journal of Political Science*, 32/4: 745–61.

Birch, S., Millard, F., Popescu, M., and Williams, K. (2002). *Embodying Democracy? Electoral System Design in Post-Communist Europe*. Basingstoke: Palgrave Macmillan.

Black, J. H. and Hicks, B. M. (2006). 'Strengthening Canadian Democracy: The Views of Parliamentary Candidates', *IRPP Policy Matters*, 7/2.

Blais, A. (1991). 'The Debate over Electoral Systems', *International Political Science Review*, 12: 239–60.

——and Bodet, M. A. (2006). 'How Do Voters Form Expectations About the Parties' Chances of Winning the Election?' *Social Science Quarterly*, 87: 477–93.

——and Carty, R. K. (1987). 'The Impact of Electoral Formulae on the Creation of Majority Governments', *Electoral Studies*, 5: 109–18.

—— —— (1991). 'The Psychological Impact of Electoral Laws: Measuring Duverger's Elusive Factor', *British Journal of Political Science*, 21: 79–93.

——and Kim, J. (2007). 'How Do Governments Terminate? How Long Do They Live? The Impact of Electoral System and Cabinet Type', Paper presented at the meeting of the European Consortium for Political Research, Pisa.

——and Massicotte, L. (1997). 'Electoral Formulas: A Macroscopic Perspective', *European Journal of Political Research*, 32: 107–29.

—— —— (2002). 'Electoral Systems', in L. LeDuc, R. G. Niemi, and P. Norris (eds.), *Comparing Democracies 2: New Challenges in the Study of Elections and Voting*. London: Sage.

——and van der Kolk, H. (2007). 'Individual Values and Citizens' Evaluations of Electoral Systems', Paper presented at the Annual Meeting of the American Political Science Association, Chicago.

——Dobrzynska, A., and Indridason, I. (2005). 'To Adopt or not to Adopt Proportional Representation: The Politics of Electoral Reform', *British Journal of Political Research*, 35: 182–90.

——Carty, R. K., and Fournier, P. (2008). 'Do Citizen Assemblies Make Reasoned Choices?', in M. Warren and H. Pearse (eds.), *Designing Deliberative Democracy: The British Columbia Citizens' Assembly*. Cambridge: Cambridge University Press.

References

Blake, D. E. (2005). 'Electoral Democracy in the Provinces', in P. Howe, R. Johnston, and A. Blais (eds.), *Strengthening Canadian Democracy*. Montreal: Institute for Research on Public Policy, pp. 269–313.

Blau, A. (2004). 'A Quadruple Whammy for First-Past-the-Post', *Electoral Studies*, 23/3: 431–53.

—— (2008). 'The Effective Number of Parties at Four Scales: Votes, Seats, Legislative Power and Cabinet Power', *Party Politics*, 14/2: 167–87.

Bogdanor, V. (1981). *The People and the Party System: The Referendum and Electoral Reform in British Politics*. Cambridge: Cambridge University Press.

Boix, C. (1999). 'Setting the Rules of the Game: The Choice of Electoral Systems in Advanced Democracies', *American Political Science Review*, 93/3: 609–62.

Boston, J. (1998). *Governing Under Proportional Representation: Lessons from Europe*. Wellington: Institute for Policy Studies.

—— and Church, S. (2002). 'The Budget Process in New Zealand: Has Proportional Representation Made a Difference?' *Political Science*, 54: 21–43.

—— Levine, S., McLeay, E., and Roberts, N. S. (1996a). *New Zealand under MMP: A New Politics?* Auckland: Auckland University Press.

—— —— —— —— (1996b). 'Why Did New Zealand Adopt German-Style Proportional Representation', *Representation*, 33: 134–40.

—— Church, S., and Bale, T. (2003). 'The Impact of Proportional Representation on Government Effectiveness: The New Zealand Experience', *Australian Journal of Public Administration*, 62: 7–22.

Bowler, S. and Farrell, D. (2006). 'We Know Which One We Prefer but We Don't Really Know Why: The Curious Case of Mixed Member Electoral Systems', *British Journal of Politics and International Relations*, 8/3: 446–60.

—— Carter, E., and Farrell, D. (2003). 'Changing Party Access to Elections', in B. E. Cain, R. J. Dalton, and S. E. Scarrow (eds.), *New Forms of Democracy? The Reform and Transformation of Democratic Institutions*. Oxford: Oxford University Press.

—— Donovan, T., and Brockington, D. (2003). *Electoral Reform and Minority Representation: Local Experiments with Alternative Elections*. Columbus: Ohio State University Press.

—— Farrell, D., and Pettitt, R. (2005). 'Expert Opinion on Electoral Systems: So Which Electoral System is Best?', *Journal of Elections, Public Opinion and Parties*, 15: 3–19.

—— Donovan, T., and Karp, J. (2006). 'Why Politicians Like Electoral Institutions: Self-interest, Values, or Ideology?', *Journal of Politics*, 68: 434–46.

Bricker, D. and Redfern, M. (2001). 'Canadian Perspectives on the Voting System', *Policy Options*, 22/6: 22–4.

British Columbia Citizens' Assembly on Electoral Reform (2004a). *Making Every Vote Count. The Case for Electoral Reform in British Columbia*. Vancouver: Citizens' Assembly on Electoral Reform.

British Columbia Citizens' Assembly on Electoral Reform (2004*b*). *Making Every Vote Count. The Case for Electoral Reform in British Columbia. Technical Report.* Vancouver: Citizens' Assembly on Electoral Reform.

Butler, D. (1963). *The Electoral System in Britain Since 1918*, 2nd edn. Oxford: Clarendon Press.

Cairns, A. C. (1968). 'The Electoral System and the Party System in Canada 1921–1965', *Canadian Journal of Political Science*, 1/1: 55–80.

Cameron, D. (2006). Speech at the Power Inquiry Conference, 6 May.

Campbell, G. et al. (2003). 'The British Columbia Citizens' Assembly: A Round Table', *Canadian Parliamentary Review*, 26/2: 4–15.

Canada, Task Force on Canadian Unity (1979). *A Future Together: Observations and Recommendations.* Ottawa: Ministry of Supply and Services.

Carroll, R. and Shugart, M. S. (n.d.) 'Parties, Alliances, and Duverger's Law in India'. Unpublished paper.

Carstairs, A. (1980). *A Short History of Electoral Systems in Western Europe.* London: Allen and Unwin.

Carty, R. K. (1981) *Party and Parish Pump: Electoral Politics in Ireland.* Waterloo: Wilfrid Laurier University Press.

——(2006) 'Regional Responses to Electoral Reform', *Canadian Parliamentary Review*, 29/1: 22–6.

Castles, F. G. (1985). *The Working Class and Welfare.* Sydney: Allen and Unwin.

Center for Voting and Democracy. Available at: http://www.fairvote.org/index.php?page=1.

Chapman, R. M. (1962). 'The General Result', in R. M. Chapman, W. K. Jackson, and A. Mitchell (eds.), *New Zealand Politics in Action: The 1960 General Election.* London: Oxford University Press, pp. 235–98.

——(1969). *The Political Scene 1919–1931.* Auckland: Heinemann.

——(1979). 'On Democracy as Having and Exercising a Clear Choice of Government', in S. Hoadley (ed.), *Improving New Zealand's Democracy.* Auckland: New Zealand Foundation for Peace Studies, pp. 85–95.

——(1989). 'Political Culture: The Purposes of Party and the Current Challenge', in Hyam Gold (ed.), *New Zealand Politics in Perspective.* Auckland: Longman Paul, pp. 14–31.

——(1992). 'A Political Culture Under Pressure: The Struggle to Preserve a Progressive Tax Base for Welfare and the Positive State', *Political Science*, 44: 1–27.

——(1999). 'New Zealand Politics and Social Patterns', in E. McLeay (ed.), *New Zealand Politics and Social Patterns: Selected Works by Robert Chapman.* Wellington: Victoria University Press.

Chhibber, P. and Nooruddin, I. (1999). 'Party Competition and Party Fragmentation in Indian National Elections: 1957–1998', in R. Roy and P. Wallace (eds.), *Indian Politics and the 1998 Elections.* New Delhi: Sage.

Colomer, J. (2004). 'The Strategy and History of Electoral System Choice', in J. Colomer (ed.), *Handbook of Electoral System Choice*. Houndmills: Palgrave Macmillan, pp. 3–80.

Cook, R. (2005). Speech to Labour Campaign in Electoral Reform. Available at: http://www.makemyvotecount.org.uk/opus24538/2_5.pdf.

Corry, J. A. and Hodgetts, J. E. (1959). *Democratic Government and Politics*. 3rd edn. Toronto: University of Toronto Press.

Courtney, J. C. (2001). 'Is Talk of Electoral Reform Just Whistling in the Wind?' *Policy Options*, 22/6: 17–21.

—— (2004). 'Reminders and Expectations about Electoral Reform', in H. Milner (ed.), *Steps Toward Making Every Vote Count: Electoral System Reform in Canada and its Provinces*. Peterborough: Broadview Press, pp. 103–15.

Cowley, P. and Stuart, M. (2004). 'From Labour Love-in to Bona Fide Party of Opposition: Liberal Democrat Voting in the House of Commons 1992–2003', *The Journal of Liberal History*, 43/2.

Cox, G. (1997). *Making Votes Count: Strategic Coordination in the World's Electoral Systems*. Cambridge: Cambridge University Press.

—— and McCubbins, M. (2005). *Setting the Agenda: Responsible Party Government in the U.S. House of Representatives*. Cambridge: Cambridge University Press.

Curtice, J. (2003). 'The Electoral System', in V. Bogdanor (ed.), *The British Constitution in the 20th Century*. Oxford: Oxford University Press, pp. 483–520.

—— and Steed, M. (1997). 'Appendix 2: The Results Analysed', in D. Butler and D. Kavanagh (eds.), *The British General Election of 1997*. Basingstoke: Macmillan.

Cutler, F. and Johnston, R. (2008) 'The BC Citizens' Assembly as Agenda Setter: Shaking Up the Vote', in M. Warren and H. Pearse (eds.), *Designing Deliberative Democracy: The British Columbia Citizens' Assembly*. Cambridge: Cambridge University Press.

Dalton, R. J. (2004). *Democratic Challenges, Democratic Choices: The Erosion of Political Support in Advanced Industrial Democracies*. Oxford: Oxford University Press.

Denemark, D. (2001). 'Choosing MMP in New Zealand: Explaining the 1993 Electoral Reform,' in M. S. Shugart and M. P. Wattenberg (eds.), *Mixed-Member Electoral Systems: The Best of Both Worlds?* Oxford: Oxford University Press, pp. 70–95.

—— (2003). 'Electoral Change, Inertia and Campaigns in New Zealand—The First Modern FPP Campaign in 1987 and the First MMP Campaign in 1996', *Party Politics*, 9: 601–18.

Denham, J. (2005). 'Without Change, Progressives Will Fight Each Other', *The Independent*, 19 May.

Dobell, W. M. (1981). 'A Limited Corrective to Plurality Voting', *Canadian Public Administration*, 7/1: 75–81.

Downs, A. (1957). *An Economic Theory of Democracy*. New York: Harper.

Dunleavy, P. (1999). 'Electoral Representation and Accountability: The Legacy of Empire', in I. Holliday, A. Gamble, and G. Parry (eds.), *Fundamentals in British Politics*. New York: St. Martin's Press, pp. 204–30.

——and Margetts, H. (1995). 'Understanding the Dynamics of Electoral Reform', *International Political Science Review*, 16/1: 9–29.

————(2001). 'From Majoritarian to Pluralist Democracy? Electoral Reform in Britain since 1997', *Journal of Theoretical Politics*, 13/3: 295–319.

————(2005). 'The Impact of UK Electoral Systems', *Parliamentary Affairs*, 58/4: 854–70.

Duverger, M. (1954). *Political Parties: Their Organisation and Activity in the Modern State*. New York: Wiley.

Eckstein, H. (1980). 'Theoretical Approaches to Explaining Collective Political Violence', in T. R. Gurr (ed.), *Handbook of Political Conflict: Theory and Research*. New York: Free Press.

Elton, D. and Gibbins, R. (1980). *Electoral Reform: The Need Is Pressing, The Time Is Now*. Calgary: The Canada West Foundation.

Farrell, D. (2001a). *Electoral Systems: A Comparative Introduction*. Basingstoke: Palgrave Macmillan.

——(2001b). 'The United Kingdom Comes of Age: The British Electoral Reform "Revolution" of the 1990s', in M. S. Shugart and M. P. Wattenberg (eds.), *Mixed-Member Electoral Systems: The Best of Both Worlds?* Oxford: Oxford University Press.

——and Gallagher, M. (1999). 'British Voters and Their Criteria for Evaluating Electoral Systems', *British Journal of Politics and International Relations*, 1/3: 293–316.

——and McAllister, I. (2006a). *The Australian Electoral System*. Sydney: University of New South Wales Press.

————(2006b). 'Voter Satisfaction and Electoral Systems; Does Preferential Voting in Candidate-Centred Systems Make a Difference?', *European Journal of Political Research*, 45: 723–49.

Fisher, S. and Curtice, J. (2006). 'Tactical Unwind? Changes in Party Preference Structure and Tactical Voting in Britain between 2001 and 2005', *Journal of Elections, Public Opinion and Parties*, 16/1: 55–76.

Flanagan, T. (1999). 'The Alternative Vote: An Electoral System for Canada', in H. Milner (ed.), *Making Every Vote Count: Reassessing Canada's Electoral System*. Peterborough: Broadview Press, pp. 85–90.

——(2001). 'The Alternative Vote', *Policy Options*, 22/6: 37–40.

Franklin, C. (2006) 'Votes, Seats and the Generic Ballot.' Available at: http://politicalarithmetik.blogspot.com/2006/08/votes-seats-and-generic-ballot.html, accessed 11 November 2006.

Ganghof, S. (2003). 'Promises and Pitfalls of Veto Player Analysis', *Swiss Political Science Review*, 9/2: 1–25.

Gallagher, M. (1991). 'Proportionality, Disproportionality and Electoral Systems', *Electoral Studies*, 10/1: 33–51.

——(1998). 'The Political Impact of Electoral System Change in Japan and New Zealand, 1996', *Party Politics*, 4: 203–28.

Gelman, A. and King, G. (1994). 'A Unified Method of Evaluating Electoral Systems and Redistricting Plans', *American Journal of Political Science*, 38: 514–54.

Gibbons, M. (2000). 'Election Programmes in New Zealand Politics, 1911–1996'. Ph.D. thesis, University of Waikato.

Grice, A. (2006). 'Labour "Can Stay in Government by Backing PR"', *The Independent*, 6 July.

Hain, P. (2004). 'Reconnecting People and Politics through the Alternative Vote'. Speech at Make Votes Count event, House of Commons, 16 March. Available at: http://www.makemyvotecount.org.uk/opus7561. html.

Hamlin, A. (2006). 'Political Dispositions and Dispositional Politics', in G. Eusepi and A. Hamlin (eds.), *Beyond Conventional Economics: The Limits of Rational Behaviour in Political Decision-Making*. Aldershot: Edward Elgar, pp. 3–16.

Hart, J. (1992). *Proportional Representation: Critics of the British Electoral System 1820–1945*. Oxford: Clarendon Press.

Helms, L. (2004). 'Five Ways of Institutionalizing Political Opposition: Lessons from the Advanced Democracies', *Government and Opposition*, 39/1: 22–54.

Howe, P. and Northrup, D. (2000). 'Strengthening Canadian Democracy: The Views of Canadians', *Policy Matters*, 1: 5.

Hunt, G. (1998). *Why MMP Must Go*. Auckland: Waddington Press.

Hyson, S. (1995). 'The Electoral Boundary Revolution in the Maritime Provinces', *Canadian Journal of Business and Current Affairs*, 25/2/3: 285–99.

Irvine, W. P. (1979). *Does Canada Need a New Electoral System?* Kingston: Queen's Studies on The Future of the Canadian Communities, Monograph No. 1.

——(1980–81). 'Power Requires Representation', *Policy Options*, 1/4: 20–6.

Jackman, S. (1994). 'Measuring Electoral Bias: Australia, 1949–93', *British Journal of Political Science*, 24: 319–57.

Jackson, K. (1978). 'A Political Scientist Looks at Parliament', in Sir J. Marshall (ed.), *The Reform of Parliament*. Wellington: New Zealand Institute of Public Administration, pp. 15–25.

——and McRobie, A. (1998). *New Zealand Adopts Proportional Representation*. Aldershot: Ashgate.

Jansen, H. (1998). *The Single Transferable Vote in Alberta and Manitoba*. Ph.D. dissertation, University of Alberta.

——(2004). 'The Political Consequences of the Alternative Vote: Lessons from Western Canada', *Canadian Journal of Political Science*, 37/3: 647–70.

Jenkins, R. (1998). *The Report of the Independent Commission on the Voting System*. London: Her Majesty's Stationery Office.

Johnston, R. and Cutler, F. (2006). 'Canada: Seats, Votes, and the Puzzle of Non-Duvergerian Equilibria', Presented to the Conference on Plurality and Multi-Round Elections at the Center for the Study of Democracy, University of California, Irvine.

—— and Koene, M. (2000). 'Learning History's Lessons Anew: The Use of STV in Canadian Municipal Elections', in S. Bowler and B. Grofman (eds.), *Elections in Australia, Ireland, and Malta under the Single Transferable Vote. Reflections on an Embedded Institution.* Ann Arbor: The University of Michigan Press, pp. 205–47.

—— and Vowles, J. (2006). 'The New Rules and the New Game in New Zealand Elections: Implications for the Campaign', in H. E. Brady and R. Johnston (eds.), *Capturing Campaign Effects.* Ann Arbor: University of Michigan Press, pp. 280–306.

Justice Department (2007). *The Governance of Britain. CM 7170.* London: Her Majesty's Stationery Office.

Karp, J. and Banducci. S. (1999). 'The Impact of Proportional Representation on Turnout: Evidence from New Zealand', *Australian Journal of Political Science*, 34: 363–77.

—— and Bowler, S. (2001). 'Coalition Politics and Satisfaction with Democracy: Explaining New Zealand's Reaction to Proportional Representation', *European Journal of Political Research*, 40: 57–79.

—— Vowles, J., Banducci, S., and Donovan, T. (2002). 'Strategic Voting, Party Activity, and Candidate Effects: Testing Explanations for Split Voting in New Zealand's New Mixed System', *Electoral Studies*, 21: 1–22.

Katz, R. (1980). *A Theory of Parties and Electoral Systems.* Baltimore: The Johns Hopkins University Press.

—— (1999). 'Electoral Reform Is Not As Simple As It Looks', in H. Milner (ed.), *Making Every Vote Count: Reassessing Canada's Electoral System.* Peterborough: Broadview Press, pp. 101–8.

—— (2001). 'Reforming the Italian Electoral Law, 1993', in M. S. Shugart and M. P. Wattenberg (eds.), *Mix-Member Electoral Systems.* Oxford: Oxford University Press.

—— (2005). 'Why Are There So Many (or So Few) Electoral Reform?', in M. Gallagher and P. Mitchell (eds.), *The Politics of Electoral Systems.* Oxford: Oxford University Press, pp. 57–76.

Kendall, M. G. and Stuart, A. (1950). 'The Law of Cubic Proportion in Electoral Results', *British Journal of Sociology*, 1: 183–97.

Kim, J. and Ohn, M. (1992). 'A Theory of Minor-Party Persistence: Election Rules, Social Cleavages, and the Number of Political Parties', *Social Forces*, 70: 575–99.

King, G. (1990). 'Electoral Responsiveness and Partisan Bias in Multiparty Democracies', *Legislative Studies Quarterly*, 15: 159–81.

Kinnock, N. (2005). Speech at Makes Votes Count fringe meeting of Labour party conference, Brighton.

Knight, T. (1999). 'Unconstitutional Democracy? A Charter Challenge to Canada's Electoral System', *University of Toronto Faculty of Law Review*, 57/1: 1–42.

Laasko, M. and Taagapera, R. (1979). 'Effective Number of Parties: A Measure with Application to West Europe', *Comparative Political Studies*, 12: 3–27.

Lamare, J. and Vowles, J. (1996). 'Party Interests, Public Opinion, and Institutional Preferences: Electoral System Change in New Zealand', *Australian Journal of Political Science*, 31: 321–46.

Law Commission of Canada (2004). *Voting Counts. Electoral Reform in Canada.* Ottawa: Law Commission of Canada.

Lijphart, A. (1984). *Democracies: Patterns of Majoritarian and Consensus Government in Twenty-One Countries.* New Haven, CT: Yale University Press.

—— (1987). 'The Demise of the Last Westminster System? Comments on the Report of the Royal Commission on the Electoral System', *Electoral Studies*, 6: 97–104.

—— (1990). 'Size, Pluralism, and the Westminster Model of Democracy: Implications for the Eastern Caribbean', in J. Heine (ed.), *A Revolution Aborted: The Lessons of Grenada.* Pittsburgh: University of Pittsburgh Press, pp. 321–40.

—— (1994). *Electoral Systems and Party Systems. A Study of Twenty-Seven Democracies 1945–1990.* Oxford: Oxford University Press.

—— (1999). *Patterns of Democracy: Government Forms and Performance in Thirty-six Countries.* New Haven: Yale University Press.

Lovink, J. A. A. (2001). 'In Canada, Proportional Representation Should Be a Hard Sell', *Policy Options*, 22/10: 50–4.

Marsh, M. (2000). 'Candidate Centered but Party Wrapped: Campaigning in Ireland under STV', in S. Bowler and B. Grofman (eds.), *Elections in Australia, Ireland, and Malta under the Single Transferable Vote: Reflections on an Embedded Institution.* Ann Arbor: The University of Michigan Press.

Massicotte, L. (1994). 'Parliament: The Show Goes On, But the Public Seems Bored', in J. P. Bickerton and A. G. Gagnon (eds.), *Canadian Politics*, 2nd edn. Peterborough: Broadview Press, pp. 328–43.

—— (2001). 'Changing the Canadian Electoral System', *Choices*, 7/1: 1–29.

—— (2002). 'Un mode de scrutin à revoir', *Relations*, 678: 32–5.

—— (2004a). 'Les institutions démocratiques', in R. Bernier (ed.), *L'État québécois au XXIe siècle.* Montreal: Presses de l'Université du Québec, pp. 383–401.

—— (2004b). *In Search of a Mixed Compensatory System for Quebec. Working Document.* Québec: Secrétariat à la réforme des institutions démocratiques.

—— (2005). 'La réforme du mode de scrutin: l'unanimité des partis est-elle indispensable?' *Éthique publique*, 7/1: 38–47.

—— and Bernard, A. (1985). *Le scrutin au Québec: Un miroir déformant.* Montreal: Hurtubise/HMH.

—— and Blais, A. (1999). 'Mixed Electoral Systems: A Conceptual and Empirical Survey', *Electoral Studies*, 18/3: 341–66.

————— and Yoshinaka, A. (2004). *Establishing the Rules of the Game: Election Laws in Democracies.* Toronto: University of Toronto Press.

McLeay, E. and Vowles, J. (2006). 'Redefining Constituency: The Roles of New Zealand MPs', *Regional and Federal Studies,* 17: 71–95.

McRobie, A. (1993). *Taking It to the People: The New Zealand Electoral Referendum Debate.* Christchurch: Hazard Press.

Milner, H. (1994). 'Obstacles to Electoral Reform in Canada', *The American Review of Canadian Studies,* 24/1: 39–5.

Mitchell, P. (2005). 'The United Kingdom: Plurality Rule under Siege', in M. Gallagher and P. Mitchell (eds.), *The Politics of Electoral Systems.* Oxford: Oxford University Press, pp. 157–84.

Monièze, D. (1987). 'Pour un nouveau mode de scrutin. Le vote unique transferable', *L'Action nationale,* 76/8: 685–90.

Morgan, E. S. (1989). *Inventing the People: The Rise of Popular Sovereignty in England and America.* New York: Norton.

Mulgan, R. (1980). 'Palmer, Parliament, and the Constitution', *Political Science,* 32: 171–7.

——— (1990). 'The Changing Electoral Mandate', in M. Holland and J. Boston (eds.), *The Fourth Labour Government,* 2nd edn. Auckland: Oxford University Press, pp. 11–21.

——— (1992). 'The Elective Dictatorship in New Zealand', in H. Gold (ed.), *New Zealand Politics in Perspective,* 3rd edn. Auckland: Longman Paul, pp. 513–32.

——— (1995). 'The Democratic Failure of Single-Party Government—The New Zealand Experience', *Australian Journal of Political Science,* 30: 82–96.

Nagel, J. (1994). 'How Many Parties Will New Zealand Have Under MMP', *Political Science,* 46: 139–60.

——— (1998). 'Social Choice in a Pluralitarian Democracy: The Politics of Market Liberalization in New Zealand', *British Journal of Political Science,* 28: 223–67.

New Brunswick, Commission on Legislative Democracy (2005). *Final Report and Recommendations.* Fredericton.

Nohlen, D. (1984). 'Two Incompatible Principles of Representation' in A. Lijphart and B. Grofman (eds.), *Choosing an Electoral System: Issues and Alternatives,* New York: Praeger.

Palmer, G. W. R. (1979). *Unbridled Power?: An Interpretation of New Zealand's Constitution and Government.* Wellington: Oxford University Press.

Palmer, M. S. (1995). 'Toward an Economics of Comparative Political Organization: Examining Ministerial Responsibility', *Journal of Law, Economics and Organization,* 11/1: 164–88.

Pilet, J.-B. (2007). *Changer pour gagner? Les réformes des lois électorales en Belgique.* Bruxelles: Éditions de l'Université de Bruxelles.

Pilon, D. (1997). 'Proportional Representation in Canada: An Historical Sketch', Paper presented at the Annual General Meeting of the Canadian Political Science Association, St. John's (Nfld).

References

Pilon, D. (1999). 'The History of Voting System Reform in Canada', in H. Milner (ed.), *Making Every Vote Count: Reassessing Canada's Electoral System*. Peterborough: Broadview Press, pp. 111–21.

Plant, R. (1992). *Working Party on Electoral Systems, Second Interim Report of the Working Party on Electoral Systems*. London: Labour Party.

Pontusson, J. (2006). 'The American Welfare State in Comparative Perspective: Reflections on Alberto Alenisa and Edward L. Glaeser, *Fighting Poverty in the US and Europe'*, *Perspectives on Politics*, 4: 315–26.

Powell, G. B. (2000). *Elections as Instruments of Democracy*. New Haven: Yale University Press.

Prince Edward Island, Commission on PEI's Electoral Future (2005). *Final Report*. Charlottetown.

Rahat, G. (2004). 'The Study of the Politics of Electoral Reform in the 1990s—Theoretical and Methodological Lessons', *Comparative Politics*, 36: 461–79.

Ratner, R. S. (2004). 'British Columbia's Citizens' Assembly: The Learning Phase', *Canadian Parliamentary Review*, 27/2: 20–6.

Reed, S. and Thies, M. (2001). 'The Causes of Electoral Reform in Japan', in M. Shugart and M. Wattenberg (eds.), *Mixed-Member Electoral Systems: The Best of Both Worlds?* New York and Oxford: Oxford University Press, pp. 152–72.

Reynolds, A., Reilly, B., and Ellis, A. (2005). *Electoral System Design: The New International IDEA Handbook*. Stockholm: International Institute for Democracy and Electoral Assistance.

Richardson, L. and Cooper, C. (2003). 'Descriptive Representative in Multi-Member District Legislatures 1975–2002', Paper presented at the Midwest Political Science Association Conference, Chicago.

Riker, W. (1986). *The Art of Political Manipulation*. New Haven: Yale University Press.

Rokkan, S. (1970). *Citizens, Elections, Parties: Approaches to the Comparative Study of the Process of Development*. Oslo: Iniversitetsforlaget.

Russell, A. and Sciara, M. (2006). 'Why Does the Government Get Defeated in the House of Lords? The Liberal Democrats as a Pivotal Group', Paper presented at the Political Studies Association Conference, University of Reading.

——Cutts, D., and Fieldhouse, E. (2007). 'National-Regional-Local: The Electoral and Political Health of the Liberal Democrats in Britain', *British Politics*, 2/2: 191–214.

Sakamoto, T. (1999). 'Explaining Electoral Reform—Japan versus Italy and New Zealand', *Party Politics*, 5: 419–38.

Schattschneider, E. (1960). *The Semi Sovereign People: A Realist's View of Democracy in America*. New York: Holt, Rinehart and Winston.

Schmeckebier, L. (1941). *Congressional Apportionment*. Washington, DC: Brookings Institution.

Seidle, F. L. (2002). *Electoral System Reform in Canada: Objectives, Advocacy and Implications for Governance*. Ottawa: Canadian Policy Research Networks. Research Document F/29 Family Network, October 2002.

Serré, P. (2002). *Deux poids, deux mesures. L'impact du vote des non-francophones au Québec*. Montreal: VLB Éditeur.

Shugart, M. (2001a). 'Electoral "Efficiency" and the Move to Mixed-Member Systems', *Electoral Studies*, 20: 173–93.

——(2001b). 'Extreme Electoral Systems and the Appeal of the Mixed-Member Alternative', in M. Shugart and M. Wattenberg (eds.), *Mixed-Member Electoral Systems: The Best of Both Worlds?* New York and Oxford: Oxford University Press, pp. 25–51.

——and Wattenberg, M. P. (2001a). *Mixed Electoral Systems. The Best of Both Worlds?* Oxford: Oxford University Press.

————(2001b). 'Mixed-Member Electoral Systems: A Definition and Typology,' in M.S. Shugart and M.P. Wattenberg (eds.), *Mixed-Member Electoral Systems: The Best of Both Worlds?* Oxford: Oxford University Press, pp. 9–24.

——Moreno, E., and Fajardo, L. E. (2007). 'Deepening Democracy through Renovating Political Practices: The Struggle for Electoral Reform in Colombia,' in C. Welna and G. Gallon (eds.), *Peace, Democracy, and Human Rights in Colombia*. Notre Dame: Notre Dame University Press.

Shvetsova, O. (2003). 'Endogenous Selection of Institutions and Their Exogenous Effects', *Constitutional Political Economy*, 14: 191–212.

Siaroff, A. (2003). 'Spurious Majorities, Electoral Systems and Electoral System Change', *Commonwealth and Comparative Politics*, 41/2: 143–61.

Sridharan, E. (2002). 'The Fragmentation of the Indian Party System, 1952–1999: Some Competing Explanations', in Z. Hassan (ed.), *Parties and Party Politics in India*. New Delhi: Oxford University Press.

Sweeting, O. (1956). 'John Q. Tilson and the Reapportionment Act of 1929', *The Western Political Quarterly*, 9/2: 434–53.

Taagepera, R. (1986). 'Reformulating the Cube Law for Proportional Representation Elections', *American Political Science Review*, 80/2: 489–504.

——and Grofman, B. (1985). 'Rethinking Duverger's Law: Predicting the Effective Number of Parties in Plurality and PR Systems: Parties Minus Issues Equals One', *European Journal of Political Research*, 13: 341–52.

——and Shugart, M. S. (1989). *Seats and Votes: The Effects and Determinants of Electoral Systems*. New Haven: Yale University Press.

Tsebelis, G. (1990). *Nested Games: Rational Choice in Comparative Politics*. Berkeley: University of California Press.

——(2002). *Veto Players: How Political Institutions Work*. Princeton: Princeton University Press.

Uhr, J. (1999). 'Why We Chose Proportional Representation', in M. Sawer and S. Miskin (eds.) *Representation and Institutional Chance: 50 Years of Proportional Representation in the Senate*. Canberra: Department of the Senate.

219

References

Vowles, J. (1989). 'Playing Games with Electorates: New Zealand's Political Ecology in 1987', *Political Science*, 41: 18–34.

—— (1995). 'The Politics of Electoral Reform in New Zealand', *International Political Science Review*, 16: 95–115.

—— (1997). 'Waiting for the Realignment: The New Zealand Party System 1972–1993', *Political Science*, 48: 184–209.

—— (2000). 'Introducing Proportional Representation: The New Zealand Experience', *Parliamentary Affairs*, 53: 680–96.

—— (2002). 'Offsetting the PR Effect? Party Mobilisation and Turnout Decline in New Zealand, 1996–99', *Party Politics*, 8: 587–605.

—— (2004). 'Electoral Systems and Proportional Tenure of Government: Renewing the Debate', *British Journal of Political Science*, 34: 166–79.

—— (2005). 'New Zealand: Consolidation of Reform?', in M. Gallagher and P. Mitchell (eds.), *The Politics of Electoral Systems*. Oxford: Oxford University Press, pp. 295–312.

—— Banducci, S., and Karp, J. (2006). 'Forecasting and Evaluating the Consequences of Electoral Change in New Zealand', *Acta Politica*, 41: 267–84.

—— Aimer, P., Catt, H., Lamare, J., and Miller, R. (1995). *Towards Consensus? The 1993 General Election and Referendum in New Zealand and the Transition to Proportional Representation*. Auckland: Auckland University Press.

—— —— Banducci, S., and Karp, J. (eds.) (1998). *Voters' Victory? New Zealand's First Election under Proportional Representation*. Auckland: Auckland University Press.

—— —— Karp, J., Banducci, S., Miller, R., and Sullivan, A. (2002). *Proportional Representation on Trial: The 1999 Election in New Zealand and the Fate of MMP*. Auckland: Auckland University Press.

—— —— —— —— —— (eds.) (2004). *Voters' Veto: The 2002 Election in New Zealand and the Consolidation of Minority Government*. Auckland: Auckland University Press.

Ward, L. (1998). 'Second-Class MPs? New Zealand's Adaptation to Mixed-Member Parliamentary Representation', *Political Science*, 49: 125–52.

Weaver, R. K. (1997). 'Improving Representation in the Canadian House of Commons', *Canadian Journal of Political Science*, 30/3: 473–512.

Index